Praise for

"When I was a girl, books were my teachers, my friends. They gave me hope, dreams, direction, and eventually power—power to become who I wanted to be. This guidebook, compiled by a knowledgeable, story-spirited woman, will allow adults to help girls find the great books that nourish the spirit. I recommend it for all those who want girls to grow up strong, free, bold, and kind."

—MARY PIPHER
Author of *Reviving Ophelia*

"With superb literary taste and an eye for books depicting strong-minded girls and women, [Odean] recommends more than six hundred outstanding titles."

—U.S. News & World Report

Praise for *Great Books About Things Kids Love*

"An invaluable resource for both fiction and nonfiction."

—Minneapolis Star-Tribune

"[Odean's] choices are superb. An excellent book."

—The Sacramento Bee

"Kathleen Odean's compilation *Great Books About Things Kids Love* is an excellent resource for home and school libraries."

—The Denver Post

"A strong parent's resource that also belongs on the professional shelf."

—Booklist

By Kathleen Odean

Great Books for Girls
Great Books for Boys
Great Books About Things Kids Love
Great Books for Babies and Toddlers

Great Books for Babies and Toddlers

More Than 500
Recommended Books for
Your Child's First Three Years

Kathleen Odean

Ballantine Books
New York

A Ballantine Book
Published by The Random House Ballantine Publishing Group

Copyright © 2003 by Kathleen Odean

All rights reserved under International and Pan-American Copyright
Conventions. Published in the United States by The Random House
Ballantine Publishing Group, a division of Random House, Inc.,
New York, and simultaneously in Canada by Random House of
Canada Limited, Toronto.

Ballantine and colophon are registered trademarks of Random House, Inc.

www.ballantinebooks.com

Library of Congress Control Number: 2003090307

ISBN 0-345-45254-2

Cover design by Derek Walls

Manufactured in the United States of America

First Edition: April 2003

1   3   5   7   9   10   8   6   4   2

Dedicated with love
to Martha Wellbaum,
who truly appreciates
children and books

CONTENTS

Acknowledgments   ix

Introduction   1

1. Nursery Rhymes, Fingerplays, and Songs   38

2. Picture-Story Books for the Very Young   70

3. Resources and Tips for Parents   288

    Favorite Picks   288

    Tips on Reading Aloud   293

    Activities with Books   295

    Music Resources   298

    Books in Spanish   300

    Locating Books   303

    Keeping Up with What's New in Children's Book
      Publishing   306

    Organizations and Web Sites Concerned with Babies,
      Toddlers, and Books   308

CONTENTS

Further Reading for Parents	310
Further Reading for Librarians	312
Author and Illustrator Index	315
Title Index	323
Subject Index	333

Acknowledgments

I want to give my warm thanks to the following people: my wonderful nieces and nephews, who enjoyed books from the very start; my fellow librarians and other friends in the children's book world, who are dedicated to connecting children with great books; my agent Lisa Ross and my editor Allison Dickens, for their support and advice; my friends and colleagues Lisa Falk, Roxanne Feldman, Carla and Alison Grady, K. T. Horning, JoAnn Jonas, Vaunda Nelson, Elizabeth Overmyer, Ken Setterington, and Vicky Smith, for sharing their ideas about books for babies and toddlers. Thanks also to the ever-cordial staff at the Barrington Public Library for filling so many interlibrary loan requests. And, most of all, thanks to my husband, Ross Cheit, for his love and support.

Great Books
for Babies
and Toddlers

Introduction

The single most important activity for building the knowledge required for eventual success in reading is reading aloud to children.

— NATIONAL ACADEMY OF EDUCATION,
BECOMING A NATION OF READERS

The ideal time to begin sharing books with children is during babyhood, even with children as young as six weeks.

— NATIONAL RESEARCH COUNCIL,
STARTING OUT RIGHT

As a parent, you want to give your child the best possible start in life. At the same time, you want to enjoy every moment you can with him or her and create wonderful memories. One of the simplest, most effective ways to do all three is also one of the most rewarding—to read aloud to your child, beginning

1

early and continuing for years to come. A host of benefits flows from the practice of reading regularly, yet you don't need to work at achieving them. In fact, the key is for both of you to have fun, to relax and enjoy the lilt of language and the pleasure of pictures. If you make books as much a part of your daily routine as meals, play, hugs, and happiness, your child will soak up information about language and books while you're having warm, happy times together.

The best way to make reading aloud a cherished routine is to read wonderful books. And the most wonderful books are those that entertain parents as well as children, since as a parent, you may very well be reading these early books again and again. The best books use language that appeals to the ear and illustrations that appeal to the eye, and often include touches of humor for parents, without losing sight of their child audience.

The goal of this guide is to make reading aloud easy by identifying the best books for a child's first three years. In the last decade, the number of books for the very young has expanded enormously, providing thousands of choices, some excellent, some not. Outstanding writers and illustrators have turned their talents to creating books perfectly suited to the attention spans of babies and toddlers. But other new books, thrown together quickly to reach a growing market, make the experience of reading aloud tedious rather than satisfying. Some books, even for the very young, are designed mainly for promoting a product. This guide brings together more than five hundred top-notch books that have illustrations and text created with an understanding of what young children need and like.

What will your child gain from hearing and seeing books early in life? First, the powerful pleasure of being with you in an activity you both like. Sharing books is an excellent way to spend time together in a busy world, a time apart. During the enjoyable experience of listening, your child is immersed in language, which is how babies learn to understand words and then speak them. It's critical that babies hear spoken language, but parents sometimes run out of things to say to someone who doesn't respond in words. Reading is a great way to supplement conversations, with the added pleasures of artwork, rhythm, and rhyme.

By reading aloud, you communicate your enthusiasm about books, sending the message that you—the most important adult in your child's life—believe reading is important. Your child learns that books are entertaining, interesting, and comforting. Reading to young children also sets them on the path of emergent literacy, a term that sums up all the ways children become at home with language, reading, and writing well before they can decipher or print a recognizable word. They start to see how books work and what they are for. They take pride in learning to turn pages and come to realize that it advances the story. Toddlers begin to connect the black printed marks with the words you speak, their first glimmerings of the power of the printed word. You'll see toddlers pretending to read to themselves and their stuffed animals, showing off their new understanding about pages, print, and how the pictures help tell a story.

Enjoying books is one of many related pleasures in a child's life. Babies and toddlers also need to explore their physical world—indoors and outdoors—play with toys, listen to songs and sing along, crawl and walk and climb, splash in water and dig in sand, interact with people and pets, and much, much more. Reading is a significant ingredient in a rich mix of play and activities that acquaints children with their world.

Babies and Language

Recent research on babies and language reveals that far more is going on in babies' minds than scientists previously believed. Amazingly, babies just two days old can tell the difference between the language they heard while they were in the womb and a foreign language, according to *How Babies Talk*, by Drs. Roberta Golinkoff and Kathy Hirsh-Pasek, a fascinating study of language acquisition in the first three years of life.[1] Newborns recognize their language from hearing it as a fetus, and for the same reason, babies who are seventy-two hours old can distinguish their mother's voice from a stranger's.[2]

Babies start out with a remarkable facility for learning language. One study showed that four-month-old infants can discriminate among the sounds used in all different languages, but around ten months, they focus on those sounds peculiar to the language they hear around them and lose their ability to distinguish sounds they won't need. Canadian babies responded at six months to sounds specific to Hindi that Canadian adults can't hear, but by twelve months, the babies could no longer distinguish the Hindi sounds.[3]

Not surprisingly, babies and toddlers who live in a setting where they are exposed to a lot of conversation, reading, and nursery rhymes acquire a greater vocabulary than those who don't. "Study after study shows that a child's vocabulary can be predicted from the number of words that the child hears. . . . Toddlers who have had more stimulating language environments in the first two years tend to have larger vocabularies and

---

1. Roberta Michnick Golinkoff and Kathy Hirsh-Pasek, *How Babies Talk: The Magic and Mystery of Language in the First Three Years of Life* (New York: Dutton, 1999), 8–9.

2. Ibid., 21–22.

3. Alison Gopnik, Andrew N. Meltzoff, and Patricia Kuhl, *The Scientist in the Crib: Minds, Brains, and How Children Learn* (New York: Morrow, 1999), 107.

more complex sentence structures when they are three years of age. In short, children *learn language by hearing language*."[4] Speaking and reading to babies and toddlers supply the vocabulary and sentence structure that they need to acquire long before they can say their first word.

Scientists have concluded that the way parents naturally speak to their children, labeled motherese, is especially adapted to helping babies learn language. Parents use shorter, simpler sentences when speaking to babies than when speaking to adults. They also frequently repeat the same thing over again with slight variations. Parents use "basic-level" words—words that fall between general and specific, such as *dog* instead of *animal* or *Pekingese*. Basic-level words are shorter than other words, and research shows that, as you might expect, babies have an easier time learning short words than long ones. The basic-level words babies learn first in English are often for objects, like *car*, *ball*, *shoe*, and *kitty*. Good books for babies reflect these attributes of motherese by using many basic-level words, names for objects, short sentences, and lots of repetition, reinforcing the very vocabulary that babies and toddlers learn most easily.

Emergent Literacy: The Process That Leads to Reading and Writing

Children who have a strong vocabulary are at an obvious advantage when the time comes to learn to read. Each time they encounter a word in print that they've heard before and perhaps used in conversation, it will be far easier to read than if

4. Golinkoff and Hirsh-Pasek, *How Babies Talk*, 146–147.

the word is entirely new. But vocabulary is only one aspect of emergent literacy, those behaviors related to reading and writing during the years before a child can technically read and write in the conventional sense. Most adults think of reading as *beginning* when a child can first decode printed words and understand their meaning. In fact, the process starts much earlier.

What takes place in the emergent literacy process of babies and toddlers? A lot of seemingly small things that adults take for granted but that turn out to be essential. For example, young children begin to understand the physical properties of a book. Starting very young, they learn that books have covers, pages, text, and pictures and must be right side up to be read. Pages are turned from right to left, while the words are read from the left to the right of the line and from the top to the bottom of the page, in English and other Western languages. These conventions of print don't need to be taught as lessons because children absorb them through contact with books as you read to them. For children to start school, as some do, with no knowledge of how books work puts them significantly behind others who've been read to as babies and toddlers.

Through listening to books and looking at the pictures, young children observe that written language is different than spoken language: the words in a book remain the same, in the same order every time, unlike conversations. The squiggly black markings that are print—which have blank spaces between them, unlike spoken words—convey meaning, often telling a story. Those stories have a common form, with a beginning, a middle, and an end. With enough exposure to books, children begin to see that stories have structure and sequence and that some can be predicted. Predictable books, which are common among books for the very young, reinforce this learning process. Stories for the very young also encompass at the most elementary level the themes that infuse all of literature, such as family, friends, journeys, simple conflicts and resolutions, and emotions like fear and love.

In listening to books and poems, children become familiar with rhyme, which does more than entertain, according to those who study how children learn to read. Children who are sensitive to rhyme, having developed what linguists call "phonemic awareness," eventually do better at reading and spelling than those who aren't, leading researchers to recommend that parents include rhyming books when they read aloud, which is easy enough in view of the books available.

Books play a key role in emergent literacy, but so does other print. Children in print-rich environments learn that the printed language conveys meaning and is used for many purposes: grocery lists, cookbooks, street signs, menus, phone books, newspapers, and television listings, to name a few. Children benefit from seeing their parents read and use print in different contexts like these. Studies confirm that children raised in homes with lots of print material, where they see their parents read, learn to read more easily and do better in school.

Although exposure to print clearly benefits young children, formal instruction in reading does not. Most child development experts advise against hurrying a child into reading independently. Even anxiety about young children's knowing the alphabet is misplaced. According to Mary Lee Griffin, an education professor at Wheaton College, "Learning the alphabet [as] isolated letter recognition is perhaps one of the least essential prereading skills for preschoolers."[5] She stresses instead other aspects of emergent literacy such as learning the conventions of print and starting to understand story structure

5. Mary Lee Griffin, "Focus on Alphabet Would Rob Pupils," *Providence Journal*, April 21, 2002.

and sequence, which parents can facilitate by reading aloud and creating print-rich environments.

The best things, then, that parents can do to encourage babies and toddlers on their path of literacy are the most enjoyable—reading aloud, having conversations (even before a child can speak), supplying toddlers with writing and drawing materials, and creating a safe, happy environment in which children can explore and learn. Under these optimal conditions, very young children naturally develop their abilities while having a good time, the best of both worlds.

Creating a Family Chord

In the end, perhaps the greatest benefits—and the most difficult to quantify—of reading to your young child are emotional. Your child comes to associate books with happy times you've shared and develops good feelings about reading. When he or she later faces the potentially difficult task of mastering reading mechanics, the knowledge that books are pleasurable will provide motivation. The combination of being read to and liking books sets children on the road to a lifetime of reading pleasure, thanks to their parents. As a librarian who speaks frequently to the public about children's books, I often have adults tell me that their happiest memories—sometimes sixty or seventy years later—are of their parents reading aloud to them when they were young.

But reading aloud isn't just about improving a child's future, important as that is. It's about enjoying the present. Good books enrich a child's life, bringing the magic of story, the satisfaction of acquiring information, and the joy of looking at art.

Sharing well-loved books also brings parent and child

closer together in the present. In *Babies Need Books*, a tribute to the importance of reading to young children, Dorothy Butler discusses how books create a parent-child bond. "It is my belief that there is no 'parents' aid' which can compare with the book in its capacity to establish and maintain a relationship with a child. Its effects extend far beyond the covers of the actual book, and invade every aspect of life. Parents and children who share books come to share the same frame of reference. Incidents in everyday life constantly remind one or the other—or both, simultaneously—of a situation, a character, an action, from a jointly enjoyed book, with all the generation of warmth and well-being that is attendant upon such sharing."[6]

Writing in the *Horn Book Magazine*, children's author Cynthia Voigt reminisced about just such a warm, shared experience of a book. She described reading *The Runaway Bunny* to her children when they were very young, a book that ends with the mother bunny saying to her little bunny, "Have a carrot." Because she and her children shared the story many, many times, that line now "constitutes a family chord," carrying a special meaning for all of them. As Voigt writes about her grown children, "Have a carrot, I say to my children, and they understand everything I mean. I mean, everything, including love."[7]

6. Dorothy Butler, *Babies Need Books*, rev. ed. (Portsmouth, N.H.: Heinemann, 1998), xii.
7. Cynthia Voigt, "Have a Carrot," *Horn Book Magazine*, March/April 1997, 147.

Books at Different Ages

Babies and toddlers respond to books as individuals. One baby may find a book enchanting, while another has no interest in it. Like nearly everything else about child development, the responses of very young children to books fall into general categories by age, but in reality, they vary from child to child. So although this section maps out what kinds of books work well in each of the first three years, you may find that not everything applies to your child. For example, traditional wisdom recommends simple pictures for one-year-olds, yet your child may especially like detailed illustrations. Some very young children are mesmerized by trucks and cars, some love books with lots of labeled objects, and others don't like either. Follow your child's lead whenever possible to maximize his or her excitement about listening to books and nursery rhymes.

Children with special needs may have different milestones in their interactions with books, but books should absolutely be a part of every child's life. Whether developmentally delayed, hearing-impaired, visually impaired, or whatever their situation, children benefit from interacting with their parents and books in whatever ways are possible: hearing stories and poems, looking at pictures, handling books and exploring their physical properties, participating in fingerplays and action rhymes, and snuggling up to their reading parents.

Books for Babies

"Babies love human voices and faces more than anything," note the authors of *The Scientist in the Crib: Minds, Brains, and*

How Children Learn.[8] No wonder newborns respond to nursery rhymes, fingerplays, songs, and simple books: they get to hear your voice and see your face at the same time, two of their favorite things in life. Most of the books listed with an age range of "Newborn and up" are Mother Goose collections, single nursery rhyme books, and songbooks, all of which you can immediately share with your new baby.

One of the first tasks of parenthood is to make babies feel calm and secure, and a major instrument is your voice—speaking, reading, and singing. You could, theoretically, talk about anything or read any book to a baby, and your infant might enjoy it. The point isn't the meaning of the words, it's the way they sound. But research into language shows that humans actually have an affinity for rhyme, which explains the popularity of nursery rhymes and songs. This guide offers many choices for Mother Goose collections plus a handful of fine songbooks to remind you of old favorites and introduce you to new ones.

Traditional fingerplays and other rhymes that incorporate actions also delight babies. Collections of fingerplays show parents how to move their fingers and hands while chanting or singing a rhyme to entertain infants and toddlers. Parents of newborns can start right away with fingerplays and observe as time goes on how their child responds differently, and joins in, as she gets older. Fingerplays zero in on exactly what babies are most attuned to in their small world: their faces, feet, hands, toes, and, of course, you. Such interactions are so effective that *patty-cake* and *peekaboo* are among the first words that babies nine to twelve months understand, if parents play these with little games with them.[9]

---

8. Gopnik, Meltzoff, and Kuhl, 64.
9. Golinkoff and Hirsh-Pasek, *How Babies Talk*, 79.

For the first four or five months, infants are very near-sighted and focus best on objects about a foot from their eyes, according to *Scientist in the Crib*, which also reports that babies turn toward patterns with high contrast and away from those with little contrast.[10] Babies need uncluttered, high-contrast pictures if they are going to discern shapes and colors, a fact that well-designed books for babies respect. Such books typically show one object in a picture, illustrated in a bright color that stands out against the background. A handful of books take advantage of the preference for contrast by using black against white and white against black in their pictures.

To share books with babies, hold them within your child's visual range and turn the pages slowly. Babies like books with flaps that you can hold close to them and open the flaps while reading the simple words. Many babies also like to see photographs of other babies, just as they like to see themselves in mirrors.

Once a baby can reach out and grasp a book, board and cloth books come into play. Babies will treat these as toys for playing with and chewing on, which is fine. Although not many cloth books are published, recent years have produced hundreds of books made of sturdy cardboard. Some of these board books are excellent, based on the needs of babies, while others cram too many details and words onto the pages. Sometimes a book that works beautifully for babies in its original hardcover format is shrunk into a board book, making the pictures too small for very young viewers. Publishers have also taken books appropriate for older children and needlessly put them into board book format. The annotations in this guide will alert you to which board books truly suit their audience

10. Gopnik, Meltzoff, and Kuhl, 28.

and which ones should be passed over in favor of the larger, original versions.

Books for One-Year-Olds

Children in their second year of life are expanding their interests and abilities, and the books for them reflect that. One-year-olds can understand many words, even though they are just learning to talk, so the texts start to be a bit longer and more complex. But most children during this year continue to have a short attention span and won't sit still for long.

One-year-olds like little books they can hold easily, such as board books that will endure their energetic handling. But it's also time for more hardcover and paperback books with larger illustrations that go beyond one or two objects on a page. These larger books work for lap reading as well as for children who insist on sitting next to parents rather than on their laps.

Their own bodies intrigue one-year-olds, who enjoy books that reflect this interest by talking about facial and body features. They also tend to be fascinated by animals and join enthusiastically in making animal sounds. They enjoy looking at pictures and photographs of children their own age and of infants. Some children develop an interest in vehicles and can't get enough books on trucks, fire engines, trains, and the like. Most of the illustrations for this age group are still bright and uncluttered, although some start to offer more detail, especially on informational topics like vehicles and dinosaurs.

During this year, children start to enjoy simple plots, with a preference for books that relate to their own lives and activities. Rhyme and repetition are very appealing to them and make listening easier. They also like pointing to familiar objects and having the adult say the object's name, which eventually the child will imitate. Some children can spend hours with the kind of "first word" books that have no plot but just show pictures or photographs with labels underneath. For this age group, concept books like alphabet and counting books lend themselves to pointing and labeling rather than providing instruction in concepts.

One-year-olds start participating more with books. Many insist on turning pages and love to open flaps. They continue to take pleasure in fingerplays and other action rhymes, but now they appreciate the meaning of the words more and can join in with the movements, giving them a sense of accomplishment. Mother Goose collections still get a lot of use, and singing is almost as natural as talking for this age group.

Books for Two-Year-Olds

Children keep learning at an amazing pace during this year, all without formal teaching. Two-year-olds are absorbing language and information with every game they play, every conversation an adult has with them, every song they sing, and every book to which they listen. A two-year-old may develop strong preferences for types of books as well as the need to hear a specific book many times, if he hasn't already. This is also the stage at which many children insist on hearing a book word for word, with no changes or omissions.

Illustrations are increasingly detailed, leading some children to pore over a book for a long time, studying the pictures and perhaps asking questions. The wider range of illustration styles in the books for this age group initiates children into many years of looking at wonderful art in their books.

Two-year-olds still respond strongly to books related to their own lives, and the books aimed at them reflect this. These stories are often presented in short, clear sentences that don't rhyme, even though up until this age the majority of books for young children are told in rhyme. As parents read such books, which usually have uncomplicated plots, like *Benny Bakes a Cake* (see page 224) and *Mr. Gumpy's Outing* (see page 101), children may start predicting what comes next, based on the pattern in the story or remembering it from an earlier reading. Repetition, which helps children learn to predict stories, still figures in many plots, which rely on patterns such as different animals doing the same thing one after another.

Many two-year-olds start to be intrigued by concepts like colors, shapes, opposites, basic counting, and the alphabet. While parents shouldn't worry about teaching these topics, if a child does show an interest, concepts can be explored in books as well as elsewhere in her world. Almost any book offers a chance to talk about colors and shapes and do some simple counting.

Poetry, songs, and action rhymes continue to be popular with two-year-olds. Many can recite nursery rhymes as well as perform movements for fingerplays. Two-year-olds can sing simple songs and will enjoy looking at single illustrated versions of favorites like *Old MacDonald* (see page 64) and *Twinkle, Twinkle, Little Star* (see page 57).

When, Where, and How to Read to Your Young Child

There is no one right way to read a book with a child.
—WILLIAM TEALE, COAUTHOR OF *EMERGENT LITERACY*

When and Where to Read

Read to your child every day, if possible, just as you talk to and play with him every day. Books for this age group are extremely short and easily fit into any routine. Beyond making it a regular part of life, there is "no one *right* way" to read to your child, and no designated time or place that's best. In fact, trying different arrangements at different times in your child's first three years will probably be the most successful approach.

For babies, any time that you would talk to your child is also a time you can read to her and share nursery rhymes. Since these short poems are easy to remember, you can incorporate them into nursing, changing diapers, riding in the car, and other daily activities. You might also prop open a poetry book beside you when you are rocking your baby, so you can read without using your hands. When your child starts to sit in a high chair for meals, you can recite rhymes as you feed him and also share simple books with your captive audience.

Books belong everywhere. Bring them with you to the doctor's office or a relative's home. Keep some in the car and your diaper bag. Put board books in your child's crib and playpen, if you use one. Have a basket or low shelf of durable books that your child can reach and look at on his own. (You can store other books that you hope to preserve for a long time on a high shelf, putting them back out of your child's reach when the reading session is finished.)

Bedtime is a traditional time to read aloud, with books as part of a calming evening ritual. You might want to set a limit on the number of books in the routine, lest the reading go on too long—or not, if you're happy reading until your child nods off. At some stages, your child might insist on a specific bedtime book every night, while a variety will work best at other times.

Bedtime reading doesn't catch on in every household. If you have a number of children to put to bed, or if your child feels cranky at bedtime and too tired to pay attention, that's fine. Look for other times that work better for your family.

Reading just before naptime can offer advantages similar to bedtime rituals. An energetic toddler might have wound down enough to sit still and snuggle up for a book, so that reading becomes an effective transition from play to rest. But as with bedtime, naptime might pose problems if your child is too tired.

You don't want to limit reading to only designated times. Add in some spontaneous sessions as well. For most children, any given session will be brief, due to their naturally short attention span. So read for as long as they are enjoying it and then stop and try again sometime later. On certain days in certain moods, your child might want to hear a number of books, while other days bring a short attention span. Nursery rhymes, poems, and songs can be worked into any part of a day, especially once you've memorized them (which will happen in some cases with no effort on your part).

When your child gets old enough to indicate through words ("Book!") or actions (thrusting a book at you) that she wants to be read to, seize the moment if at all possible. If you stop what you're doing and read, you will convey in a powerful way that you think reading is important. In cases where you can't set aside what you're doing, suggest that your child "read" the book to herself or to a stuffed animal or toy, then try to join her as soon as you can.

If you have more than one child, it's sometimes good to read to everyone at once, especially if your children are similar in age. If your toddler has a friend over to visit, you might read to both of them if they are in the mood. But try to read one-on-one frequently, if not daily, with each of your children to make the most of the benefits of reading aloud.

Share the pleasure of reading with as many people in your child's life as you can. Encourage older siblings, grandparents, aunts and uncles, and other relatives to read aloud. Make sure any child-care environment your child enters has lots of books and scheduled time every day for reading aloud. If your child goes to a baby-sitter or child-care center, tell the caregivers what books he likes and find out what books the children hear during the day.

Again, there is no one right time or place. Nor should it be a cause for guilt if daily reading isn't possible, as long as books are an important part of your child's life. This is about adding pleasure, not one more obligation on a parental checklist. There are lots of right times and places, and others that just don't work out (even if they did the day before). If one time or place doesn't work, try another. Expect some sessions to be brief and others longer. Have books with you and around you, as familiar as the furniture and as treasured as favorite toys.

How to Read to Your Baby or Toddler

Read with pleasure and enthusiasm. If you are not used to reading aloud, making your debut with a baby or toddler is a good way to start. She will often just be pleased to hear your voice, sit in your lap, and have you to herself for the duration of the books.

Slow down if you are a naturally fast speaker. Babies and toddlers need a little extra time to absorb language. Reading slowly, though, doesn't mean using a monotone. Be expressive. Get into the fun of imitating animals and chanting rhymes. Make your voice softer, then a little louder. Draw out suspenseful parts and bounce your voice through rhythmic ones. If it's bedtime or naptime, aim for a quiet, soothing tone.

Amuse yourself by adding variety. Any given book can be read a number of different ways, even with babies. You could read your infant *Goodnight Moon* (see page 95) while holding the pages close enough for him to see the pictures. Or you could read it just for the sound of the words, without sharing the illustrations. You could read a line or two and then stop and comment on the pictures in a conversational voice—even to a newborn. "Look, there's a little bunny in a bed, and you're in your bed. Let's see what else is in the room." You could point to an object as you read about it or gently take your baby's finger and point it at the picture.

Reading to toddlers offers similar variations. Sometimes, you'll read a book from cover to cover without stopping, and that will be just what your child wants. Other times, stop, comment, and ask questions. Even if your child doesn't talk yet, you can pause for an answer, getting into the spirit of what will happen when she's older and can respond. Try to vary your voice for these combined reading-and-talking sessions, so

19

that one voice is a more formal reading voice and the other is a more casual, conversational tone.

Conversations can be confined to the book and its topics, or you can connect the book to your child's life. "This girl has red rubber boots just like yours," or, "Look at that teddy bear. Does it look like your teddy bear?" You might want to stop sometimes and fetch the real-life item to compare it to the fictional one.

Some two-year-olds love "first word" books made up entirely of individual pictures with name labels. *My First Word Book* (see page 272) is filled with photographs of many familiar things—animals, toys, clothes, and more—identified by name. Reading books like this will involve a lot of pointing and naming, first by you and later by your growing child. If your child naturally repeats the label after you, that can be fun, but don't turn it into a test. Many conversations can also spring from looking at the pictures as your child absorbs new information and asks questions or links the object or activity to his life.

Pointing to labels under such pictures makes a connection in a child's mind between the black shapes that are print and the pictures they name. This doesn't teach a child to read as such but does prepare her gradually for learning to read when the time is right. You should sometimes run your finger under the print in a storybook as you are reading to a toddler. You don't need to explain what you're doing; simply add in this "walk-and-talk" feature now and then to indicate the link between your words and the print.

Just for fun, some illustrators add a small animal throughout the book that may never be mentioned in the text, a feature that will generate pointing and conversation. *In the Small, Small Pond* (see page 137), for example, shows a frog on every page, although the text is about other animals. Let your child be the first to point out the frog and then enjoy the excitement of finding it again and again. Some days, finding the frog may be the main activity instead of reading the words.

During some readings like the frog search, you may never get to the text at all. The pictures serve instead as a spring-board for conversations—a valuable aspect of sharing books. The repeated question "What's that?" from your child may lead to a session of naming objects, and not just in "first word" books. Or you can spend your entire time making animal or ve-hicle noises with your child and naming the animals or types of vehicle. These are all fine ways of "reading" together.

Books That Invite Children to Join In

Any book can be read in a way that involves a child's active participation, but some books especially lend themselves to children's joining in verbally. Even before your child can talk, you will notice he anticipates certain lines in a book, particu-larly refrains or other repeated patterns. Some books ask direct questions, to be answered by you and your child, when he can speak. Still others inspire participation through their rhyme scheme. Children start filling in the last word in a sentence, knowing it rhymes with the sentence before. By changing the inflection of your voice when you read and pausing a little, you send a signal to your child to join in.

Many folk songs that we sing with children incorporate re-frains, so it's not surprising that well-written books do, too. Singing "E-I-E-I-O" over and over makes it easy for children to remember that part. In a book such as *Just Like Daddy* (see page 77), the phrase "Just like Daddy" occurs again and again until the very end, where tables are turned and it becomes "Just like Mommy," a funny surprise. *Oh No, Anna!* (see page

143) combines flaps and a repeated phrase for children to say. Each time the incorrigible Anna makes a new mess, a flap opens to show the minor disaster and the memorable words "Oh no, Anna!"

Other books have no specific refrain but use repetition or rhyme in a way that nudges children to join in. *The Lady with the Alligator Purse* (see page 67) has variations on the same sentence, "In comes the doctor, in comes the nurse, in comes the lady with the alligator purse." After you've read it aloud a number of times, start pausing a little before you say, "the lady with the alligator purse," and toddlers may supply the phrase or say it with you.

Questions pull in listeners, too. In *Who Hops?* (see page 120), the story asks that question, then shows three hopping animals to name. But the fourth animal is a cow, a humorous mistake that will cause the audience to laugh or object, or both. The book goes on to ask who swims, flies, and crawls. You can read the book straight through or pause with each question to talk with your child before going on to the book's answers.

Spots, Feathers, and Curly Tails (see page 256) also asks questions about animals, supplying clues to the answers in large pictures. "Who has spots?" shows enough of a black-and-white cow that a toddler might get it right the first time, and probably will the next. Knowing the answer, though, is no deterrent to wanting to read the book again. If anything, the triumph of getting it right makes the book all the more attractive.

Wordless or nearly wordless books ask you and your child to supply the whole story, with the freedom to make it different every time. *Good Night, Gorilla* (see page 223) and *Do You Want to Be My Friend?* (see page 104) offer enough material in the illustrations to come up with more than one story. You can use simple questions to encourage your child, such as, "What are the animals doing now?" Wordless books don't offer the pleasures of rhyme or witty language, but they can make a good change and strongly appeal to certain children.

Books That Invite Movement

While some books inspire young children to join in the words, others invite physical response. At the simplest level of physical participation, "touch-and-feel" books incorporate textures for young children to feel, like the furry cloth, scratchy paper, and shiny mirror surface in *Pat the Bunny* (see page 186). These can provide hours of entertainment at certain stages in a child's life.

Books with moving flaps and tabs to pull delight young children. You will captivate babies by reading them flap books and moving the flaps, while older children will reach out to help. These books aren't as durable as books without moving parts, but while they last, books like *Where's Spot?* (see page 159) and *Dear Zoo* (see page 103) raise the level of excitement about reading. Many ask the child to guess what's under the flap, but a lot of children can't wait for the question, much less give an answer, before they reach to open the flap. No problem. Let them learn patience in other situations where it matters more.

Some flap books also have pop-up pages, which tend to be more fragile than flaps, so you might want to keep them in a special place. You wouldn't want a steady diet of reading pop-ups and flap books, but you also wouldn't want your child to miss the fun. For a pop-up book that will grab the attention of a crowd of wiggly toddlers, try *Dinosaur Stomp!* (see page 251). And for sheer artistry, read Paul Zelinsky's *Wheels on the Bus* (see page 69).

Fingerplays and other action rhymes entertain babies and toddlers, enticing them to join in the movements as soon as they are old enough. Certain picture-story books, like *Toddlerobics* (see page 211) and *From Head to Toe* (see page 105), resemble extended action rhymes. Their illustrations show children and animals flapping their arms, jumping, stretching, and bending down to touch their toes—and encourage listeners to do the same. Don't read this kind of book unless you are ready for action, but if you and your child are in the mood to play, books like these are perfect.

In a less explicit way, other stories prompt children to add movements as they listen. *Caps for Sale* (see page 246) is a charming tale of a peddler and some monkeys. Several times, the peddler shakes his finger and calls out, "You monkeys you. You give me back my caps." In response, the monkeys shake their fingers at him and say, "Tsz, tsz, tsz." Expect to have toddlers join in the phrase and shake their fingers, too. The words "you monkeys you" may well become part of your family folklore.

Extending Books into Everyday Life

Adults who love books refer to them in conversations and talk about them in book groups. They browse in bookstores, use libraries frequently, and give books as gifts. Books are a vital part of their lives. This pleasure can be true for young children, too, with your help. Having books in lots of different places—crib, car, diaper bag, relative's house—is one aspect of this. Research shows that children who become strong readers typically come from homes where books and magazines are in evidence and they see their parents reading.

Besides talking about books when you're reading, mention books at other times if they relate to what you're doing. If you've read *The Carrot Seed* (see page 186), bring it up the next time you buy or eat carrots together. Going out into the snow may remind you or your child of Ezra Jack Keats's wonderful book *The Snowy Day* (see page 183); make snow angels together or just walk through the snow and admire your footprints as Peter does.

You can be deliberate about extending books into other activities. If your child sees a cardinal in the yard and you own the modern classic *Brown Bear, Brown Bear, What Do You See?* (see page 194), take a moment to read it together and make the connection with the red bird in it. Did an ice cream truck ring its bells to get your child out for an ice cream cone? Follow that pleasure up with *Sidewalk Trip* (see page 167), an upbeat book about that very experience.

You can also read a book and plan an activity afterward to go with it, especially as your child gets older. Such plans need not be elaborate. Many babies will happily take the lead of the charming book *Pots and Pans* (see page 166) and play on the kitchen floor with noisy pots and pans. If you garden, read *Ten Seeds* (see page 97) or *Growing Vegetable Soup* (see page 128) and plant a few simple flowers or vegetables with your child. Read *Round Is a Mooncake* (see page 258) or *What Is Round?* (see page 124), then take a trip around your home looking at shapes.

Planning is good, but so is spontaneity. At any time during the day, you could start chanting a line from a book in conjunction with what's happening or just out of the blue. "Chicka chicka boom boom. Will there be enough room?" you might ask as you put your baby into a crib, echoing the incomparable *Chicka Chicka Boom Boom* (see page 195). The nonsense lyrics from *Charlie Parker Played Be Bop* (see page 222) work anytime: "Boomba, boomba. . . . Boppity, bibbitty, bop. BANG!" If only you and your child are present, you don't need to feel self-conscious, and you'll be infusing her with a love of language that lasts a lifetime.

Introducing New Books and Rereading Familiar Ones

Aim for a balance of new and familiar books when reading aloud. Some children take eagerly to new books, while others want them introduced gradually. For those who prefer the gradual approach, you might look at the cover together one day, leaf through the book the next, add the first page, and so on, to ease into it. Very young children often find it confusing to hear a new book every day, so mix the new ones with books you know your child already likes.

As soon as your child starts to indicate which books he prefers, which will happen well before he starts speaking, try to follow his lead. If a baby wants to look over and over again at books filled with photographs of babies' faces, make sure he has a good supply. If your toddler loves a certain series, like Kipper (see page 174) or Maisy (see page 114), realize how exciting it is that he's developing preferences. Encouraging your child's excitement about certain books is a great path to building up enthusiasm about reading.

Following your child's enthusiasms naturally leads to a lot of rereading of favorites, which is not usually a problem. But sometimes a child insists on hearing the same book over and over to the exclusion of every other story. What do you do the hundredth time your child wants you to read *Green Eggs and Ham* (see page 239) and you have long since grown tired of it? Why does a child want to hear the same book over and over, even once he or she has it memorized? First, rest assured that the day will come when you won't have to read this book constantly. Then, think about the benefits repetition offers to a young child. One is the comfort of familiarity. Life as a baby and toddler is full of new experiences over which the child has little or no control. Imagine, under those circumstances, finding something you like and enjoying it again and again. That's one thing that makes rereading valuable. Another is the mastery of vocabulary and other content.

Hearing books over and over is vitally important because it gives a child the chance to understand the words and pictures completely. The first time through, everything is new and she understands only some of it, especially if it's at a challenging level. She slowly absorbs information, new vocabulary in context, and details in the illustrations, distinguishing characters and elements in the setting. Once a child understands all the content, she can revel in her sense of accomplishment and enjoy the book because she has mastered it.

The television show for preschoolers *Blue's Clues* has become popular precisely because it taps into children's need for repetition. The same episode airs for five days in a row. On the first day, young viewers can answer only a few of the questions the episode poses. By the end of the week, most viewers know all the answers and yell them out, proud of having solved the mystery. The same joy of expertise applies to books, with the additional pleasure for the child of having her parent all to herself for the duration of the reading.

Finally, some books that your child wants to hear repeatedly fill an emotional need for him that you may never understand. In any event, try to stay good-natured about requests for the same book, knowing that this, too, shall pass. At the same time, keep trying to introduce other books into the reading routine. See if you can negotiate a trade—the child's choice and then yours, expanding the repertoire without rejecting the current favorite.

Not Always as Easy as It Sounds

The idyllic vision of parent and child snuggled happily together with a book does reflect reality, but not always. What about the times when reading aloud doesn't work well? When your child won't sit still or grabs the book or turns the pages quickly to the end? What's the right response?

It's best not to insist on reading if your child definitely doesn't want to listen. You can try a few tricks, and if they don't work, plan to read another time when she's feeling more receptive. Before stopping, you could start a favorite story or a flap book or put on your most dramatic voice for a "scary" book like *A Dark, Dark Tale* (see page 96). You could read aloud to yourself, without urging your child to join you, and see if that pulls her in. Another technique some parents try, which is more powerful if used sparingly, is to incorporate your child's name into the story. Rename one of the characters with her name and see if that draws her interest.

In *The Read-Aloud Handbook*, Jim Trelease suggests a method for very reluctant listeners.[11] If he won't listen to books at all, start telling a child stories that include a character with his name. After a few days, also add a character from a book you have, such as the dog from *Where's Spot?* (see page 159). A week of this leads up to reading *Where's Spot?*, which will be all the more intriguing thanks to the earlier stories. Telling such stories is a technique to use sparingly as an entrée into books rather than a way to replace them.

11. Jim Trelease, *The Read-Aloud Handbook*, 4th ed. (New York: Penguin, 1995), 68.

But generally, if your child isn't in the mood for listening, follow her lead. The idea is to make reading a pleasure, not an obligation. Running around, playing with toys, going for walks, and the other activities your child might feel more like doing at the moment are as important as reading. In fact, reading is less effective without real-life experiences to make sense of the words—reading about "hot" and "cold," for instance, makes no sense without having experienced those sensations.

Often a baby or young toddler will seem happy you are reading yet grab at the book or turn the pages in clumps. Grabbing and throwing things has an irresistible appeal at some stages, and fighting it isn't in your best interests. One approach is to supply your child with something else to hold or throw, like a rattle. Or have two books on hand, one to give to your baby and another for you to read. If he grabs the one you have, just switch your reading to the second book.

One advantage of books for the very young, especially the ones that rhyme, is that they are so easy to memorize. You may find you know the words without even trying to remember them, which makes it easier to proceed when a book migrates from your hands into your child's. Once a child has discovered the fun of turning pages, you will often find yourself several pages ahead in a story, having skipped the ones in between. Just improvise if you don't know the words. Until the day comes when your child insists on word-for-word renditions, the text isn't sacred. Skip parts, change parts, repeat parts—it's up to you.

Just as the specific words of a book aren't sacred, neither is the physical object. Parents raised with a few, precious books may find it unsettling to watch their baby chew on a board book or their toddler turn pages roughly. But babies equate books with toys, which is good, while toddlers' fine motor skills typically aren't up to turning thin pages with care. This isn't a reason to keep books away from them. Fortunately, board books are relatively inexpensive, very durable, and can be cleaned with a damp cloth.

So you can let your child have free rein with board books and keep the more easily damaged books out of her reach if you feel strongly about torn pages. Rather than chastise your child about book care, convey a message through how you handle books yourself. Occasionally comment on how you are reaching up to the right-hand corner of the page and turning it with care. The idea will sink in over time when your child's understanding and physical skills are up to it.

Don't avoid books with flaps and tabs to pull just because they don't last long. Buy at least a few, if you can afford it, and assume they'll have a short but much-appreciated life span. You can sometimes check out flap books and pop-ups at a local library, but the selection is usually limited because the books get damaged quickly.

The Library Link

Your local library can be a valuable partner in helping you raise a child who loves books. A medium or large public library will have many of the books listed in this guide or can get them for you through a simple borrowing process. It will also have books that are older and out of print, as well as videos, music tapes, and audiobooks. Check out the parenting section, too, if your library has one. And if you can, get to know a children's librarian who can recommend promising books at each new stage in your child's life.

You can bring home a lot of books at once, new ones and ones you've checked out before. You'll probably want to keep them all in the same place, out of your child's reach when you're not reading if she's likely to tear pages or feed a book to the dog. As you read library books, you'll run across some that your child adores. If you can afford to build up a home library—children love to have their own books—using the public library will allow you to try books out before you buy them.

Many public libraries offer storytimes for babies and toddlers, which are wonderful ways to learn about new books, hear new songs and fingerplays, and meet other parents who value reading. Attending a library storytime sends your child the message that people get together socially around books, which is a lovely notion to convey. Checking out books and going to a storytime are steps in making libraries part of your child's life, a habit associated with strong readers and one that can bring a lot of pleasure over a lifetime.

Making the Choices

The last decade has brought an explosion of books for the very young. When today's parents were growing up, *their* parents had a very limited number of books to read to a child under three. Now the choices are overwhelming. In deciding on which ones to include in this guide, I chose favorites from the past, but the majority of books listed have been published since 1990. I looked for books with well-chosen words and excellent illustrations, with a careful eye toward how children develop physically, mentally, and emotionally as babies and toddlers. My goal was to give parents a wide choice of books with strong selections for every stage in a child's first three years. To that end, the guide provides more than five hundred annotations, some of which discuss more than one book, with a total of more than six hundred books.

I read or reread every book on the list as well as a few hundred that I chose not to include. I read many of them aloud to young children and consulted frequently with parents about what books their babies and toddlers liked best. I drew on my seventeen years of experience as a children's librarian in schools and public libraries and also elicited ideas from librarians, teachers, friends, and children. I searched through reference books, publishers' catalogs, and lists from libraries; browsed through bookstores and library collections; and surfed the Internet. I have included only books that were in print in either hardcover, paperback, or board book as I was doing my research, so that parents can buy copies of favorite books.

How to Use This Guide

The guide is divided into two main chapters that describe books: "Nursery Rhymes, Fingerplays, and Songs" and "Picture-Story Books for the Very Young." Each book entry contains the author, title, illustrator, publishing information, an age range, and a description. The publishing information includes the original year of publication in the United States and the publishers of whichever editions are currently in print—hardcover, paperback, board book, or all three. (Since publishing status changes rapidly, check with a bookstore for updated information if you want to buy a book.) If the book has sequels or related books, I listed those or alerted readers to the series.

In designating age ranges, I drew on advice from parents about their children's preferences, recommendations from librarians who interact with many young children and their parents, and published book reviews. These sources concur on the age range for some books like Mother Goose collections, which everyone agrees are for newborn infants through preschoolers. For other books, however, the recommendations vary enormously, usually with parents suggesting younger ages and book reviewers, older ones. Some parents start reading *Brown Bear, Brown Bear, What Do You See?* (see page 194) shortly after birth with great success, while other sources consider it a book for children aged two and older. In reviewing *There's a Cow in the Cabbage Patch* (see page 90), one respected journal pegged it at "6 months through 4 years," while another said, "2 through 6." In the face of such varied feedback, I combined my own experience with the opinions I gathered and assigned each book an age range that will work for many, but not all, children.

INTRODUCTION

Some of the parents I checked with had two-year-olds who, especially toward the end of that year, were ready for the longer, more complex books usually recommended for three- and four-year-olds. Most of these children had an affinity for books and had been read to since birth. While this guide does include many books that appeal to preschoolers, parents of such children might also like to consult my other guides—*Great Books for Girls*, *Great Books for Boys*, and *Great Books About Things Kids Love*—which have more suggestions. A short list on page 292 of this guide also points parents to series popular with preschoolers.

For the most part, the age ranges included with each annotation are open-ended, such as "18 months and up," because the book in question appeals to both toddlers and children over two. A book like *Color Zoo* (see page 126) by Lois Ehlert, for example, will amuse an eighteen-month-old with its die-cut holes and poster-bright colors but also interest a four-year-old who is ready for the complicated geometrical shapes. Many of the books labeled "2 years and up," like *Max's Dragon Shirt* (see page 270), will be satisfying for several more years, even into early elementary school. The range "6 months through 2 years" includes two-year-olds. Typically, these are books with almost no plot that are too simple for many three-year-olds.

The annotations include the phrase "Good for groups" if a book works especially well with a group of children, as recommended by librarians who conduct storytime programs. Many of these books have large pictures that can be seen well from a distance and the sort of inviting rhyme or rhythm that secures the attention of very young children. This information will be of use to librarians and child-care providers, but parents might also incorporate books like these into parties or family gatherings to entertain a group of young children.

34

Because books for the very young are sometimes published in related sets, a number of entries describe more than one book. For example, the small books *Gentle Rosie* and *Wild Rosie* (see page 208) show two sides of the same mouse girl and are more effective if read at the same time. The outstanding board books *All Fall Down*, *Clap Hands*, *Say Goodnight*, and *Tickle, Tickle* (see page 215), were all published at the same time and show the same wonderful babies in action. They are extremely short and work well read together. While any of the multiple titles can be read separately, reading them all at once adds another dimension.

The last chapter in this guide gives more ideas and resources about books for the very young and related topics. The first section, "Favorite Picks," highlights books in useful categories like "Baby Shower Gifts" and "Favorite Bedtime Books." This is followed by tips on reading aloud, suggested activities to pair with books, resources for finding musical recordings, and a list of recommended books in Spanish. Readers will also find information about locating books through bookstores and libraries; keeping up with children's book publishing; organizations and Web sites concerned with the very young; recommended reading for parents; and books for librarians who do programming for young children and their parents.

My Hopes

The most important thing, I believe, about books for ba-
bies and very young children is that they are shared be-
tween the child and a caring adult. It is a time for physical
closeness and comfort, of quiet and harmony, of sharing
ideas and emotions, laughing and learning together. The
learning and benefit that take place are not only enjoyed by
the child. Any adult who takes time to share books with
small children will be rewarded, enriched, and revitalized
by it, every time.

—JAN ORMEROD

In this quotation, Ormerod, a talented author-illustrator for young children, beautifully expresses the joys for parents of reading aloud to their young children.[12] The harmonious time together makes life better for both parent and child, while it creates a clear link in a child's mind between pleasure and books. My goal in writing this guide is to make that process easier and more enjoyable by steering parents to wonderful books.

The learning that Ormerod mentions—and pairs with laughter—takes place naturally, as I have stressed in this intro-duction. Reading aloud is not about formally teaching young children to read. A child who learns to read as a preschooler gains no advantage over a child who learns in early elemen-

---

12. Jan Ormerod, quoted in Ellin Greene, *Books, Babies, and Libraries: Serving Infants, Toddlers, Their Parents, and Caregivers* (Chicago: American Library Association, 1991), 172.

tary school, any more than a child who walks early necessarily becomes a better athlete.

I like to think of reading aloud to young children as akin to singing. Parents don't sing to babies and toddlers to teach them the basics of music. Songs are entirely for pleasure—the singer's and the listener's. I hope parents will adopt that joyful spirit for reading, too. Delight in introducing your baby to the incomparable magic of books, savor the pleasures of language and art with your toddler, and know that when you read aloud, you are sharing an experience that will change your child's life—and your own—forever.

1

Nursery Rhymes, Fingerplays, and Songs

You will want to have some of the books in this chapter on hand when your baby is born to move seamlessly into the habit of reading aloud. A collection of nursery rhymes is a must. These time-tested verses trip off the tongue, thanks to years of being polished through oral tradition. You will soon have memorized some of them—if you don't already remember some from your childhood.

Turn to nursery rhymes at any time of day. Some will come to mind at certain moments, like "One, Two, Buckle My Shoe" while slipping on booties and "Wee Willie Winkie" at bedtime. But any favorite rhyme will entertain your child, especially if you say it with enthusiasm. Since nursery rhymes are so popular with very young children, not many collections of other poems are published for this age group. *Ride a Purple Pelican* (see page 62) and *Read-Aloud Rhymes for the Very Young* (see page 62) are two exceptions that will add variety to your reading for toddlers.

The term *fingerplays* covers a host of different types of

rhymes accompanied by actions. You will find a number of collections and single versions of such action rhymes to captivate your child from birth through preschool. Many parents and grandparents will recall "This Is the Church," "Eeensy-Weensy Spider," and others, but most collections will also give you new ideas and lead to new favorites.

These books show gentle movements for you to entertain your baby by counting his fingers and toes, as in the familiar "This Little Piggy." Although they can't join in, babies like watching performances of fingerplays in which you move your fingers in conjunction with rhymes. When they get a bit bigger and sturdier, babies are ready for jogging rhymes, in which you bounce them gently on your knees to words such as "To market, to market, to buy a fat pig." You can initiate hand-clapping rhymes like "Pat-a-Cake" by moving your baby's hands before he can clap them himself.

Toddlers respond enthusiastically to all different action rhymes. They keep trying movements and eventually master them for verses like "Head, Shoulders, Knees, Toes" and "I'm a Little Teapot." Dozens of other action rhymes and fingerplays are waiting for you to try with your toddler and pre-schooler, some of which are certain to delight you both.

Songs work the same way. In this chapter, you will find soothing lullabies to incorporate into naptime and bedtime routines. Many nursery rhymes have tunes that go with them, while other folk songs like "Old MacDonald" appeal to babies, too. Most of the single versions of songs to sing to babies and toddlers have illustrations with too many details for babies, but toddlers will enjoy looking at the pictures sometimes during the song. If you are at all musical, it's great to own one of the longer collections of songs, which have simple music for piano and guitar. A good songbook will carry you from your child's birth through elementary school and beyond.

Beaton, Clare. *Mother Goose Remembers.* **2000. Hardcover: Barefoot Books. Good for groups. Ages newborn and up.**

Stunning clothwork art distinguishes this collection of nursery rhymes from the many available. Beaton combines antique fabrics, bric-a-brac, and embroidery to create textured pictures with a three-dimensional feel. Humpty Dumpty perches roundly on a wall of stitched brown bricks, above yellow-and-green flowers that incorporate buttons into their design. The Queen of Hearts glows in her red felt dress and yellow crown, surrounded by a cunning border of hearts and dots. Even the first lines of the nursery rhymes are made from stitches. Forty-six rhymes, most of them familiar, provide just the right playful subject for the wonderful art.

Bedtime/Playtime. **1999. Board book: Candlewick. Ages 3 months and up.**

These unusual board book anthologies bring together several stories and rhymes for very young children, with a variety of authors and illustrators. Both include a nursery rhyme illustrated by Rosemary Wells and a double-page spread by Catherine and Laurence Anholt with labeled pictures. *Bedtime* has five other short poems and stories, ending with a bedtime poem illustrated by Marc Brown. *Playtime* leans toward livelier rhymes that children can act out, such as "Heads and Shoulders, Knees and Toes." This provides a good introduction to some fine illustrators for the young, which could lead you to more of their books.

Benjamin, Floella, collector. *Skip across the Ocean: Nursery Rhymes from around the World.* **Illustrated by Sheila Moxley. 1995. Hardcover: Orchard. Ages newborn and up.**

If you are looking to expand beyond the usual repertoire of nursery rhymes, here is an intriguing collection of thirty-two poems from around the world. Many are printed in their original language and English, and some provide directions for movements to go with the rhymes. The choices come from Poland, Puerto Rico, Sri Lanka, Sweden, and Nigeria, among other places. A rich palette characterizes the illustrations, which expand the international settings and characters. An attractive gift for new parents with a global outlook.

Brown, Marc. *Finger Rhymes*. 1980. Hardcover: Dutton. Paperback: Puffin. Good for groups. Ages newborn and up.

The author-illustrator of the well-known Arthur and D.W. books provides a service to parents in this and his other action rhyme books, listed below. Each double-page spread, illustrated with attractive black-and-white pictures, spells out a rhyme to say to young children while performing hand movements. Small boxes by each line of the verse show the hand movements and when to do them. Some of the fingerplays may be known to parents although perhaps only vaguely remembered, such as "The Eensy, Weensy Spider," "Five Little Pigs," and "Where Is Thumbkin?" Others will probably be unfamiliar. Try them out and see what amuses your child. As the child gets older, he or she will start imitating your hand movements and joining in the rhymes. These simple activities provide wonderful ways to interact with babies while exposing them to the pleasures of rhythmical language, invaluable for child-care providers as well as parents and grandparents. *Party Rhymes*, now out of print, looks similar but gives words and music for simple folk songs like "Skip to My Lou" and "The Muffin Man."

Brown, Marc. *Hand Rhymes*. 1985. Hardcover: Dutton. Paperback: Puffin. Good for groups. Ages newborn and up.

Like *Finger Rhymes* above, this helpful book introduces

fourteen fingerplays to entertain young children. Again, each double-page spread, illustrated here with tidy colored pictures, spells out a rhyme to say to young children while performing hand movements. Small boxes by each line of the verse show the hand movements and when to do them. Parents and other adults may recognize the rhymes that open "This is the church" and "Two little monkeys fighting in the bed," but most will probably be new. Pick and choose among them to see what suits your child, who may join in the words and movements as a toddler. Not only do these little games entertain children one-on-one, but they are indispensable for working with groups of young children, guaranteed to catch the attention even of restless ones.

Brown, Marc. *Play Rhymes*. 1987. Paperback: Puffin. Good for groups. Ages newborn and up.

Like *Finger Rhymes* and *Hand Rhymes*, described above, this collection of rhymes includes small boxed pictures to illustrate movements that go with the verses. Unlike the previous two books, the movements go beyond hands to include the whole body. The illustrations, which are more inventive than in the earlier books, are too detailed for the very young, but parents will enjoy their humor and coziness. Several of the rhymes can be sung, with simple music provided at the back of the book, including "The Noble Duke of York," "Do Your Ears Hang Low?" and "Wheels on the Bus." This collection can lead to hours of playtime for parent and child over a number of years. Those who work with groups of children will also find it a real asset.

Calmenson, Stephanie. *Good for You: Toddler Rhymes for Toddler Times*. Illustrated by Melissa Sweet. 2001. Hardcover: HarperCollins. Good for groups. Ages 18 months and up.

An appealing collection of rhymes addresses daily life for

young children from the potty to the playground, from blocks to bedtime. Eye-catching illustrations in a kaleidoscope of colors show a multicultural array of little kids having a good time. In the poem "First Things," for example, a boy admires his first haircut, a girl holds up her first toothbrush, while another shows her first letter, from her grandmother. The verses rely on lots of lively word sounds, like "bumpity, bumpity" in a poem about a bus and "Tumble! Rumble! Blocks in a jumble!" Some short poems provide simple riddles to guess, with clues in the pictures. This is a book you and your child will want to browse in rather than read from cover to cover.

Carter, David A. *If You're Happy and You Know It, Clap Your Hands: A Pop-Up Book.* **1997. Hardcover: Scholastic. Ages 12 months and up.**

In this variation on the popular folk song, the lyrics and pop-up illustrations introduce new actions for children to imitate. The first line is the traditional "If you're happy and you know it, clap your hands." When you pull on a tab, a smiling cat claps her hands. The next instruction, to "wag your tail," shows a dog whose tail wags when the tab is pulled. A skunk pats its head, a chicken flaps its wings, an owl winks its eye, and a mouse touches its toes before the final picture, where all the animals pop up in a group and "shout hooray." Well-constructed pop-ups with movements that invite listeners to participate make this an excellent choice for groups or individuals. Also try Carter's *Old MacDonald Had a Farm*, which has a similar pop-up and tab format.

Chorao, Kay. *Knock at the Door and Other Baby Action Rhymes.* **1999. Hardcover: Dutton. Ages newborn and up.**

Flowery illustrations fill each page of this useful collection of fingerplays and bouncing games. The twenty action rhymes, wonderful for entertaining the very young, range from well-known examples like "This Little Piggy" and "Pat-a-Cake" to the lesser-known "Here's a Ball for Baby" and "Bunnies' Bedtime." Nicely displayed, the verses appear in large type, with a small box next to each line that shows the finger movements or ways to bounce the baby on your knees. Some suggest easy movements for the child, such as clapping or covering eyes. Others, for younger children, are carried out by the adult, such as "Slowly, Slowly," where you creep your hand—"a little mousie"—up your baby's arm to tickle under the neck. The illustrations are too detailed for very young children but will appeal to toddlers and adults who lean toward pastels and coziness.

Cole, Joanna, and Stephanie Calmenson, compilers. *Pat-a-Cake and Other Play Rhymes.* **Illustrated by Alan Tiegreen. 1992. Paperback: Mulberry. Good for groups. Ages newborn and up.**

This valuable resource for parents and educators brings together a lot of fingerplays and other interactive rhymes. It's divided into six sections: "Finger-and-Hand Rhymes," "Toe-and-Foot Rhymes," "Face Rhymes," "Tickling Rhymes," "Knee-and-Foot Riding Rhymes," and "Dancing Rhymes." For each of the thirty rhymes, a series of pictures shows an adult interacting with a young child, with a line from the rhyme under each illustration. Extra instructions use arrows to offer more details on how to move hands, feet, and the rest. Some rhymes will be familiar, such as "Pat-a-Cake" and "This Little Piggy"; many will probably be new. The black-and-white illustrations are functional although not outstanding. For a similar book geared more to toddlers and older, look for *Eentsy, Weentsy Spider: Fingerplays and Action Rhymes,* by the same compilers.

Cony, Frances. *Old MacDonald Had a Farm.* **Illustrated by Iain Smyth. 1999. Hardcover: Orchard. Ages 12 months and up.**

Jovial, cartoonish animals and a farmer smile out from the cover of this entertaining book, which uses flaps, tabs, and pop-ups in its ten pages. The familiar song diverges from the traditional mainly by adding a tractor "with a chug-chug here and a chug-chug there" to the list of noisemakers. As the song goes on, a flock of sheep pops up from a double-page spread, a tab makes a line of pigs' heads move, and another moves cows' eyes in a comical way. The final spread pops up to show all the animals around the tractor. This old song endures as a popular one with children because of its animal sounds and "e-i-e-i-o" refrain. The movable features in this version add to the fun.

Cousins, Lucy. *Humpty Dumpty and Other Nursery Rhymes/ Jack and Jill and Other Nursery Rhymes/Little Miss Muffet and Other Nursery Rhymes/Wee Willie Winkie and Other Nursery Rhymes.* **1996/1997. Board book: Dutton. Ages newborn and up.**

Illustrated with the bright, thick paints that resemble children's art, these four board books each bring together fourteen pages of nursery rhymes. Figures outlined with black and set against solid backgrounds illustrate the rhymes without unnecessary details. "Jack be nimble, / Jack be quick, / Jack jump over / The candlestick" uses a simple white candle in a red holder, with blue and yellow panels behind it. The pages vary in design, and the nursery rhymes, most of which will be familiar to many parents, range from four lines to twelve. This set serves as a good way to introduce nursery rhymes, with sturdy cardboard pages and pictures that babies can enjoy.

Delacre, Lulu. *Arroz con leche: Popular Songs and Rhymes from Latin America.* **1989. Hardcover: Scholastic. Good for groups. Ages 12 months and up.**

If you are looking for Spanish songs and rhymes for your child, try this cheerful book, even though only a handful of these songs and rhymes are specifically for very young children. It gathers songs, rhymes, and singing games from Latin America, given in Spanish with the English translation, and provides music for most of them. Several give directions for adding movement when using with infants. Once your child is a preschooler, the singing games can be added to the repertoire. Illustrations in pastel colors accompany every rhyme. Not everyone likes the cassette that can be bought with the book, but the book itself does a nice job of sharing traditional folklore.

dePaola, Tomie. *Tomie dePaola's Mother Goose.* **1985. Hardcover: Putnam. Ages newborn and up.**

If you like Tomie dePaola's tidy illustrations, as many do, this is a wonderful Mother Goose collection to give as a present or own yourself. The illustrator drew mainly on classic versions of the nursery rhymes, as collected by folklorists Peter and Iona Opie. Like other collections that stick to the originals, this one includes the woman in the shoe whipping her children and Tom the Piper's son getting beaten. The large, beautifully designed book offers more than two hundred rhymes, each illustrated in delicious colors, with coziness and humor. One of many fine Mother Goose books for a child's first exposure to poetry.

Dunn, Opal. *Hippety-Hop, Hippety-Hay: Growing with Rhymes from Birth to Age Three.* **Illustrated by Sally Anne Lambert. 1999. Hardcover: Henry Holt. Good for groups. Ages newborn and up.**

This outstanding collection sets out to teach and reassure new parents about talking with their babies. Dunn, an expert on early childhood language, has assembled a group of rhymes good for interaction and participation. She divides them by age group—two to twelve months, twelve to twenty-four months, and twenty-four to thirty-six months—with useful advice at the beginning of each chapter about what children are capable of doing at different ages in terms of listening and language acquisition. Many of the dozens of well-chosen rhymes, illustrated by amusing watercolors, have instructions about accompanying movements, and the last two pages include music for several of them. A terrific gift, especially for parents who haven't spent a lot of time around babies and toddlers. Also excellent for child-care providers.

Dyer, Jane. *Animal Crackers: A Delectable Collection of Pictures, Poems, and Lullabies for the Very Young.* **1996. Hardcover: Little, Brown. Ages newborn and up.**

Jane Dyer's wonderful senses of color and pattern infuse this lovely collection of poems, songs, and nursery rhymes. The large book has charming watercolors on every page of children, adults, and animals, cozy things and places. Grouped by topic, the verses touch on seasons, food, animals, and bedtime, with a section of nursery rhymes and another of action rhymes. As a resource, this will endure from early years, when babies will enjoy hearing the nursery rhymes and bedtime poems, through toddler years, with more poems and action rhymes. An excellent book to give as a gift or add to your home collection. Dyer has also created three attractive board books with material from this collection; each is titled *Animal Crackers*, with subtitles of *Nursery Rhymes*, *Bedtime*, and *Animal Friends*.

Emerson, Sally. Music arranged by Mary Frank. *The King-fisher Nursery Rhyme Songbook*. Illustrated by Colin and Moira Maclean. 1992. Paperback: Kingfisher. Good for groups. Ages newborn and up.

Here is one of the few books that offer a wide collection of songs to sing to your baby and to teach your toddler. A British import, it brings together more than forty songs, some familiar and some not, with piano music and guitar chords. It opens with fingerplays and action rhymes to sing, such as "Row, Row, Row Your Boat," "Duke of York," and "Wheels on the Bus." Then come musical versions of nursery rhymes and popular folk songs, including "Sing a Song of Sixpence" and "Pop Goes the Weasel." The final ten songs are lullabies. Cute watercolor illustrations add color to the pages of this book, which will be useful at home and in child-care centers.

Griego, Margot C., et al. *Tortillitas para Mamá: And Other Nursery Rhymes, Spanish and English*. Illustrated by Barbara Cooney. 1981. Hardcover: Henry Holt. Paperback: Henry Holt. Good for groups. Ages newborn and up.

Lovely paintings by Caldecott Medal–winning artist Barbara Cooney grace this collection of traditional rhymes. Collected from the Spanish community in the Americas, as the introduction explains, these are presented in their native Spanish and translated into English. Notes with some describe hand gestures to add. The verses can be chanted to babies with the gestures, while toddlers can join in the words and movements. As with Mother Goose rhymes, a few of these may bother some parents. In one, a girl will be beaten if she soils her dress; in another, the father gets the good tortillas and the mother gets the burned ones. An attractive collection drawn from oral tradition.

Hague, Michael. *Mother Goose: A Collection of Classic Nursery Rhymes*. 1984. Hardcover: Henry Holt. Ages newborn and up.

While the characteristic Michael Hague illustrations have too many details for a very young child, many parents will find them a treat to look at as they read to their baby. For those who like his style, this also makes a fine gift book. It contains many well-known nursery rhymes that adults will recall from their own childhood, such as those starting with the phrases "Jack be nimble," "Jack and Jill," "Rub-a-dub-dub," "Hickory dickory dock," "Humpty Dumpty," and many more. Not toned down, the old woman in the shoe still whips her children and the farmer's wife cuts off the mice's tails. Children and animals in old-fashioned dress illustrate the rhymes, mostly in half-page pictures. A solid collection for Hague fans.

Hague, Michael. *Teddy Bear, Teddy Bear*. 1997. Board book: Morrow. Ages 12 months and up.

This classic jump rope rhyme becomes an activity for the young to do as shown by a furry little bear. With Hague's typical pretty watercolors, this creates a homespun little world in which the bear demonstrates various movements, starting with "Teddy Bear, Teddy Bear, turn around" and ending with "Teddy Bear, Teddy Bear, say good night." In between, his mother chides him in the pictures for dragging in mud and later tucks him gently into bed. First published as a larger hardcover book, this is now available only as a small board book. Adults working with groups of children can look for a library copy of the larger book to read aloud and get children moving along with the rhyme.

Hale, Sarah Josepha. *Mary Had a Little Lamb*. Photographs by Bruce McMillan. 1990. Paperback: Scholastic. Good for groups. Ages 12 months and up.

Fine photographs update the story of a little girl whose lamb follows her to school. In colorful shots, an African American girl, who incidentally wears glasses, cuddles a darling white lamb. The setting is a one-room schoolhouse in the country, complete with an old-fashioned bell. The rhyme sticks to the traditional one many parents will already know, while a note at the back gives the history of the poem and some information about how reading was taught in the past. A particularly thoughtful and attractive way to change our perception of a well-known poem.

Hillenbrand, Will. *Down by the Station*. 1999. Hardcover: Harcourt. Ages 18 months and up.

If you aren't familiar with this old song, start at the back of the book, where there's a simple version of the music. "Down by the station early in the morning. See the little puffer-bellies all in a row," it starts off. In the pictures, which create a story not told in the song, a young woman boards the train, where a driver starts up the intriguing engine, a colorful vehicle with a smiling steam whistle. "Puff, puff / Toot, toot, / Off we go!" The book's wide format allows the train to stretch out as it heads to pick up its first passenger, a baby elephant. The "puff, puff" refrain adds verses as one baby animal after another boards the train on its way to a children's zoo. Your child will soon be humming, if not singing, along with you.

Ho, Minfong. *Hush: A Thai Lullaby*. Illustrated by Holly Meade. 1996. Hardcover: Orchard. Paperback: Orchard. Ages 2 years and up.

Striking illustrations of cut-paper collage enhance this Thai lullaby. In lyrical language, a young mother admonishes a series of animals, telling them to "Hush!" because her baby is sleeping. What readers will notice, which the mother doesn't, is that the child awakens and starts to crawl out of the hammock. Humorous touches fill the pictures, such as the mother trying to catch a frog and holding her nose as she scolds the pigs. The sounds each animal makes will captivate young listeners—the frog's "Op-Op, Op-Op" and the pig's "Uut-Uut, Uut-Uut." Meanwhile, the child crawls back into the hammock, and finally the mother herself falls asleep. A delightful book from a writer who grew up in Thailand and is a talented illustrator.

Hort, Lenny. *The Seals on the Bus*. Illustrated by G. Brian Karas. 2000. Hardcover: Henry Holt. Good for groups. Ages newborn and up.

Here's one to sing to your baby and share the pictures with your toddler. Sung to the tune of the familiar "Wheels on a Bus," these lyrics incorporate animal sounds as a bus stops and picks up animal after animal, to the surprise of a family on board. The seals, tigers, geese, monkeys, snakes, sheep, and skunks all make noise—"The seals on the bus go errp, errp, errp"—while the rabbits go "up and down," for a little variation. Soon the bus is crowded with frolicking creatures in the zany illustrations, and the bus pulls in at a festival for everyone, human and animal, to enjoy. A song version that lends itself to hamming it up and adding more animal noises to the rhythmic, repetitive verses.

Hush, Little Baby. Illustrated by Shari Halpern. 1997. Hardcover: North-South Books. Ages newborn and up.

Delightful mixed-media collages of cut paper and cloth adorn this traditional folk song, familiar to many, that begins, "Hush, little baby, don't say a word, Mama's going to buy you a mockingbird." The book's unvarying pattern presents a small picture and the words on the left, opposite a square illustration bordered like a quilt, with a picture of the child and a gift mentioned in the song. The lively pictures move toward bedtime, with the final scene of the mother and child in a rocking chair. Piano music with guitar chords appears on the last two pages of this nicely designed book.

Jaramillo, Nelly Palacio. *Grandmother's Nursery Rhymes/ Las nanas de Abuelita.* Illustrated by Elivia. 1994. Paperback: Henry Holt. Good for groups. Ages newborn and up.

With the subtitle "Lullabies, Tongue Twisters, and Riddles from South America," this attractive volume pairs jaunty Spanish verses with their English translations. Like other nursery rhymes, these can be read aloud—in English or Spanish— to infants, who will enjoy the sounds well before they will appreciate the meaning. The riddles, which read like short poems, also work as short poems, although they are too difficult for young ones to solve yet. The flowing, impressionistic watercolors add form and color without overwhelming the nursery rhymes. A fine collection, especially welcomed by parents who speak Spanish.

Keats, Ezra Jack. *Over in the Meadow.* 1971. Hardcover: Viking. Paperback: Viking. Good for groups. Ages 18 months and up.

This folk counting rhyme, collected in Appalachia in the 1800s, has the polished rhythm of oral tradition. "Over in the meadow, in the sand, in the sun, / Lived an old mother turtle and her little turtle one," it begins, illustrated with pleasing collages that combine paint and cut handmade paper. The second set of animals shown, fish, have two little ones, while the bluebird has three. Each group of young ones gets an instruction from the mother. With the muskrats, the rhyme proceeds, " 'Dive!' said the mother. / 'We dive,' said the four. / So they dived and they burrowed, / In the reeds on the shore." The numbers go up to ten, ending with fireflies glowing against the night. Although young children won't understand all the words, the sounds will beguile them and the pictures are quite beautiful.

Kenyon, Tony. *Pat-a-Cake*. 1998. Board book: Candlewick. Ages newborn and up.

This board book supplies illustrations that add action and characters to the well-known hand rhyme "Pat-a-Cake." In old-fashioned pictures, a little girl requests a cake from a baker clad in a white jacket and hat. Her hands demonstrate the actions to the rhyme while he mixes up ingredients and puts the cake in the pan and oven. For a moment, the girl looks disconcerted when the word *baby* summons up an infant crawling into the room, but the final picture shows the girl and baby happily sharing the cake, much of it on the baby's head. Not necessary for enjoying the rhyme, but this bright little book adds to the fun.

Kirk, Daniel. *Hush, Little Alien*. 1999. Hardcover: Hyperion. Board book: Hyperion. Good for groups. Ages 12 months and up.

If you prefer retro to cozy, you'll enjoy this snappy adaptation of the traditional lullaby "Hush, Little Baby." Instead of buying his baby a mockingbird, this green-skinned space alien is going to catch a "goonie bird." If the bird doesn't sing, the alien father has lots of possible gifts for the baby—a shooting star, an astronaut, a satellite, and a laser beam. The amusing illustrations use rounded shapes and glossy colors with an airbrushed look to them. Outer-space fans will especially love this unusual but warm song about a father's love for his baby. No music is given, but the text reads well as a rhyme, too.

Lamont, Priscilla. *Playtime Rhymes*. 1998. Hardcover: DK. Paperback: DK. Good for groups. Ages newborn and up.

This British import offers old favorites and some new fingerplays to amuse babies and toddlers. "This Little Pig Went to Market" and "Itsy-Bitsy Spider" are well known to many, whereas "There's a Wide-Eyed Owl" and "Two Little Men in a Flying Saucer" may not be. The pages combine large typeface, sprightly watercolor illustrations, and small photographs demonstrating the actions that accompany the rhymes. The photos, which are quite effective in conveying the movements, show children and parents from different ethnic groups and include infants and toddlers. The pen-and-watercolor pictures add humor and color; unlike the photographs, they show mainly white characters. A useful guide in an attractive package.

Lear, Edward. *The Owl and the Pussycat*. Illustrated by Jan Brett. 1991. Hardcover: Putnam. Paperback: Putnam. Board book: Putnam. Good for groups. Ages 12 months and up.

Jan Brett places this famous poem in a Caribbean setting that suits her ornate illustration style. Lear's words are a joy to read aloud, with a compelling rhythm that will appeal to children too young to appreciate the pictures. The poem tells the story of an owl and a pussycat who sail away "for a year and a day." They get married by a turkey, having obtained a ring from the nose of a pig, who was willing to sell it for one shilling. Brett dresses her characters in colorful island clothing and adds lush vegetation to the land and colorful fish to the sea in this popular version of a well-loved poem. Read this in the full size, not board book, or you will miss the cunning details in the pictures.

Linch, Tanya. *Three Little Kittens.* **2001. Hardcover: Sterling. Ages 18 months and up.**

Chunky, wide-eyed kittens look guilty as they confess to having lost their mittens in this traditional nursery rhyme, familiar to many parents from their own childhood. The mother cat, clad in a pink-and-white apron, looks quite annoyed and dishes up the well-known punishment, "You shall have no pie!" The loss of pie provides the incentive for the three kittens, each one smaller than the next, to figure out just where they left their mittens. Eating the pie with mittens on leads to washing them and putting their busy mother in a good mood once again. An old-fashioned lesson updated with bright pictures, pretty borders, and a little mouse enjoying all the action.

Lobel, Arnold, selector and illustrator. *The Arnold Lobel Book of Mother Goose.* **1997 reissued edition. Hardcover: Random House. Ages newborn and up.**

Outstanding illustrator Arnold Lobel has compiled and illustrated more than three hundred nursery rhymes, some well known, others more obscure. His delightful pencil-and-watercolor pictures amplify every rhyme, adding personality and humor, with animals and humans in old-fashioned clothing who act out the verses. The nursery rhymes are grouped loosely by themes, such as love, weather, journeys, and the like.

Published previously as *The Random House Book of Mother Goose*, this wonderful collection is bound to become a family favorite and makes an excellent gift at a baby shower.

Long, Sylvia. *Hush Little Baby*. 1997. Hardcover: Chronicle. Board book: Chronicle. Ages newborn and up.

As Sylvia Long explains in an opening note, she was always bothered by the traditional words to "Hush, Little Baby," because they describe buying a series of items to quiet a baby. She has rewritten the words to celebrate the natural world and illustrated them with pictures of a mother and baby rabbit dressed like humans. Standing on a porch, the mother cradles the baby in her arms and says, "Hush, little baby, don't say a word, / Mama's going to show you a hummingbird," replacing the original line about buying a mockingbird. If the hummingbird flies away, the mother will show the baby the evening sky, spread out in glorious sunset colors. She also offers crickets, shooting stars, a lightning bug, and a harvest moon. The pen-and-watercolor illustrations will appeal to those who like pictures ornamented with details. No music is included, but many adults may already know the tune, and the words also read like a poem.

Long, Sylvia. *Sylvia Long's Mother Goose*. 1999. Hardcover: Chronicle. Ages newborn and up.

Familiar nursery rhymes get new life in Sylvia Long's cozy vision, in which mice wear pinafores and sheep have picnics. Each poem is set on a different page, with lots to study in the picture that surrounds it. Adults will enjoy the artwork while reading aloud to infants, and toddlers will enjoy it on their own as well. Long brings together seventy-five rhymes, only altering the old woman in the shoe, who now kisses her children instead of whipping them. A lovely book to give as a present or keep for your child's own collection.

Long, Sylvia. *Twinkle, Twinkle, Little Star: A Traditional Lullaby.* **2001. Hardcover: Chronicle. Ages 12 months and up.**

The traditional song extends beyond the first, well-known lines in this bedtime book. Sylvia Long creates her characteristic pictures with animals in clothes, in a homey setting with old-fashioned touches. A lamplighter is making his rounds as a group of assorted animal children watch the sunset from a hill and then return to their village. Parents welcome the youngsters home, feed, bathe, and tuck them into bed to the rhythms of the rhyming lines. A bedtime book with a lot to look at and a soothing sound.

Manning, Jane. *My First Baby Games.* **2001. Board book: HarperCollins. Ages newborn and up.**

This handy little board book offers seven time-tested rhymes perfect for chanting to infants while performing the matching movements. "This Little Piggy" and "Pat-a-Cake" may be remembered from many childhoods, while "Jeremiah, Blow the Fire" and "Slowly, Slowly" may not. The actions range from pointing to the baby's eyes, ears, nose, and other features in "Eye Winker, Tom Tinker" to rocking the baby and lifting him or her in the air in "Mix a Pancake." The pleasant pictures, which illustrate some of the movements, show pairs of adults and babies from different ethnic groups, all smiling as they interact. A good introduction to how to play with a baby using language and simple, gentle actions.

Manning, Jane. *My First Songs.* **1998. Hardcover: Harper-Collins. Ages newborn and up.**

This book serves as a handy reminder to have on hand for parents who heard these folk songs in their own childhood and may have forgotten the words. Since it doesn't provide the music, it will only work for those who remember the tunes to "Old MacDonald," "The Eentsy, Weentsy Spider," "Row, Row, Row Your Boat," "London Bridge," and a few more. The design sets the words on the right-hand page and a colorful picture on the left, using a multicultural cast of children and adults. A useful, simple gift for new parents.

Manning, Jane. *This Little Piggy.* **1997. Hardcover: Harper-Collins. Ages 6 months and up.**

Sure, it's gimmicky to have a book shaped like a foot, but it's also a lot of fun. In this rendition of the well-known nursery rhyme, each foot-shaped page has a verse on the left-hand foot and a picture on the right side. For each foot, one of the toes bends down. For the final toe, the pinkie toe who cried "Wee, wee, wee" all the way home, the toe pulls out like a tab and the piggy leaps off the page toward a little pop-up house. A pop-up book for the very young that delights babies and fascinates toddlers.

Marshall, James. *Old Mother Hubbard and Her Wonderful Dog.* **1991. Paperback: Farrar, Straus & Giroux. Good for groups. Ages 6 months and up.**

Babies like this for the sound, toddlers will find a lot to look at and join in phrases, and parents will notice hilarious details in the pictures that only an adult will appreciate. The incomparable James Marshall creates a dog like no other, with a deadpan expression, witty side remarks in balloons, and a remarkable wardrobe. Each verse comes to life with the old woman and dog in different costumes from the Wild West and the flapper era, among other settings. Chickens and mice pop up in many of the pictures, voicing their astonishment about a dog who can stand on his head, play the flute, and ride a goat. An original, colorful interpretation of a jaunty rhyme, not to be missed.

Opie, Iona. *Humpty Dumpty and Other Rhymes/Little Boy Blue and Other Rhymes/Pussycat Pussycat and Other Rhymes/ Wee Willie Winkie and Other Rhymes.* **Illustrated by Rosemary Wells. 1997/2001. Board book: Candlewick. Ages newborn and up.**

While the large Mother Goose collections created by Opie and Wells are stunning, and their size enhances the illustrations, parents may also like to have these smaller, more easily handled board books, which draw from the collections. Each presents eight nursery rhymes with smaller, although charming, illustrations that won't be as easy for little children to appreciate. However, for reading aloud, these work well and fit small hands much better. Many of the rhymes are familiar and well loved; some are less familiar but stand out for their wordplay. The colors are delicious, and the small, plump animals that people the books are irresistible.

Opie, Iona, editor. *My Very First Mother Goose.* **Illustrated by Rosemary Wells. 1996. Hardcover: Candlewick. Ages newborn and up.**

For this gem among Mother Goose books, noted British folklorist Iona Opie has chosen more than sixty familiar and lesser-known Mother Goose rhymes. In an oversize format, with large print, charming watercolors illustrate the verses. Rosemary Wells's characteristic endearing rabbits mingle with well-dressed pigs, cats, and plump people. She gives new images to old poems, such as rabbits in an old-fashioned roadster who are driving an urbane pig for the rhyme "To market, to market, to buy a fat pig." Everything about this large book is amusing or cozy. Young children will want to hear it and look at it again and again. A top-notch baby gift, but sure to please toddlers, too. The companion volume *Here Comes Mother Goose* is also delightful.

Orozco, José-Luis. *De colores and Other Latin-American Folk Songs for Children.* Illustrated by Elisa Kleven. 1994. Hardcover: Dutton. Good for groups. Ages 2 years and up.

If you are looking for Spanish songs to sing to your child, this collection is a treasure-house. Orozco, who was raised in Mexico and has traveled around the world as a performer, drew on his own family's songs and those he learned on his travels. He presents them with simple piano music and guitar chords, with the words in Spanish and English. The twenty-seven tunes start with a morning song and end with a lullaby, with lots of songs about animals and other high-interest topics in between. Pleasing borders grace every page, while wonderful frequent full-page collage illustrations make this a very attractive book. A welcome addition to Spanish material available for the young.

Orozco, José-Luis. *Diez deditos: Ten Little Fingers & Other Play Rhymes and Action Songs from Latin America.* Illustrated by Elisa Kleven. 1997. Hardcover: Dutton. Paperback: Puffin. Good for groups. Ages 2 years and up.

Singer Orozco has brought together more than thirty fingerplays and action songs from his own childhood and his travels in Latin America. Most have small boxes that show the movements for the rhymes or songs, which are given in Spanish and English. A few of the songs have a paragraph of instruction about the movements. The choices alternate between fingerplays and songs, with music provided and guitar chords indicated for the songs. Enchanting collage illustrations full of strong colors and patterns lift this above most fingerplay and song books. A lively compilation for inspiring kids to sway, clap, and chant along, the songs are also available on a CD by Orozco.

Paxton, Tom. *Going to the Zoo.* **Illustrated by Karen Lee Schmidt. 1996. Hardcover: Morrow. Good for groups. Ages 15 months and up.**

If you don't know this toe-tapping tune, you'll want to add it to the songs you sing with your child. "Daddy's taking us to the zoo tomorrow, zoo tomorrow, zoo tomorrow. Daddy's taking us to the zoo tomorrow. We can stay all day." The appealing topic gets an energetic interpretation in comical pictures about a father and his three children at the zoo. The antics of the animals and a goofy-looking female zookeeper make the scenes lively, in keeping with the upbeat song. With easy piano music and guitar chords on the endpapers, you'll be able to learn this and soon have young ones singing along.

Peek, Merle, adapter. *Mary Wore Her Red Dress and Henry Wore His Green Sneakers.* **1985. Hardcover: Houghton. Paperback: Houghton. Good for groups. Ages 18 months and up.**

"Mary wore her red dress, red dress, red dress. Mary wore her red dress all day long." So starts this song, which works equally well as a chant. The name, color, and clothing item change from verse to verse, but the mesmerizing rhythm remains the same. Henry wore his green sneakers, Katy wore her yellow sweater, Ben wore his blue jeans—all day long. The cheerful but not outstanding pictures show different animals dressing and acting like humans, gathering for a birthday party. The text appears in boxes filled with the color that the words mention. After the story, a simple version of the music appears along with an author's note suggesting other ways to play with these verses. Although the pictures won't appeal to the very young, turn the rhyming scheme into verses using your child's name and watch his or her face light up.

Prelutsky, Jack. *Read-Aloud Rhymes for the Very Young.* **Illustrated by Marc Brown. 1986. Hardcover: Knopf. Ages 18 months and up.**

If you are ready to add other short poems to your Mother Goose routine, here is a large, well-illustrated collection to dip into. While the vocabulary will be above a toddler's head, the sounds and rhythms will make up for that. The pictures by the illustrator of the popular Arthur and D.W. books will also satisfy young children while helping them follow the action in the verses. More than two hundred poems, many from popular children's poets, are loosely arranged by well-chosen topics, such as teddy bears, holidays, food, and more. This attractive volume makes a wonderful gift that will be opened again and again.

Prelutsky, Jack. *Ride a Purple Pelican.* **Illustrated by Garth Williams. 1985. Hardcover: Morrow. Paperback: Mulberry. Good for groups. Ages 12 months and up.**

In this attractive collection, popular children's poet Jack Prelutsky has crafted short poems with the polish and appeal of nursery rhymes. He infuses the verses with bouncing rhythms and wonderful words to amuse child and adult alike. Even though children won't recognize many of the words, they will enjoy the music of the language. The poems are set in large typeface against a white page, with a picture on the opposite page by Garth Williams, known for illustrating *Charlotte's Web* and the Little House books. The illustrations, which combine black line drawings with oil paintings, incorporate different animals. A welcome addition to the home library, as is its companion volume *Beneath a Blue Umbrella*.

Raffi. *Down by the Bay*. Illustrated by Nadine Bernard West-cott. 1987. Paperback: Crown. Board book: Crown. Good for groups. Ages newborn and up.

You can start singing this catchy tune to your infant and keep singing it as the years go on. Both the words and the pictures, when your child is old enough to appreciate the visual details, are highly entertaining. Very simple music, including guitar chords, appears on the final page. The whimsical watercolors show a boy and girl eating watermelon together in view of a bay of water. They share their humorous concern that if they go home, their mothers will ask them absurd questions, such as, "Did you ever see a goose kissing a moose, down by the bay?" Westcott excels at drawing expressive, funny creatures, which are in full force in this tune: "Did you ever see a bear combing his hair, down by the bay?" The song lends itself to making up new lines, so feel free to improvise and have a good time. You might also want to get the recording by Raffi and sing along with that.

Raffi. *Raffi Children's Favorites*. 1993. Paperback: Homeland Publishing. Good for groups. Ages newborn and up.

If you can read music, play piano, or strum easy guitar chords, this large paperback collection is a gold mine of songs to sing to and with your child. The well-known children's entertainer Raffi has written or adapted more than fifty songs that kids love. From the traditional "The More We Get Together" and "This Little Light of Mine" to songs Raffi has made popular like "Baby Beluga" and "Willoughby, Wallaby, Woo," there's something for everyone who likes to sing. The collection will expand your choices of what to sing to your baby and provide great songs to teach to your toddler. An excellent resource for child-care providers, too.

Roll Over: A Counting Song. Illustrated by Merle Peek. 1981. Hardcover: Clarion. Paperback: Clarion. Board book: Clarion. Good for groups. Ages newborn and up.

This song, a favorite for older children to sing on their own, will also entertain infants with its rhythm and repetition. It begins, "10 in the bed and the little one said, 'Roll over! Roll over!' They all rolled over and one fell out," moving on each time to the next lower number. The cozy illustrations, in blues and yellows, show a child in bed, crowded on each side by animals. The animals fall out of the low bed one by one and find other places in the room to sleep. The monkey sleeps on a bench, the bear on a rug, and the parrot on a chair. When the child has the whole bed at last, the illustrations show the animals painted on a frieze on the bedroom walls. Music including guitar chords appears on the last page, if you don't know this one from your childhood.

Schwartz, Amy. Old MacDonald. 1999. Hardcover: Scholastic. Good for groups. Ages newborn and up.

Why not sing this old favorite to your baby and later introduce the large, charming illustrations? The music, which appears on the last page, is infectious, and your child will love the repetition and sounds. The gouache illustrations show a friendly farmer and his capable, enthusiastic daughter performing their farm chores, then going on a picnic with mother and baby. They encounter animals galore: rooster, cats, chicks, cow, sheep, ducks, horse, goat, pigs, and dogs, with extra noise coming from a tractor and the "yakkity yak" of neighbors.

Seeger, Laura Vaccaro. I Had a Rooster: A Traditional Folk Song. 2001. Hardcover: Viking. Good for groups. Ages 2 years and up.

Here is a catchy folk song to add to your favorites, with

lively illustrations and a CD of Pete Seeger's rendition. The spiral-bound book uses a clever design in which the pages get increasingly small in a way that adds each verse to the previous ones. The singer in the illustrations appears as a tow-headed child who happily acquires animal after animal, all making their characteristic animal noise. While you could certainly sing this to a baby, the format will especially intrigue older toddlers. Final pages include simple music, while the foreword by Pete Seeger suggests other activities to incorporate into the song. A fine, durable book for family songfests.

Skidamarink: A Silly Love Song to Sing Together. **Illustrated by G. Brian Karas. 2001. Hardcover: HarperCollins. Paperback: HarperCollins. Ages 18 months and up.**

A chunky polar bear and an energetic penguin, both clad in skates, serenade each other in this short book. The winsome illustrations show the bear and penguin skating, almost like a dance, as they sing to each other. The penguin even draws a heart on the ice with its skates. Karas has made good use of flaps that open twice, once to give the next line or syllable, and then again for the final one. The movement of turning the flaps cleverly matches the song's rhythm. It helps if you know the tune, which isn't included but is very simple. Short, silly, and adorable.

Taback, Simms. *I Know an Old Lady Who Swallowed a Fly.* **1997. Hardcover: Viking. Good for groups. Ages 12 months and up.**

Many adults will remember the tune to this silly folk song, which is unusually easy to sing with expression, if not goofiness. The illustrations in this Caldecott Honor Book perfectly capture that spirit and provide extra jokes for adults while fascinating young children. Taback cleverly uses die-cut holes in the old lady's stomach to show what she has swallowed, holes that children will want to poke their fingers through. As the old lady swallows animal after animal, she gets bigger and so do the holes. Not every parent will be comfortable with the ending, where "She died, of course!" although it's hard to resist the moral, "Never swallow a horse." Pure entertainment with great pictures.

Titherington, Jeanne. *Baby's Boat*. 1992. Hardcover: Greenwillow. Board book: Morrow. Ages newborn through 2 years.

The words in this bedtime book come from a nineteenth-century song, to which some parents may know the tune. The music isn't included here, but the book can be read as a poem and enjoyed for its pictures. In a slightly surreal atmosphere, a baby is rowing a boat with a big spoon, with a teddy bear and blanket nearby. Hazy stars fill the purple sky, and the waves form from glowing white fabric. More toys appear, and the baby catches a toy fish before finally settling down to sleep in the boat. The lyrics move along gently, with two verses that both end "Sail, baby, sail, Out upon that sea, / Only don't forget to sail Back again to me." The shimmery, pastel illustrations appeal greatly to some parents, while others find them a bit static.

Wells, Rosemary. *The Bear Went over the Mountain/BINGO/ The Itsy-Bitsy Spider/Old MacDonald*. 1998/1999. Board book: Scholastic. Ages newborn and up.

Here are four familiar songs to sing to your child and share the cozy pictures as your baby gets old enough to enjoy them. A toddler who has learned the song lyrics will be able to pretend that he or she is reading the short books in this Bunny Reads Back series. *BINGO*, unlike the others, uses a realistic-looking dog throughout the song and changes the lyrics to say,

"And BINGO was her name-o," instead of the traditional "his name-o." The other three feature Wells's usual cuddly animals dressed as humans. Old MacDonald is a plump rabbit in denim overalls, while the bear who goes over the mountain wears plaid overalls. In *Itsy-Bitsy Spider*, a duck watches mesmerized as a small spider climbs, falls, and climbs again. A merry, singable quartet of small board books.

Westcott, Nadine Bernard, adapter. *The Lady with the Alligator Purse*. 1988. Paperback: Little, Brown. Board book: Little, Brown. Good for groups. Ages 6 months and up.

"In comes the doctor, in comes the nurse, in comes the lady with the alligator purse," sounds the refrain of this old jump rope rhyme, brought to life in whimsical illustrations. Tiny Tim has swallowed a lot of soap, to his mother's distress, so she calls for help. When the three answer her call, the lady with the alligator purse prescribes a remedy that most children adore: pizza. The whole family, including cat and dog, gather around a recovered Tiny Tim, all scarfing down pizza. The many funny aspects of the pictures complement the light-hearted rhyme. A lark to read aloud, this works well in board book as well as paperback format, for babies and toddlers. You'll have it memorized in no time and so will your child.

Westcott, Nadine Bernard. *Peanut Butter and Jelly: A Play Rhyme*. 1987. Paperback: Viking. Good for groups. Ages 18 months and up.

You might start at the back of this book, which explains gestures to use in conjunction with the lines. But it can also just be read, chanting it like a jump rope rhyme and poring over the amusing pictures, which go far beyond the text. The words and actions tell how to make a peanut butter and jelly sandwich, returning every two lines to the refrain "Peanut butter, peanut butter. Jelly, jelly." In the exaggerated illustrations, a girl and boy sit at a table with their dog and stuffed rabbit, envisioning a peanut butter and jelly sandwich. A baker comes in and mixes a huge amount of bread dough and bakes a gigantic loaf. "First you take the dough and / Knead it, knead it." Then come elephants to crack and mash the peanuts to make the peanut butter. It's a wild scene, which gets wilder when they squash grapes for jelly. Amuse your younger children by acting out the rhyme as you chant it, and they will join in as they get older. And, of course, make the real thing together.

Winter, Jeanette. *The Itsy-Bitsy Spider/Twinkle Twinkle Little Star*. 2000. Board book: Harcourt. Ages newborn and up.

Among the smaller board books published, these two versions of folk songs are attractive and practical. With just a few words on each page, they can be sung while you turn the pages. The palette is especially lovely in the small paintings, with artwork finer than most board books offer. Expect to sing these over and over again. They are also sturdy enough, with rounded corners, to give to a young child to look at and chew.

Wright, Blanche Fisher. *The Real Mother Goose*. 1916. Hardcover: Scholastic. Board book: Scholastic. Ages newborn and up.

Many parents will recognize and like the old-fashioned illustrations in this popular collection, which has been in print for more than eighty years. It can also be found in shorter versions, some in board book format. The longer volume brings together more than two hundred nursery rhymes, with many small illustrations and some full-page ones. While lots of the rhymes will be familiar, others probably won't be. No one has toned these down for modern ears: the old woman in the shoe whips her children, Tom "was beat" for stealing a pig, and an old man who wouldn't say his prayers is thrown down the stairs. But if you don't mind some surprises—and an all-white cast in the pictures—you may enjoy taking a trip down memory lane while choosing rhymes to read aloud.

Zelinsky, Paul O. *The Wheels on the Bus*. 1990. Hardcover: Dutton. Good for groups. Ages 12 months and up.

Zelinsky, a Caldecott Medal–winning illustrator, turns his talents to a pop-up book with predictably great success. He takes the popular children's song and transforms it into an unusually clever creation, with turning wheels, flaps, tabs to pull, and even windshield wipers that swish, as described in the song. The bus doors open, the driver's hand and arm motion riders to the back, a bus window opens and shuts, and mothers soothe their wailing babies, all with clever touches in the rest of the illustrations, too. The back cover gives the simple music, including guitar chords. Sturdy paper and thoughtful engineering help this book endure as you and your child make it move to your singing. An outstanding pop-up book.

2

Picture-Story Books for the Very Young

Picture-story books, which are the heart of literature for young children, typically have a simple plot, with illustrations on every page or two. The pictures are integral to the stories and add information not given in the words. By eighteen months, and often earlier, children can follow a brief plot, especially if it reflects aspects of their own lives. Parents may recognize some old favorites for the upper end of the age range from their own childhoods, such as *Harold and the Purple Crayon* (see page 178) and *Harry the Dirty Dog* (see page 286).

A number of these books, which are sometimes called "concept books," emphasize topics like the alphabet, counting, colors, shapes, and opposites. Such books often incorporate information about concepts into a plot, like *The Very Hungry Caterpillar* (see page 106), which tells a story but also works in colors, numbers, and days of the week. For this age group, such books are not meant to be teaching tools but rather pleasure reading. If your toddler starts identifying colors and shapes, the books are low-key ways to explore the concepts without turning the process into a lesson. In this chapter, you will also find several "first word" books, made up of photographs or individual illustrations labeled with their names, which lend themselves to "point-and-say" activities.

Age designations for each book are approximate, and most are open-ended. Note that if your child is two, you should continue to try books with the age ranges "12 months and up" or "18 months and up," not just confine your choices to "2 years and up." The same book can appeal to babies for certain reasons and toddlers for other reasons. Babies revel in the sound of your voice and respond strongly to rhythm and rhyme, so feel free to read your baby a rhyming book that has an older age designation. For example, *The Piggy in the Puddle* (see page 220) has a tongue-twisting text, which some parents have found mesmerizes their baby, although the pictures are too detailed for a baby to appreciate. Toddlers like this terrific book for its pictures as well as its words—as do parents themselves.

If your two-year-old has an affinity for books and has built up a long attention span, you could start adding in books aimed at slightly older children while still returning to old favorites. The "Favorite Picks" section in the final chapter has a list of popular series for preschoolers to try with toddlers who are ready for longer sessions or more complex stories. Look for more suggestions in the companion books to this guide, *Great Books for Girls*, *Great Books for Boys*, and *Great Books about Things Kids Love*.

The annotations indicate whether the book is one in a series, so you can seek out the others if your child likes the first book. So, too, look for other books by an author or illustrator whose work appeals to you. Public libraries are a great place to explore authors and series. Bring home a lot of books and see which ones appeal to the tastes and interests of your baby or toddler.

Acredolo, Linda, and Susan Goodwyn. *Baby Signs at Meal-time/My First Baby Signs.* **Photographs by Penny Gentieu. 2002. Board book: HarperCollins. Ages newborn through 2 years.**

Whether or not you think teaching your baby hand signs is a good idea, these two board books can serve as entertainment with their excellent photographs of babies. Few board books have such clear, crisp photos of a cast of cuddly babies from different ethnic groups. The mealtime book combines familiar words and phrases such as *all gone* and *more* with a picture of a child and a few smaller shots of cereal, a bowl, a cup of apple juice, and the like. The other book shows a ball, hats, a dog and cat, books, and flowers. The children are demonstrating the signs, but the gestures are unobtrusive. Your child can enjoy the photographs without realizing they are meant to be a lesson.

Ahlberg, Janet and Allan. *Baby Sleeps/Blue Buggy/Doll and Teddy/See the Rabbit.* **1998. Board book: Little, Brown. Ages 12 months through 2 years.**

Four board books with a British touch show familiar objects and babies in everyday settings. *Baby Sleeps* has a picture on every page of one or more babies, many with droll expressions, and two words of text, such as "Baby bounces" and "Baby hides." In *Doll and Teddy*, illustrations of recognizable items are set in uncluttered pages and named in the text. The other two books offer a guessing game, with the text naming something, usually fairly easy to spot, found somewhere in the picture. Parents will appreciate the humorous aspects of the pictures in this appealing quartet.

Alborough, Jez. *Hug.* **2000. Hardcover: Candlewick. Board book: Candlewick. Good for groups. Ages 12 months and up.**

It's impossible not to like the friendly little chimp on this book's cover, who is shouting in bright red letters, "HUG." The word *hug* is repeated again and again as the chimp sets off through the jungle one day and encounters different animals hugging. On most pages, a voice balloon from the chimp contains the single word, while the expansive illustrations show him looking sadder and sadder as he realizes he wants a hug, too. Finally, perched on the elephant's trunk and surrounded by giraffes, tigers, hippos, and other animals, the little chimp calls the word as loudly as he can. Imagine everyone's surprise when a large chimp in a tree shouts, "Bobo." "Mommy," calls the little chimp, running to his mother for a hug, of course. A moving story told in very few words. The words and pictures translate fairly well into the small board book, but for full appreciation of the animals' expressions, take a look at the original hardcover version.

Alborough, Jez. *Where's My Teddy?* 1992. Hardcover: Candlewick. Paperback: Candlewick. Good for groups. Ages 18 months and up.

In this original variation on the theme of a lost toy, a boy named Eddie goes searching for his teddy bear Freddie in the woods. He is a tiny boy, and the woods are huge and dark. Listeners may feel a bit scared until Eddie finds his teddy bear. But strangely enough, Freddie has grown huge, to Eddie's disappointment. " 'You're too big to huddle and cuddle,' he said, 'and I'll never fit both of us into my bed.' " As it turns out, this teddy belongs to a huge bear who has found Eddie's teddy and thinks his own has grown small. In a funny encounter, the bear scares the boy and the boy scares the bear. They switch teddies and dash off to their own cozy beds. The jaunty rhyme, clever story, and amusing pictures add up to a winner. Also look for the other books in the series, *My Friend Bear* and *It's the Bear*.

Aliki. *One Little Spoonful.* **2001. Hardcover: HarperCollins. Ages 6 months through 2 years.**

A crying baby and a frazzled mother rush to a high chair as this attractive little book opens. With the mother holding a small bowl of food, the fun begins. "One little spoonful for your toes," and in goes the first spoonful of something green as the baby reaches for its stuffed monkey's toes. Then, "One little spoonful for your nose." The baby in the picture, and probably your baby at home, points a finger at its nose. Although a bit of the food has eluded the baby's mouth, it's only after four spoonfuls and a sip of a drink that the food inevitably starts flying around as the baby's hand bangs into the spoon. After a bit more chaos and a burp, the patient mother takes her plump, smiling baby off to play. Parents will soon know the simple verse and can add it to mealtime routines. Right on target.

Aliki. *Welcome, Little Baby.* **1987. Hardcover: Greenwillow. Ages newborn through 18 months.**

Pastel colors and rounded shapes characterize the watercolor-and-crayon illustrations in this sweet book. A mother is taking care of her newborn baby and talking to her, as parents do. The pictures show the long-haired mother bathing and nursing her child, then putting her into her bassinet to sleep. They go to the park together, where bigger children are playing, and the mother tells her baby, "You'll learn to walk, to run, to talk, to read." The text is short, simple, and warmhearted, opening and closing with the words "Welcome to our world, little baby." Parents who are feeling understandably sentimental about their newborn will especially enjoy this hymn of welcome.

Allen, Pamela. *Who Sank the Boat?* **1983. Paperback: Putnam. Good for groups. Ages 18 months and up.**

Five friends—a cow, a donkey, a pig, a sheep, and a

mouse—decide to go for a row in the bay one sunny day. Rhyming couplets with a strong rhythm ask about each animal, "Do you know who sank the boat? Was it the cow who almost fell in, / when she tilted the boat and made such a din?" It wasn't the cow, though. One by one, the big animals tentatively climb into the little rowboat. Children will chant the recurring question "Do you know who sank the boat?" along with the reader, until they reach the end. Watercolor illustrations with pen outlines and cross-hatching create funny animals with exaggerated expressions, adding to the amusing expedition.

Appelt, Kathi. *Bubbles, Bubbles*. Illustrated by Fumi Kosaka. 2001. Hardcover: HarperCollins. Good for groups. Ages 2 years and up.

Standing in only her underpants, a toddler who is covered with dirt happily declares, "Dirty fingers, dirty toes, / dirty shoulders, dirty nose. / All my dirty deeds are done. / Time to have some bubble fun." An extravagantly bubbly bath awaits her, and she climbs in with her frog and yellow duck. The exuberant pictures show them reveling in the bath, scrubbing, shampooing, and playing with the bubbles. Happy to have been dirty, now she is happy to be clean. Clothed in her pajamas, she's off to bed: "Flannel bottoms, flannel shirt—good-bye bubbles, good-bye dirt." An appealing celebration of a routine not all children embrace so enthusiastically.

Appelt, Kathi. *Rain Dance*. Illustrated by Emilie Chollat. 2001. Hardcover: HarperCollins. Good for groups. Ages 12 months and up.

Simple and effective, this short book shows how some different animals react when it starts raining, using numbers from one to ten. "Water drops. 1 Froggie hops," it opens, and goes on in kind. The well-chosen rhymes flow naturally, making it fun to read, while the slightly stylized pictures are uncluttered, showing large, familiar animals such as chickens, cows, and pigs. Raindrops splatter every page, leading up to the final "10 Ponies prance, Rain dance!" The numbers help supply the rhythm, but the book can be enjoyed fully by those who aren't ready to learn to count. Sturdy pages will help this book endure in the hands of the very young. The notes on the back suggest sharing the book at bath time and staging your own rain dance, a splendid idea.

Appelt, Kathi. *Toddler Two-Step*. Illustrated by Ward Schumaker. 2000. Hardcover: HarperCollins. Good for groups. Ages 18 months and up.

Toes will start tapping and toddlers start dancing when you read this jaunty book. Counting in twos from one to ten and back again, the fast-moving text describes movements for children to imitate. "Three, four / Clippity-clop. Cross the floor / Hippity-hop. Five, six / Zippity-zoom. Now a kick / Uh oh! Ka-boom!" The illustrations show round-faced children jumping and hopping but don't offer precise directions. While children will make up their own interpretation of some of the actions, others like "clap, clap, clap" are unmistakable. In either case, this is an irresistible invitation to combine reading and lively activity.

Arnosky, Jim. *Rabbits & Raindrops*. 1997. Hardcover: Putnam. Paperback: Putnam. Ages 2 years and up.

Soft watercolors paint a realistic setting at the edge of a lawn where a mother rabbit and her five babies live under a hedge. The babies, out of their nest for the first time, hop after their mother into the sunlight. They meet other small creatures, which young listeners will point out and identify. When it starts raining, they head back to the hedge, where more creatures join them. The lovely illustrations switch from greens and yellows before the rain to grays and blues, then back to a light-drenched scene when the sun returns and the bunnies "play rabbit tag" on the lawn. A straightforward story told in few words, this will nevertheless enchant young children with its glimpse into the natural. Also look for other wonderful books by Arnosky about nature, some of them out of print but available at libraries, such as *Come Out, Muskrats*, and *Deer at the Brook*.

Asch, Frank. *Bear's Bargain*. 1985. Paperback: Simon & Schuster. Ages 2 years and up.

This story of friendship starts with Bear and Little Bird shaking hands over their bargain: to teach each other something important. Little Bird wants to learn how to be big, and Bear wants to learn to fly. But Little Bird's work with tiny barbells doesn't make him grow, so Bear concocts another scheme, carving Little Bird's picture on a pumpkin. When the pumpkin grows huge, so does the picture, to Little Bird's joy. Teaching Bear to fly the traditional way doesn't work either, so Little Bird thinks of another answer, one that will make readers smile. A gentle story with simple, appealing pictures, about friends who want to make each other happy. Also see *Bear Shadow*, *Mooncake*, and others.

Asch, Frank. *Just Like Daddy*. 1980. Paperback: Aladdin. Good for groups. Ages 18 months and up.

A bear child, dressed like its father but not identified as a boy or girl, imitates all the father's actions throughout the morning as the family prepares to go fishing. "Just like Daddy," goes the refrain. But the twist at the end of this simple story has the little bear catch a large fish, "just like Mommy," while

Daddy catches a tiny one. Most children will be surprised the first time they hear the end and see the picture of the mother and child with a big fish and the father with a tiny one. A welcome tribute to mothers.

Baer, Gene. *Thump, Thump, Rat-a-Tat-Tat*. Illustrated by Lois Ehlert. 1989. Paperback: HarperCollins. Good for groups. Ages 12 months and up.

The rhythm of a parade band infuses the text of this striking book. "Rat-a-tat-tat / Rat-a-tat-tat / THUMP, THUMP / THUMP, THUMP," it opens, and continues, "Distant drums / Chirping horns / Rat-a-tat-tat / Rat-a-tat-tat." Small geometrical figures in bold colors can be seen approaching from a distant truck labeled "Marching Band." The words continue in the same vein, the marching sounds paired with short descriptions of the band as it gets closer and louder. Bright oranges, pinks, and reds form the boxy figures of the marchers, with the first wave carrying flags and the rest playing instruments. Soon they fill the page and then start marching away, eventually back to the bus. A visual feast with equally engaging words.

Baker, Alan. *Little Rabbit's First Word Book*. 1996. Hardcover: Kingfisher. Ages 15 months and up.

Like other "first word" books, this organizes pictures by subject, with each object labeled with its name. But unlike most similar books, it engages children by adding characters, showing rabbits and a mouse on every page. The topics reflect children's interests and everyday life: clothes, toys, animals, colors, shapes, and such. The illustrations are colorful and well designed, with white space surrounding most items to make them easy to identify. The author suggests possible activities to enhance the reading, such as having your child find the mouse on every page and identifying the colors. One in a series of attractive books that combine rabbits and concepts.

Baker, Keith. *Big Fat Hen.* **1994. Hardcover: Harcourt. Paperback: Harcourt. Board book: Harcourt. Good for groups. Ages 6 months through 2 years.**

This delightful book, which opens with the words "1, 2, buckle my shoe," serves as a nursery rhyme rather than a lesson in counting. The very young will learn to count eventually, but right now they can simply enjoy this rhyming text with engaging pictures. An assortment of large hens and their chicks glow with color against a reddish-gold background, as the hens peer nearsightedly at worms, snails, and other small creatures. Meanwhile, the chicks hatch from their eggs and explore their surroundings. The final pages burst with the crowd of hens and dozens of hatched eggs. Popular with groups and for reading one-on-one, this is a treat.

Baker, Liza. *I Love You Because You're You.* **Illustrated by David McPhail. 2001. Hardcover: Scholastic. Ages 2 years and up.**

A cozy mother fox, clad in a long dress, reassures her son of her love from beginning to end in this gentle book. She describes in short sentences all the times she loves him—when he's happy, sleepy, silly, frightened, and even when he's angry and wild. The winsome illustrations, set against a white background, show the two of them together in their different moods, adding details not given in the story, such as a droll owl doctor who visits when the fox boy is sick. This charmer offers a range of emotions that can help young children understand what they are feeling. But best of all, the story affirms the message every child needs to hear, of being loved "because you're you," as the final line declares.

Bang, Molly. *The Grey Lady and the Strawberry Snatcher.* 1980. Hardcover: Four Winds. Paperback: Simon & Schuster. Ages 2 years and up.

This Caldecott Honor Book has a highly original look. The main characters are the grey lady, whose figure is mainly negative space plus her face and hands, and the strawberry snatcher, a strange creature with blue skin, big blue feet, and a long blue nose. After the grey lady buys a basket of strawberries, the strawberry snatcher pursues her, dressed in a purple hat and a red and lime green cloak. Although this is a wordless book, the plot is quite clear. She saves her strawberries when he snatches at them, then she flees and boards a bus. He trails the bus on his skateboard and follows her through some scary woods, where she eludes him in an unexpected way. This unusual book encourages you and your child to supply the story and dialogue, making it an interactive experience that's different every time.

Bang, Molly. *Ten, Nine, Eight.* 1983. Hardcover: Greenwillow. Board book: Tupelo. Good for groups. Ages newborn through 2 years.

In this modern classic, a small black girl and her father count down together from ten to one at bedtime. Sitting in a big rocking chair, they start with her ten toes, then her nine animal friends, on through to "1 big girl all ready for bed," when she is tucked into her crib. The paintings in this Caldecott Honor Book use rich, lustrous colors set off against the intriguing patterns of the wallpaper and chair upholstery, to charming effect. Even the very young will recognize familiar elements, such as shoes, crib, cat, and kisses. Warm and reassuring, this is a lovely way to close the day.

Bang, Molly. *When Sophie Gets Angry—Really, Really Angry* . . . 1999. Hardcover: Scholastic. Good for groups. Ages 2¹/₂ years and up.

This Caldecott Honor Book takes on the topic of childhood anger. As the story opens, Sophie's sister grabs a stuffed animal from Sophie, and their mother agrees it's the sister's turn. A double-page spread with an angry red background shows a close-up of Sophie's face: "Oh, is Sophie ever angry now!" She kicks and screams and roars. "Sophie is a volcano, ready to explode." Reds and oranges in frenzied shapes express her fury, until she dashes out of the house, slamming the door. Then greens and browns of outdoors reflect Sophie's feelings as she gradually calms down. When she climbs a tree, "The wide world comforts her." Home again, her family welcomes her back. The many children who recognize the feelings in this powerful book may take comfort in knowing that they are not the only children to get angry and that the anger does go away.

Bang, Molly. *Yellow Ball*. 1991. Hardcover: Greenwillow. Ages 18 months and up.

In this lovely book, a yellow ball takes a long trip starting at a beach. Three people are playing with the yellow ball on a crowded beach, but when they quit paying attention, it starts to float out past the swimmers. The perspective in the illustrations shifts, so the reader is looking back at the beach from a distance, and then there is no beach in sight. With another shift, we look down from the sky at the ball in four different places. Children will have to search for the ball on some pages, where it is one of many objects on a beach or looks like a speck far below on the ocean. On other pages, it takes center stage. Just a few words appear on each page, leaving the focus on the outstanding illustrations. The satisfying end brings the ball ashore and into the hands of a delighted child.

Banks, Kate. *Baboon*. Illustrated by Georg Hallensleben. 1997. Hardcover: Farrar, Straus & Giroux. Ages 2 years and up.

A philosophical air infuses this story, originally published in French, about a young baboon exploring the world. When he opens his eyes, the young baboon sees a great, green forest and observes to his much larger mother, "So, the world is green." "Some of it," she replies. Large, striking paintings with black outlines and heavy brushstrokes depict the baboon's world as he and his mother proceed. He sees a huge turtle and concludes the world is slow, then a bushfire and concludes the world is hot. The pace is leisurely and reassuring, with little drama despite encounters with a herd of elephants, a crocodile, and a rhinoceros. As night falls and the pictures darken, the feeling gets even quieter, until the mother finally agrees with her sleepy child, "Yes, the world is big."

Barner, Bob. *Bugs! Bugs! Bugs!* 1999. Hardcover: Chronicle. Good for groups. Ages 18 months and up.

Collage illustrations in festive colors introduce insects through one short, rhyming sentence per page. "Friendly daddy longlegs that never bite," reads one double-page spread with harmless-looking spiders, followed by a smiling grasshopper and the line "Grasshoppers hop, hop, hopping out of sight." While the pictures are more playful than realistic, children will recognize some familiar bugs, like ladybugs and bees. At the back, in a thoughtful touch, one page shows the insects in their actual sizes. For older children, a page labeled "Bug-O-Meter" answers simple questions about each insect, such as "Where does it live?" Sure to be a hit with those fascinated by creepy-crawlies.

Barrett, Mary Brigid. *Leaf Baby/Snow Baby*. Illustrated by Eve Chwast. 1998. Board book: Harcourt. Ages 6 months through 2 years.

In *Leaf Baby*, one of two board books about enjoying the seasons, a grandfather, dog, and small child stroll to the park together, where the "leaf baby" twirls, swings, plays with the dog, and hides in the leaves, with the relaxed grandfather nearby. Then they head home, where the child falls to sleep on Daddy's lap. In *Snow Baby*, the adults are female. A mother bundles up a little child, who goes out into the wintry landscape with Gram. They walk up a snowy hill, make snow angels, and ride a sled before returning to the warm, light-filled house. The block prints, with their rich colors and simple shapes, give a palpable sense of the seasons in these small adventures. Also look in your library for *Beach Baby* and *Mud Baby*, now out of print.

Barton, Byron. *Airport*. 1982. Hardcover: HarperCollins. Paperback: HarperCollins. Good for groups. Ages 18 months and up.

Simple words and large, colorful pictures introduce children to different aspects of an airport. Starting with passengers as they arrive in cars and buses, the illustrations show them checking in, sitting in the waiting room, boarding the plane, and fastening their seat belts. Interspersed are pictures of the plane getting checked and loaded, pilots preparing in the cockpit, workers in the control tower, and finally, the plane taking off. A double-page cross section of the plane's interior shows the cargo hold, fuel tanks, and cockpit. Children who are about to fly or those interested in large vehicles will enjoy this brightly illustrated book.

Barton, Byron. *Boats/Planes/Trains/Trucks*. 1998. Board book: HarperCollins. Ages 15 months and up.
Young vehicle fans will be delighted by these four small books. With bold colors and black outlines, Barton explores the variety in each category. The boats range from a single person in a sailboat to a ferryboat filled with passengers. The main focus for the planes is a passenger jet, although smaller planes such as a seaplane and crop duster also appear. The trains include passenger and freight, while the trucks revolve around those a child might see in daily life: garbage truck, tow truck, and even an ice cream truck. These were originally issued as larger hardcovers, now out of print, and lose some of their effect in the small board book size, but they will still capture the interest of many young children.

Barton, Byron. *Dinosaurs, Dinosaurs*. 1989. Hardcover: HarperCollins. Paperback: HarperCollins. Board book: HarperCollins. Good for groups. Ages 18 months and up.
This candy-colored introduction to dinosaurs hits just the right note for the very young, focusing on the dinosaurs' main features, with sentences like "There were dinosaurs with horns and dinosaurs with spikes." A fierce-looking, purple dinosaur with its little ones wears the horns, while a long, orange one flaunts its spikes, both set against bright, simple backgrounds. For more information, the endpapers show the dinosaurs with name labels. A surprisingly sweet ending makes this a possible bedtime book as it describes "Very tired and very, very sleepy dinosaurs. Dinosaurs, dinosaurs, a long time ago."

Barton, Byron. *I Want to Be an Astronaut.* **1988. Hardcover: HarperCollins. Paperback: Trophy. Good for groups. Ages 18 months and up.**

Simple in text and pictures, this book uses bold colors and thick, black outlines in its illustrations of outer space and life in a space shuttle. After blasting off, the shuttle gains altitude, with the illustrations showing what happens on board. Various astronauts, including females and characters with dark skin, work at a control panel, put on a space suit, and sleep in zero gravity. Then astronauts walk in space in order to fix a satellite and build a factory in orbit. The story starts out with the declaration by a woman, "I want to be an astronaut," and ends on almost the same note. Some words may be difficult for listeners, but children who love vehicles will be fascinated with this trip to outer space.

Barton, Byron. *My Car.* **2001. Hardcover: Greenwillow. Good for groups. Ages 18 months and up.**

Eye-catching colors set against a cheerful yellow background introduce Sam and his car, which resembles a Volkswagen Beetle. Sam loves his red car with its purple tires and green hubcaps. In brief text, Sam explains how he cares for it: "I keep my car clean. My car needs oil." A purple-clad woman changes his oil, then Sam fills the gas tank. Young vehicle fans will enjoy the picture that separates the car out into its basic parts, with labels attached. The book follows Sam as he drives at night and in rain. In an unexpected twist, when he drives to work, it turns out that Sam is a city bus driver. Although simple, the illustrations vary enough to stay interesting. An outstanding book, not just for toddlers fascinated by cars.

Barton, Byron. *The Three Bears*. 1991. Hardcover: Harper-Collins. Paperback: HarperCollins. Board book: HarperCollins. Good for groups. Ages 18 months and up.

This beautifully simplified version, with its childlike paintings and honed-down text, is a great introduction to the well-loved story. The three bears first appear, brown and sturdy, across a double-page spread, while Goldilocks appears later, also boxy and slightly bewildered. Most of the backgrounds are bold, solid colors, which give the book an inviting appearance. The story follows the traditional format, with a comfortable rhythm and traditional phrases to repeat, like "It was just right." Goldilocks wakes up and runs away, just on schedule, "And the three bears never saw little Goldilocks again." Barton has also retold and illustrated *The Little Red Hen* with equal success.

Bauer, Marion Dane. *My Mother Is Mine*. Illustrated by Peter Elwell. 2001. Hardcover: Simon & Schuster. Good for groups. Ages 12 months and up.

In this gentle celebration of mothers, a sentence or two on each page praise an attribute of an animal mother, reflected in a related painting. A giraffe and its child illustrate the line "My mother is tall and tall and tall." Next come a duck and duckling, "But she doesn't mind that I am small." The large typeface is set against a light-colored background, while the illustrations, created from pastels, have a fuzzy, soft-edged feeling. The rhyming text concludes with a human mother and child, standing outdoors together. A brief, reassuring book for bedtime reading.

Beaton, Clare. *One Moose, Twenty Mice*. 1999. Hardcover: Barefoot Books. Paperback: Barefoot Books. Board book: Barefoot Books. Ages 18 months and up.

Unusual felt and appliqué illustrations grace this entertaining book. Although basically a counting book, children will most enjoy looking for the hidden cat on every page. "One moose, but where's the cat?" it opens, showing a large felt moose with a goofy smile and a cat half hidden behind the number "one." Then, "Two crabs, but where's the cat?" The crabs are in a bucket, and the cat's underneath with its tail showing. The pattern doesn't vary, announcing the next number and asking where the cat is. But children won't mind, since the fabric artwork—which incorporates buttons, beads, sequins, and other decorations—is so much fun to look at. Those who can't count yet can name the animals and find the orange cat. Great fun.

Bennett, David. *One Cow Moo Moo!* Illustrated by Andy Cooke. 1990. Hardcover: Henry Holt. Good for groups. Ages 2 years and up.

Large pictures and animal sounds make this cumulative tale a hit with groups as well as individual children. A tousle-headed boy narrates the action, looking small as a huge cow zooms by. "I saw one cow go running by. / It said, 'Moo Moo!' / I wonder why." Next come two horses, filling the oversize pages, then three donkeys, who hee-haw as they pass. "They chased the horses / that chased the cow / that said, 'Moo Moo!' " Funny details not mentioned in the text appear in the frenetic pictures, which eventually come together in a scene that shows all the animals—just before the surprise ending. An exciting tale to look at, listen to, and join in.

Berends, Polly Berrien. *I Heard Said the Bird.* Illustrated by Brad Sneed. 1995. Paperback: Puffin. Ages 18 months and up.

A bright-eyed bird informs the barnyard animals, "There's a NEW ONE coming." Large, sculpted animals with deadpan expressions puzzle over the bird's meaning. A horse, cow, hen, and goose accompany the bird to ask the duck if the NEW ONE is a duckling. When the answer is no, the duck goes with them to ask the pig, and the group keeps growing. Meanwhile, near a house in the background, a family emerges from a car, carrying something. Finally, a boy comes out to the animals and clears up the mystery, leading them to the window to see the NEW ONE, a baby boy. Full of inviting repetition and rhyme, tied together with lovely watercolor illustrations.

Berger, Barbara. *Grandfather Twilight.* **1984. Hardcover: Philomel. Paperback: Paperstar. Ages 12 months and up.**

This is one of the more mystical bedtime books for children. Although it doesn't appeal to everyone, its fans love the calm tone and magical illustrations as a mysterious old man places the moon in the nighttime sky. He lives in a fairy-tale forest, where he takes a single pearl from a strand in a wooden chest. As he carries the pearl—a journey shown without words—his luminous figure starts to trail a shimmering cloud, and the pearl grows larger. At a shore, he lifts the white sphere into the sky, where its light glows on the water below. Then he returns home with his dog, where he goes to sleep in his outdoor bed. The positive image of a gentle grandfather adds another dimension to this peaceful book.

The Big Book of Baby Animals. **1998. Hardcover: DK. Ages 2 years and up.**

Many adults like to leaf through a glossy magazine, just looking at the photographs. Children, too, enjoy colorful photographs of subjects that interest them. This attractive book, suitable for an older child as well, has dozens of clear, color photographs, set against white backgrounds, that show baby animals and their parents. No need to read all the words, just explore the pictures together, such as a joey in a kangaroo's pocket, a baby koala on its mother's back, and a monkey clinging to its parent's underside. The well-designed, oversize pages are organized by topic, including a large double-page spread of seven kittens and another of five wild cat babies. A pleasure for browsing.

The Big Book of Things That Go. 1994. Hardcover: DK. Ages 18 months and up.

While this book is aimed at older children, toddlers who love vehicles will love the photographs in it. You can skip over the text and just name the "things that go," unless you want to get into details. An unusually large book, it features a different kind of vehicle on each large double-page spread. For example, the pages titled "On the Farm" show ten different tractors and other farm machinery in crisp, colorful photographs. Other titles are "At the Roadworks," "In the Air," "On the Building Site," "Firefighters," and many more. A treat for those who can't help but stop and stare at a backhoe or truck.

Blackstone, Stella. _Baby Rock, Baby Roll._ Illustrated by Denise & Fernando. 1997. Hardcover: Holiday House. Good for groups. Ages 18 months and up.

Three babies rock and roll their way through these cheerful pages, putting a variety of verbs into action. Three phrases occur on each page, such as "Baby rock, Baby roll, Baby move" and "Baby boogie, Baby clap, Baby groove." The pictures show the three sturdy toddlers—one white, one black, and one Asian—putting the words into effect, rocking on a wooden horse, clapping, and dancing, with a gray cat somewhere on every page. Listeners won't know all the words, but the compelling rhythm will keep them involved in the story. And while the illustrations are a bit pedestrian, they offer enough for children to look at without too many details. Children in a lively mood will start imitating the actions, turning this into a performance as well as a read-aloud.

Blackstone, Stella. *Bear at Home*. Illustrated by Debbie Harter. 2001. Hardcover: Barefoot Books. Good for groups. Ages 2 years and up.

Utterly charming illustrations will captivate adult readers, while children will enjoy the pictorial details and the smiling bear. "This is bear's house, and this is the key," the story opens. Bear's gesture welcomes readers to his cheerful yellow house with its bright red roof and red tulip-filled window box. With a black-and-white cat frolicking in every picture, the book takes bear through cleaning the kitchen, eating honey in the dining room, enjoying toys in the playroom, napping in the living room, and continuing to visit every room in the house until bedtime. The rhyming text works well, but the whimsical pictures steal the show. The final pages feature a plan of the house's two floors, showing each room from above. One of several attractive stories about the same bear.

Blackstone, Stella. *There's a Cow in the Cabbage Patch*. Illustrated by Clare Beaton. 2001. Hardcover: Barefoot Books. Paperback: Barefoot Books. Good for groups. Ages 12 months and up.

Exceptional artwork sewn from colored felt and decorated with embroidery stitches combines with a fresh approach to barnyard animals in this fine book. An irresistible cloth cow gazes out from the first large page, with the words "The cow is in the cabbage patch, moo, moo, moo! She should be in the dairy, what shall we do?" The two farmers, male and female, are only at the beginning of their troubles. In the dairy, they find a dove—"coo, coo, coo"—that should be in the birdhouse, where there's an owl that should be in the old barn. "What shall we do?" echoes the refrain. The well-crafted rhyming text and the expressive felt animals will delight listeners all the way to the satisfying end. Don't miss this delightful book.

Blos, Joan. *Bedtime!* Illustrated by Stephen Lambert. 1998. Hardcover: Simon & Schuster. Ages 12 months and up.

In this variation on a theme, a little boy doesn't want to go to bed when his grandmother announces, "Bedtime!" Chalk pastels in lovely, muted colors show him busy playing with blocks and his three toy friends, Bear, Clown (who is really a monkey), and Tiger. But after a while, the boy suggests that, although he isn't sleepy, maybe Bear is. "So do you know what that grandma did?" She tucked the teddy bear into bed and gave him a kiss, with the boy looking on. And so it goes with the other two toys and the patient grandmother. The grandmother sits down to read a story to the stuffed animals, and the boy climbs on her lap to see the pictures. Then he announces, in his own time, that he is ready for bed. With so many grandparents raising young children, this portrayal of an understanding grandmother is especially welcome.

Bornstein, Ruth. *Little Gorilla.* 1976. Paperback: Houghton. Board book: Clarion. Good for groups. Ages 15 months and up.

This deceptively simple book speaks so directly to children that it has endured for more than two decades. It begins, "Once there was a little gorilla, and everybody loved him." Large illustrations in jungle greens and oranges show that animals throughout the jungle, from Lion to Old Hippo, love Little Gorilla. "Then one day something happened . . . ," the same thing that happens to all children: Little Gorilla began to "grow and Grow and GROW." After a few pages that don't show Little Gorilla, he suddenly appears, now so big that he fills a double-page spread. But happily, everybody comes to a birthday party for him, "And everybody still loved him." A reassuring theme, presented in effective pictures and simple words. Avoid the board book of this, which doesn't do justice to the illustrations.

Bowie, C. W. *Busy Toes.* **Illustrated by Fred Willingham. 1997. Hardcover: Whispering Coyote Press. Paperback: Charlesbridge Publishing. Board book: Whispering Coyote Press. Good for groups. Ages 18 months and up.**

Here's a tribute to toes, an important body part, especially for the youngest. Realistic paintings show many possibilities of what toes can do and what can be done to them, all at a child's level. Toes can wave, and toes can be tickled. Toes can rub a dog's tummy, and they can be counted. With only a phrase on each page, the pictures show a child, often African American or Asian American, thinking about what toes can do, with an active foot in the background. Or the children are trying an activity themselves, dipping toes in water, hiding them in sand, and even putting tiny doll clothes on them. Sure to delight listeners and prompt toe activities. Choose the full-size over the board book for the sake of the pictures.

Boynton, Sandra. *Blue Hat, Green Hat/But Not the Hippopotamus/The Going to Bed Book/Moo, Baa, La La La/ Opposites.* **1982. Board book: Simon & Schuster. Ages 9 months and up.**

Parents revel in the humor of cartoonist Boynton as much as children do. These now classic board books were reissued in 1995 with updated illustrations, but the older versions that you may find at your library hold up well, too. In many of these fourteen-page books about animals, the jokes come from an animal who knows less than even a little child. In *Blue Hat, Green Hat*, three animals put on clothing the right way, while a bird does it wrong, putting its shirt on upside down, standing in its hat, and the like. In *Moo, Baa, La La La*, all the animals know their proper sound except the pigs, who say, "La La La." In the other three books, the humor springs mainly from the pictures, as animals illustrate opposites, get ready for bed, and invite a friend to join in their fun. These board books deserve their great popularity; look for Boynton's other board books as well.

Brennan, Linda Crotta. *Flannel Kisses*. Illustrated by Mari Takabayashi. 1997. Hardcover: Houghton. Ages 2 years and up.

A brief rhyming text and cheery pictures celebrate winter through the activities of two young children. After a breakfast of hot oatmeal in a cozy kitchen, the children are out the door and into a snowy yard. Together they build a snowman with a carrot nose and a wool striped cap. Back inside again, they warm up by the fire and eat hot soup. Then outside once more, the two share a tea party with their dog, teddy bear, and snowman. Paintings with a folk art feel, full of details worth examining, show a happy family playing, eating, and reading together.

Brown, Marc. *D.W. Rides Again!* 1993. Hardcover: Little, Brown. Paperback: Little, Brown. Good for groups. Ages 2 years and up.

The aardvark D.W., younger sister of Arthur, has a mind of her own, sometimes to Arthur's distress. In this entry in the series, D.W. doesn't want to waste any time in learning to ride a bike. She considers training wheels beneath her and practices until she can get rid of them. When their father takes D.W. out to test her new skills, he ends up in a creek while she stays safely on her bike. In her typical wisecracking way, D.W. offers him her training wheels now that she has finished with them. Simpler in text and smaller in format than the Arthur books, the D.W. books are high on child appeal.

Brown, Margaret Wise. *Big Red Barn*. Illustrated by Felicia Bond. 1989. Hardcover: HarperCollins. Board book: Harper-Collins. Good for groups. Ages 15 months and up.

The author of *Goodnight Moon* and the illustrator of *If You Give a Mouse a Cookie* come together in this appealing farmyard tale. Brown's straightforward but rhythmic text introduces many familiar farm animals, using words and sounds that appeal to the senses. The story opens at dawn, when a pink pig was "learning to squeal," and closes at nighttime, "While the moon sailed high / In the dark night sky." Almost all the visual groupings include baby animals in the bright pictures, which achieve just the right level of detail without being overwhelming. The board book version doesn't do justice to Bond's artwork, so stick to the larger original.

Brown, Margaret Wise. *Bumble Bee*. Illustrated by Victoria Raymond. 1999. Board book: HarperCollins. Ages 9 months through 2 years.

While not in the same class as *Goodnight Moon*, this bouncy little board book combines unusual collage illustrations with minimal text. Brown's rhyme is only forty-seven words total, arranged in curved lines that echo what they describe. The words "Drowsy Browsy Lump of a Bee" seem to sag a little, as the tired bumblebee does in the accompanying picture. The bee consists of cloth yellow and black strips with gossamer wings and prominent black-and-white eyes, an amusing look. It flies from page to page against a blue textured background studded with puffy white clouds. Finally, the bumblebee zooms away. Read this slight story for the pleasure of the words and the fetching pictures.

Brown, Margaret Wise. *Goodnight Moon*. Illustrated by Clement Hurd. 1947. Hardcover: HarperCollins. Paperback: HarperCollins. Board book: HarperCollins. Ages newborn and up.

Perhaps no bedtime book has captured the hearts of so many young children and their parents as *Goodnight Moon*. The perfect cadence of the words soothes babies, while the cunning details in the pictures enchant toddlers. The words mostly name objects in the room, as seen by a little bunny in bed, then go on to say good-night to each of the objects and to the "quiet old lady who was whispering 'hush.' " The room gets progressively darker until, after saying good-night to the stars and air, the book closes with the words "Goodnight noises everywhere." Incorporate this into your nightly routine to bring a final note of comfort before sleep. The board versions, one of which is smaller than the original and the other of which is larger, retain the same pictures and words, with slightly brighter colors.

Brown, Margaret Wise. *Little Donkey Close Your Eyes*. Illustrated by Ashley Wolff. 1995. Hardcover: HarperCollins. Paperback: HarperCollins. Ages 15 months and up.

Soothing rhythms and lovely illustrations combine to make this a fine bedtime choice. One after another, baby animals wind down at the end of the day, snuggling up to their parents. "Little Pig that squeals about / Make no noises with your snout. / No more squealing to the skies / Little Pig now close your eyes." With black outlines and rich colors, the cozy illustrations visit woods, farmyards, and campsites, finally looking through a window at a child tucked in for the night.

Brown, Margaret Wise. *The Runaway Bunny.* **Illustrated by Clement Hurd. 1942. Hardcover: HarperCollins. Paperback: HarperCollins. Board book: HarperCollins. Good for groups. Ages 15 months and up.**

Endearing, old-fashioned paintings alternate with black-and-white drawings in this story about a mother's love. It begins, "Once there was a little bunny who wanted to run away. So he said to his mother, 'I am running away.'" But she replies, "If you run away, I will run after you." Thus setting the theme, the story continues with the little bunny imagining ways to run away and his mother telling how she would pursue him. If the bunny becomes a rock on a mountain, the mother will be a mountain climber and climb to where he is. After several such scenes, the bunny decides just to stay home. While some parents find the mother's attitude cloying, many read the story as reassuring, with its wonderful rhythms and message of love.

Brown, Ruth. *A Dark, Dark Tale.* **1981. Paperback: Dutton. Good for groups. Ages 18 months and up.**

Even young children like to be scared sometimes—while sitting safely in their parent's lap. This brief tale with its dark illustrations builds up to a scary climax, then supplies an ending that takes away the fear. A repetitive structure leads the listener along from a "dark, dark wood," to a "dark, dark house," through a "dark, dark door," to a "dark, dark hall," and so on. Children will spot the dark cat in every illustration, even though it isn't mentioned in the story. Following the cat up the stairs, the pictures show it approaching a dark cupboard. What will be in the "dark, dark box"? It's a surprise that contrasts with whatever scary creature the listener expects. This entertaining tale begs to be read in a scary voice, if your child is up for the excitement.

Brown, Ruth. *Ten Seeds*. 2001. Hardcover: Knopf. Good for groups. Ages 18 months and up.

A child is pouring seeds from a packet on the cover of this short book about planting. The opening pages show the child's hand poking a hole in the ground, to plant the tenth seed visible in the picture. "Ten seeds, one ant," read the large words. The ant, as the pictures show, is carrying away one of the seeds. The next seed to disappear ends up in the beak of a pigeon: "Nine seeds, one pigeon." Meanwhile, the seeds begin to grow roots and sprout upward. The words change from counting seeds to counting seedlings, then shoots, then plants. Finally, a beautiful yellowish-orange flower appears in a full-size illustration. Although not a board book, this has unusually sturdy pages, as does Brown's *Snail Trail*, which will appeal to the same audience.

Browne, Anthony. *Things I Like*. 1989. Hardcover: Knopf. Paperback: Knopf. Good for groups. Ages 18 months and up.

Anthony Browne, an outstanding British illustrator, usually aims his work toward older children. But here is a sprightly book for toddlers about one of Browne's characteristic chimps. "This is me and this is what I like," the chimp announces, smiling out at the reader. Each small page shows him at an activity he enjoys, with a short description under the framed picture. He likes painting, riding his tricycle, playing with toys, dressing up, and other pastimes your child will recognize. He also likes watching TV and hearing a bedtime story. You'll find yourself smiling at the little chimp, who throws himself into everything he does. Look in your library for the companion book *I Like Books*, now out of print.

Bruss, Deborah. *Book! Book! Book!* Illustrated by Tiphanie Beeke. 2001. Hardcover: Scholastic. Ages 2¹/₂ years and up.

Bored because the farm children have gone back to school, a group of animals hikes into town one day. They see adults and children with happy faces emerging from a building labeled "Public Library," so one by one, the animals enter to find something to do. (Young listeners will especially enjoy finding the book-loving frog on every page.) The friendly librarian can't understand their neighs, moos, baaahs, and oinks, until the chicken comes in clucking "Book! Book!" Childlike illustrations glowing with rich colors follow the pleased book-bearing menagerie home, where "their sounds of delight lasted until sundown."

Buck, Nola. *How a Baby Grows*. Illustrated by Pamela Paparone. 1998. Board book: HarperCollins. Ages newborn to 2 years.

This felicitous book for the very young reviews daily life as many babies know it. "These are the things that babies do: Cry, wet, sleep, coo." Four round-faced babies with different features and skin colors demonstrate the four verbs. On the following double-page spread, slightly dazed parents stand next to a crib, near a window that looks onto a yard: "These are the things a baby sees: Mommy, Daddy, window, trees." By using plain backgrounds, the illustrator can fit several babies into most of the pictures without crowding, giving young children plenty of familiar sights to look at. The rhymes work unusually well and, in combination with the on-target pictures, make this an ideal choice for sharing with the very young.

Buckley, Helen E. *Grandfather and I*. Illustrated by Jan Ormerod. 1994. Hardcover: Lothrop. Paperback: Harper-Collins. Ages 2 years and up.

A special relationship between a child, who looks to be a boy, and his grandfather revolves around their leisurely walks together in this engaging book. "We walk along and walk along and stop . . . and look . . . just as long as we like," explains the child. He muses that everyone else in his life is always in a hurry and wants him to hurry, but his grandfather is always willing to examine a plant or pick flowers or stare at a squirrel. Then, when they return home, they sit together in a rocking chair and look in a natural history book to identify what they've found on their walk. The importance of treasuring daily life and the wonder of childhood pervade this book. Realistic charcoal-and-watercolor illustrations with soft edges add to its spirit of warmth.

Buckley, Helen E. *Grandmother and I*. Illustrated by Jan Ormerod. 1994. Hardcover: Morrow. Paperback: Morrow. Ages 2 years and up.

A granddaughter nestles in the lap of her grandmother, who rocks and hums in a relaxing way. As the girl explains, other people have laps, but her grandmother's lap is the best when she needs comforting. When the girl has a cold or is scared by lightning or worries about a lost cat, she finds Grandmother's lap "just right." Glowing charcoal-and-watercolor illustrations portray a gently smiling African American woman and her granddaughter, who looks like a preschooler. Other family members appear, who are clearly kind but just not as soothing as the grandmother. An especially lovely closing picture shows the two close together, with a blossoming tree branch in the foreground and the cat, now found, in the girl's arms.

Burningham, John. *Hushabye*. 2001. Hardcover: Knopf. Ages 18 months and up.

British illustrator John Burningham turns his talents to bedtime in this lovely book. Starting with the appealing cover of a baby asleep on a boat, the pictures convey the personalities of the plump baby and a number of animals. All of them— cat, baby, bears, fish, goose, frog, and the man in the moon—are tired and looking for a place to rest. On each double-page spread, the left-hand side tells the story with large typeface and a small black-and-white drawing, while the facing page introduces the characters in illustrations saturated in color. Halfway through, the tide turns and each finds the perfect place to sleep, ending with words to the listener, "You'll soon be asleep. Hushabye, hushabye, hush."

Burningham, John. *Mr. Gumpy's Motor Car*. 1973. Hardcover: HarperCollins. Good for groups. Ages 18 months and up.

In this sequel to *Mr. Gumpy's Outing*, Mr. Gumpy, a British country gentleman, is going out for a ride in his old-fashioned convertible. A combination of black-and-white pen drawings and larger colored ones shows him setting off and soon meeting the children and animals from the earlier book. Mr. Gumpy agrees to let them come along, "But it will be a squash." They pile in and are chugging merrily down an old dirt road when it begins raining. The road gets muddy, and Mr. Gumpy announces that some of them will have to get out and push. Each child and animal announces the reason he or she won't push, but eventually everyone helps out. On a happy note, the sun emerges and they have a refreshing swim. While the story isn't as strong as *Mr. Gumpy's Outing*, the illustrations are a delight, and fans of the earlier book will definitely want to read this one.

Burningham, John. *Mr. Gumpy's Outing*. 1971. Hardcover: Henry Holt. Paperback: Henry Holt. Board book: Henry Holt. Good for groups. Ages 18 months and up.

Mr. Gumpy, who lives by a river, goes out for a boat ride one morning and takes on passenger after passenger, giving directions on how they should behave. When a girl and boy ask to come along, he says, "Yes, if you don't squabble." To the pig, Mr. Gumpy says, "Yes, if you don't muck about," and to the cow, "Don't trample about." All goes well until they all ignore the directions, and the boat tips over. Wet but unharmed, they swim to shore and head across the fields to have tea at Mr. Gumpy's. The lovely, large pictures culminate in nine animals and three people sitting around a table having fruit, cake, and tea. A completely delightful British import.

Burns, Kate. *Jump Like a Frog!/Snap Like a Crocodile!* 1999. Hardcover: Levinson. Ages 12 months and up.

These two eye-catching books combine flaps with participatory activities. The batiklike illustrations in tropical colors create outdoor scenes with flaps that extend the right-hand page out, up, or down. Behind the flap, with just a small bit peeking out, is an animal. "Who is swinging in the tree?" The flap reveals the animal and the words, "Orangutan. Can you swing from your Mummy's or Daddy's hands?" Each animal suggests movement or a facial expression for a toddler to make or a parent to demonstrate to a baby in this pair of clever books. Also look for the author's *Waddle Like a Duck!* and *Blink Like an Owl!*

Burton, Jane. *My Kitten Friends/My Puppy Friends.* 2002. Board book: Simon & Schuster. Ages 12 months through 2 years.

These two board books will delight very young children who like kittens and puppies. On the left-hand page of each double-page spread, one word appears against a brightly colored background. On the opposing page, a photograph of a kitten or puppy stands out from the surrounding white space. The words, which seem almost superfluous, are mostly adjectives to describe how the baby animal looks: sneaky, shy, sleepy, snuggly. While the photos are fairly ordinary, they are cute and appealing. Since these were created as board books, not reduced from larger books as so many board books are, they fit the format well. Babies and toddlers will alternate chewing on them and staring at the photos.

Butler, John. *Whose Baby Am I?* 2001. Hardcover: Viking. Good for groups. Ages 12 months and up.

Nothing could be simpler than this book pitched toward very young children. Each right-hand page shows a baby animal, starting with a baby owl, above the question "Whose baby am I?" Turn the page and see that an adult animal has joined the baby, and the question is answered: "I am an owl baby." Most of the adorable babies will be easy to name, like the elephant and zebra. The koala might be new to some children but will quickly become familiar. The skillful acrylic and colored-pencil illustrations on plain backgrounds are realistic, with fur that looks soft enough to touch. The last double-page spread shows the baby animals on the left side and the parents on the right, with the challenge to match them up. The very last page assembles the babies again, with their proper labels, such as "owlet" and penguin "chick."

Bynum, Janie. *Altoona Baboona.* **1999. Hardcover: Harcourt. Paperback: Harcourt. Ages 2 years and up.**

A pleased baboon looks out from the basket of her hot air balloon on the cover of this jaunty book. Altoona Baboona, whose story is told in rhyme, is bored one day in her home near the beach. What better solution than to take to the sky in a hot air balloon? Color pictures show her flying to Cancun and Rangoon and later picking up a lonely loon for company. On another day, she hears music and follows it to find a saxaphone-playing raccoon, who also joins her in the balloon. With her new friends, Altoona returns home, content after her journey. Followed by *Altoona Up North.*

Cabrera, Jane. *Panda Big and Panda Small.* **1998. Hardcover: DK. Ages 12 months and up.**

Bright colors in thick paint strokes create a big panda and a small panda, who "do not like the same things at all." Parents and children may see themselves in some of the differences. Panda Big likes to be asleep "at the beginning of the day while Panda Small is awake and ready to play." When the big panda sits in front of the bamboo eating, the little one hides in the bamboo, playing peekaboo. In each picture, both pandas look happy with their choices and tolerant of each other, except the one time they are separated. Then they know that they have one preference in common: being together. Young children will point out the small animals that appear in each picture along with the pandas but aren't mentioned in the text. An attractive book with a welcome, unforced message.

Campbell, Rod. *Dear Zoo.* **1986. Hardcover: Simon & Schuster. Ages 9 months and up.**

While the sturdy flaps may not last long with young children, try this book anyway. Unlike many books that use flaps, this one integrates them perfectly into the story. Each left-hand page reads, "I wrote to the zoo to send me a pet. They sent me an . . ." The opposing page shows a yellow crate marked "Very Heavy!" Open the crate, which is formed by a flap, and see an elephant. "He was too big! I sent him back." This establishes the pattern, with the zoo sending other animals hidden behind different-colored crate doors. There is a problem with each animal, and it must be sent back. Some of the flaps have cut-out squares that form windows, giving a hint of the animal within. In the end, the zoo finally sends the right animal, a puppy. "I kept him," reads the last line. An unusually clever use of flaps, and a repetitive story that suits the very young.

Carle, Eric. *Do You Want to Be My Friend?* 1976. Hardcover: HarperCollins. Paperback: HarperCollins. Board book: HarperCollins. Good for groups. Ages 12 months and up.

This nearly wordless book opens with a jumping mouse asking, "Do you want to be my friend?" The question seems to be addressed to a tail, until you turn the page and see a horse. On the opposing page, the mouse appears again, with its head in a questioning position but no words. This time two tails extend onto the page, which turn out to be a bird perched on a crocodile. The mouse dashes away from the crocodile's open mouth, under the tail of—and here, older children will be shouting out their guess—a lion. And so it goes. Carle's characteristically sumptuous collage illustrations, set in a wide book with plenty of white space, keep the story moving along until the mouse finally finds the perfect friend.

Carle, Eric. *From Head to Toe*. 1997. Paperback: Harper-Collins. Board book: HarperCollins. Good for groups. Ages 12 months and up.

Read this outstanding book when your child is old enough and in the mood to move! "I am a penguin and I turn my head. Can you do it?" begins the series of meetings between animals and children, illustrated in vibrant collages set in generous white space. The child replies to the penguin, "I can do it!" and turns her head. The wonderfully wrought animals dominate the pages: giraffe, buffalo, seal, gorilla, cat, crocodile, and more. The actions progress from head turning and neck bending to leg kicking and foot stomping. Calming down, the final two pages show a child saying, "I am I and I wiggle my toe. Can you do it?" Be ready for arm waving and hand clapping and chest thumping. Try to get this in paperback rather than the board book for full appreciation of the pictures. Not to be missed.

Carle, Eric. *Little Cloud*. 1996. Hardcover: Philomel. Paperback: Penguin. Board book: Philomel. Good for groups. Ages 18 months and up.

Sure to stimulate your child's imagination, this oversize book plays with the shapes that clouds can make. Heavy brushstrokes create shapes using whites, grays, and blues, set against a rich blue sky. The cloud transforms into a sheep, an airplane, and a shark. On a note of silliness, it turns into an elaborate clown with stars for eyes but then goes back to being a cloud and joins its cloud companions again. Read this on a day with fluffy white clouds in the sky and see what new shapes your child sees in them. Or make cloud pictures using cotton balls, glue, and crayons or paint. Or just enjoy the book and its collage illustrations.

Carle, Eric. *Pancakes, Pancakes!* **1990. Paperback: Al-addin. Board book: Aladdin. Ages 2 years and up.**

When Jack wants pancakes for breakfast, his mother agrees but sends him out to cut wheat and take it to the miller to grind. He must also fetch an egg, milk the cow, and churn the butter before he gets his breakfast. Vibrant collages show Jack and illustrate the very simple pancake recipe. If your toddler loves pancakes, this book will be perfect. Read it before or after a pancake meal.

Carle, Eric. *The Very Busy Spider.* **1985. Hardcover: Philomel. Board book: Philomel. Good for groups. Ages 9 months and up.**

Blown onto a fence one day, a spider starts to spin a web. One by one, other animals—including a cow, goat, and dog—ask if she wants to play, but as the refrain says, "The spider didn't answer. She was very busy spinning her web." Running a finger over the page, you can feel the embossed, slightly raised, spiderweb, which fascinates young children. As usual, Carle's artwork, collage from hand-painted paper, excels in portraying animals and creating one beautiful page after another. The repetitive nature of the story and the familiar animal noises make this a fine book for making animal sounds and joining in the repeated words. Look for this one in the full size, because the spider is too small for the board book format.

Carle, Eric. *The Very Hungry Caterpillar.* **1970. Hardcover: Philomel. Paperback: Putnam. Board book: Putnam. Good for groups. Ages 12 months and up.**

In this modern classic, a tiny, hungry caterpillar is born on a Sunday morning. He looks for food and each day eats greater amounts. "On Monday he ate through one apple. But he was still hungry. On Tuesday he ate through two pears, but he was still hungry." By Saturday, he eats through a remarkable array of food. Following a stomachache, he spins a cocoon and, after a time, emerges as a beautiful butterfly. Numbers and the days of the week are introduced, but the focus is on the terrific story and pictures. The pace makes it perfect for reading aloud, and the illustrations are priceless. Small holes are punched in the pages where the caterpillar has eaten through food, which delights young children, who are also thrilled when the colorful butterfly appears. The format works best in the larger size rather than the board book. A nearly perfect book, not to be missed.

Carle, Eric. *The Very Quiet Cricket*. 1990. Hardcover: Philomel. Board book: Putnam. Good for groups. Ages 2 years and up.

Vibrant collages of hand-painted paper sweep across the pages of this wide book. Under a huge sun, a cricket hatches from an egg. A bigger cricket chirps a welcome by rubbing its wings together to chirp, but when the little cricket imitates the action, nothing happens. Different insects—including a locust, praying mantis, spittlebug, cicada, and dragonfly—greet the little cricket, who still cannot answer. Finally, to the delight of young listeners, the cricket chirps, with the sound emerging from an embedded microchip. Not Carle's most wonderful book, but still expect to read it again and again.

Carlstrom, Nancy White. *Jesse Bear, What Will You Wear?* Illustrated by Bruce Degen. 1986. Hardcover: Simon & Schuster. Paperback: Simon & Schuster. Board book: Simon & Schuster. Good for groups. Ages 12 months and up.

This modern classic flows along with a happy rhythm and lots of childlike humor. For his mother's simple questions,

"Jesse Bear, what will you wear? What will you wear in the morning?" Jesse Bear has several answers, including "my pants that dance" and "a rose in my toes." The cozy illustrations show him bounding through the morning with enthusiasm in a beautiful outdoor setting. His mother repeats the questions at lunch, substituting "noon" for "morning," and Jesse proclaims that he'll wear "carrots and peas / And a little more please," along with other foods. With the parents in traditional roles, Jesse's father comes home in the evening in a business suit and asks his son what he'll wear at night, leading to a hilarious (in the eyes of the very young) line about "ants in my pants." Ending with poetic references to moon and stars, this wraps up as perfectly as it starts. Great for groups and one-on-one, this is not to be missed, preferably in the larger version rather than the board book. The first in a series.

Carlstrom, Nancy White. *Jesse Bear's Tum-Tum Tickle*. Illustrated by Bruce Degen. 1994. Board book: Aladdin. Ages 12 months through 2 years.

This comfy board book consists of four double-page spreads plus the front cover, which shows a mother bear tickling her child. Fans of *Jesse Bear, What Will You Wear?* will recognize the family from that longer book and its sequels. Here, Jesse Bear bounces on his parents' bed in the morning to wake them: "Tum-tum tickle / Shush, boom, shake." His grinning father gets up, and Jesse Bear tickles his mother's nose. Then we see mother bear and child as he wakes up from his afternoon nap. Finally, the father bear is carrying Jesse Bear to bed at night as the little one waves good-night to the moon. Three other board books in this series are out of print, but check your libraries for them if your child likes this one.

Carr, Jan. *Dappled Apples.* **Illustrated by Dorothy Donohue. 2001. Hardcover: Holiday House. Good for groups. Ages 2 years and up.**

Oranges, reds, yellows, and browns fill the pages of this look at the pleasures of autumn. A brisk rhyming text accompanies the detailed, three-dimensional cut-paper collages crafted from handmade paper. Several children frolic among leaves, pick apples and pumpkins, and dress up for trick-or-treating, with a short verse on every page that conveys their activities and excitement. When they carve pumpkins with the help of a dog, "Teeth are zigzag / Tail goes wigwag / Seeds are slimy / Scoop the goop." Fun for reading in autumn and at Halloween. For spring, try *Splish, Splash, Spring* by the same author and illustrator.

Carter, David A. *Says Who?: A Pop-up Book of Animal Sounds.* **1993. Hardcover: Simon & Schuster. Ages 18 months and up.**

In this book with an unusually adept use of flaps and pop-ups, the listeners are presented with clues and a question. On the first page, the text in a white circle reads, "I'm big and furry and I eat berries. GRRR! Says who?" A flap that looks like a bush opens and out pops the face of a bear, with a dialogue balloon saying, "GRRR! I'm a BEAR." The hidden animals will be familiar to most young children—bees, a tiger, an owl, and more. The final double-page spread comes as a happy surprise, with all the animals incorporated into a large pop-up and the snake perched above the book itself. Admittedly, the flaps and larger pop-ups may last only a limited time due to hard wear, but they will delight young children while they do.

Cauley, Lorinda Bryan. *Clap Your Hands*. 1992. Hardcover: Putnam. Paperback: Putnam. Board book: Putnam. Good for groups. Ages 12 months and up.

As the clapping, dancing child and animals on the cover suggest, this lively book invites participation. Wide pictures throughout show a multiethnic group of children and a range of animals following directions such as, "Rub your tummy, pat your head. / Find something yellow, find something red. / Reach for the sky, wiggle your toes. / Stick out your tongue and touch your nose." While very young children won't be able to respond fully, the adults who read to them can incorporate the actions into the reading. As they get older, the children can join in and even do the somersaults like the dog, penguin, and bear do. A top-notch book for getting feet moving.

Chandra, Deborah. *A Is for Amos*. Illustrated by Keiko Narahashi. 1999. Hardcover: Farrar, Straus & Giroux. Ages 2 years and up.

A young girl, who appears on the title page in overalls and a cowboy hat, imagines that her hobbyhorse is the real thing and starts riding. Structured as an alphabet book, each page shows the two of them on their journey, with rhythmic lines such as "B for the bumpity bridge we cross. C for the clippety clop of his trot." The girl and her horse ride across pastures and fields, galloping and jumping fences. A rainstorm sends them trotting back home to the warm, dry barn. Lovely watercolors capture the day in the countryside and the many animals they meet on their energetic outing.

Charlip, Remy. *Fortunately*. 1964. Paperback: Aladdin. Good for groups. Ages 2 1/2 years and up.

One day—fortunately—Ned got invited to a birthday party, but—unfortunately—the party was hundreds of miles away.

"Fortunately a friend loaned him an airplane. Unfortunately the motor exploded." So starts Ned's series of fortunate and unfortunate incidents and near misses before he finally reaches the birthday party. Each double-page spread of a fortunate event appears in cheerful colors, while those about unfortunate happenings, such as encountering sharks and tigers, is in black and white. Listeners immediately catch on to the book's alternating use of "fortunately" and "unfortunately," and join in as the pages turn. A rollicking journey with a happy conclusion.

Charlip, Remy. *Sleepytime Rhyme*. 1999. Hardcover: Greenwillow. Good for groups. Ages newborn and up.

This ode to love will delight adults with its sentiments and babies with its sounds. "I love you. / I think you're grand. / There's none like you / in all the land," it begins, with a picture of a loving mother cuddling a baby and a cat cuddling a kitten. Circular shapes and jewel-like colors against a delicious purple background show a mother hugging and playing with a baby. The text continues to express the mother's love for every part of the baby: hair, head, chin, neck, knees, north and south. Inevitably, parents will point out, play with, or kiss their baby's nose and toes as the verses name them. Singing the words to the tune of "Twinkle, Twinkle, Little Star" works fairly well, too. With unforced rhymes and gentle rhythm, and its potential for interaction, try this for bedtime or playtime.

Christelow, Eileen. *Five Little Monkeys Jumping on the Bed*. 1989. Paperback: Houghton. Board book: Houghton. Ages 12 months and up.

This traditional rhyme not only captivates young children, it subtly introduces the idea of subtraction. But no need to worry about the math—just have a good time with these five mischievous monkeys. After a bath, it's on with the pajamas, teeth brushed, and into bed with innocent looks on their faces. But when their mother closes the door, they immediately start jumping on the bed. Then—"One fell off and bumped his head. The mama called the doctor. The doctor said, 'No more monkeys jumping on the bed!' " While the fifth little monkey stays on an easy chair with an ice pack on his head, the other four go back to their tricks, one by one bumping their heads. Energetic drawings capture the fun and consequences of being naughty. Parents will appreciate the last page, where the mama herself takes a few bounces on her bed. Followed by *Five Little Monkeys Sitting in a Tree*.

Cimarusti, Marie Torres. *Peek-a-Moo!* Illustrated by Stephanie Pearson. 1998. Hardcover: Dutton. Good for groups. Ages 3 months through 2 years.

Seven familiar animal faces and one child's face are hidden behind flaps in this successful book for young children. The book is large, and so are the faces and flaps, making it good for groups as well as one-on-one. The flaps show hands, hooves, or wings covering the faces. At the top of each page, it says, "Guess who? Peek-a-" but doesn't complete the answer. When the flap is opened, downward, the phrase is filled in with the animal sound, like "Peek-a-moo." The solid colors and cheerful pictures culminate in the final pink-skinned baby saying, "Peek-a-boo." Whether you are turning the flaps for an infant or toddlers are turning the flaps themselves, this is likely to be a big hit.

Collicutt, Paul. *This Train*. 1998. Hardcover: Farrar, Straus & Giroux. Paperback: Farrar, Straus & Giroux. Ages 2 years and up.

Train lovers will immediately be sidetracked by the endpapers of this picture book, which show clearly labeled trains from around the world. A train fills each page, with a few words that contrast the pictures opposite each other: "This train is long. This train is short." The vivid paintings show trains in all their glory, in different settings. If your young one likes trains, plan to read this again and again. Also look for the similar *This Boat, This Car,* and *This Plane.*

Cousins, Lucy. *Country Animals/Farm Animals/Garden Animals/Pet Animals.* 1990. Board book: Morrow. Ages 6 months through 2 years.

These appealing board books introduce a range of animals, with one animal on each small page. Cousins employs her usual thick paint, delicious colors, and simple forms that resemble children's own artwork. *Farm Animals* and *Pet Animals* include the creatures most familiar to the very young, who will want to make the sounds the animals make, especially on the farm. *Garden Animals* favors insects, while *Country Animals* brings together insects, birds, reptiles, and mammals. Each small book shows ten animals, with their names as the only text. A wonderful basic collection for introducing many animals.

Cousins, Lucy. *Flower in the Garden/Hen on the Farm/ Teddy in the House.* 1992. Cloth book: Candlewick. Ages newborn through 2 years.

These three wordless cloth books are bright and cheerful, as well as washable and chewable. Each consists of eight pages, with one object on the page, centered respectively around a garden, a farm, and a house. *Teddy in the House,* for example, shows objects that babies might have encountered, such as a banana, block, telephone, and cat. No story ties the pictures together, but the poster-bright hues and childlike pictures are likely to attract the very young in a format they can also play with.

Cousins, Lucy. *Maisy Drives*. 2001. Board book: Candlewick. Ages 18 months and up.

This board book about the popular mouse Maisy, who is seen on television now, shows her at the wheel of a series of vehicles. The paintings, which use rich colors in strong black outlines, begin with Maisy driving a car on the cover of the book, which itself is shaped like a car. "Maisy drives a train. Toot, toot!" reads the first page, where Maisy waves from an old-fashioned green-and-red steam engine. She goes on to drive a tractor, fire engine, and bus as well as pilot a plane and ride her tricycle. Each simple illustration includes other animals besides Maisy as passengers or onlookers. The white mouse glows with pride and pleasure in each vehicle in this spirited book, which young children will love. Look for other books in this long series.

Cousins, Lucy. *Playtime, Maisy!/Snacktime, Maisy!* 2001. Cloth book: Candlewick. Ages newborn through 2 years.

These two brightly colored books are made from hand-washable cloth with nontoxic inks. Wordless, they show the popular mouse Maisy engaged in the everyday activities of play and eating. At play, she puts sand in a toy truck, swings, slides, throws a ball, and rides a tricycle. At snacktime, she goes through basic steps of baking and ends up with cupcakes—after which, she washes the dishes. The pictures are more detailed than you might expect in a cloth book, but the colors are bright and attractive, and the cloth is durable, easy to handle, and chewable. Two other Maisy cloth books are *Bedtime, Maisy!* and *Bathtime, Maisy!*

Cowell, Cressida. *What Shall We Do with the Boo-Hoo Baby?* Illustrated by Ingrid Godon. 2000. Hardcover: Scholastic. Good for groups. Ages 12 months and up.

"For perplexed parents everywhere," reads the dedication

of this terrific book. What do you do when a baby cries? A tiny baby with a wide-open mouth is wailing, "BOO-HOO-HOO!" as a duck, cat, dog, and cow peek around a door. Their first idea, shown on a wordless page, is to offer the baby a yellow rubber ducky. A moment of peace occurs, followed by more crying. This time the dog suggests, "Feed him." The animals all bring different food, each making its traditional animal sound. But the baby cries again. Bathing him and playing with him offer only momentary respite, so "They put him to bed." In a large close-up, the baby finally looks content, and the animals fall asleep as well. Winsome illustrations of an adorable baby and concerned animals combine with the clever story to make a real winner.

Cowen-Fletcher, Jane. *Mama Zooms*. 1993. Hardcover: Scholastic. Paperback: Scholastic. Ages 18 months and up.

In this very brief story, an attractive, smiling mother zooms a young boy around on her "zooming machine." Told from the child's perspective, the story portrays the mother as adventurous and fun-loving. It's only near the end that the audience realizes the zooming machine is a wheelchair. The mother with her "very strong arms" gives her child love and excitement, all the while erasing stereotypes about the disabled.

Cowley, Joy. *Red-Eyed Tree Frog*. Photographs by Nic Bishop. 1999. Hardcover: Scholastic. Paperback: Scholastic. Ages 2 years and up.

Spectacular color photographs show a tiny red-eyed tree frog at home in the rain forest. The book opens at sunset, when many animals fall asleep and the frog awakens. A series of photographs show it hopping from branch to branch looking for food. A brief text, often just one sentence on a page, narrates the frog's action and identifies the other animals, such as a boa, katydid, iguana, macaw, and toucan. Questions and exclamations spark up the narrative, but the book's highlight is the outstanding photography. An award-winning informational book for the young.

Coy, John. *Vroomaloom Zoom*. Illustrated by Joe Cepeda. 2000. Hardcover: Crown. Paperback: Dragonfly. Good for groups. Ages 2 years and up.

Don't be put off by the amount of text on the first page—this joyful jaunt will quickly capture the interest of toddlers. On a hot August evening, a little girl named Carmela can't sleep, so her father takes her and her blankie for a ride in his little yellow car. But the effect is far from soporific. Sound effects crop up on every page, from the car noise of "Vroomaloom zoomaloom vroom zoom" to the owl in the woods—"whoo whoo"—and the sound of the city—"pell mell bell YELL." Daddy, sporting an old-fashioned leather racing helmet and goggles, gets adventurous and covers a lot of ground, from oceans to swamps to mountains. Not surprisingly, Carmela doesn't get sleepy, but they both have a terrific ride. Not one for bedtime, this combines gloriously vivid illustrations and a great spirit of fun.

Crebbin, June. *Cows in the Kitchen*. Illustrated by Katharine McEwen. 1998. Hardcover: Candlewick. Good for groups. Ages 12 months and up.

Watch out! There are cows in the kitchen, dancing around and making a marvelous mess. Oversize illustrations show three large, smiling cows kicking up their heels against a sunny yellow background. "Cows in the kitchen, moo, moo, moo," repeats the text three times. More chaos: "Ducks in the dishes, quack, quack, quack." Then pigs in the pantry, hens on the hat stand, and sheep on the sofa, all having a great time.

Where's the farmer? Asleep in the haystack. The dog rouses him, and Farmer Tom shoos the animals out, but not for long. A catchy rhythm, inviting illustrations, and a funny concept make this popular with very young children and their parents.

Crews, Donald. *Freight Train*. 1978. Hardcover: Morrow. Paperback: Morrow. Board book: Morrow. Good for groups. Ages 12 months and up.

This modern classic is a triumph of striking graphics and high child appeal. Using vibrant hues and clean lines, the book introduces a train with six cars of different colors plus a black tender and a black steam engine. Beautifully designed pages set the train against a white background, with only a few words of text. Once introduced, the train starts traveling and picking up speed, indicated by the blurring of the colors into one another and the smoke streaming back from the engine. This remarkable image passes a city, crosses a trestle, moves into darkness and daylight, "Going, going . . . gone." And so it ends, with only a tail of smoke going off the right-hand side of the picture. Children love this book, which was named a Caldecott Honor Book for its stunning artwork, as was Crews's book *Truck*, which will appeal to the same audience. They will also like the innovative board book *Inside Freight Train* by Crews, which uses sliding panels to reveal the inside of boxcars.

Crews, Donald. *Parade*. 1983. Paperback: Morrow. Good for groups. Ages 18 months and up.

You can count on Donald Crews for graphically wonderful books on topics with high appeal for toddlers. Here he combines his bright, posterlike art with a brief text, building up anticipation as the day of a parade dawns. The pictures initially have more white space than illustrations, which slowly changes as spectators gather and the parade approaches: "Here it comes! Flags flying." A marching band leads the way, with the instruments named in the text. Then come floats, antique bicycles and cars, and, to the delight of the very young, a brand-new fire engine. The pictures empty more quickly than they filled, with the last one of a road sweeper cleaning up confetti.

Crews, Donald. *School Bus*. 1984. Hardcover: Greenwillow. Paperback: Mulberry. Ages 15 months and up.

The golden yellow color of school buses fills this well-designed book, which will especially interest young children who watch their siblings board school buses. It opens with a wonderful picture of four rows of eight school buses parked next to one another. With just a sentence or phrase on each page, the book records how buses move through a town, empty at first, then stop for lines of waiting schoolchildren clad in bright colors. Off to school, then the buses return to their parking lot: "Empty buses wait." On the road again after school, buses are everywhere until children are "Home again," and so are the buses. While not Crews's most exciting book, this cheerfully celebrates a familiar sight.

Crews, Nina. *One Hot Summer Day*. 1995. Hardcover: Greenwillow. Ages 2 years and up.

An exuberant African American girl makes the most of a hot summer day in the city. Striking collage illustrations juxtapose photographs over one another, showing her trying to fry an egg on the ground, drawing with chalk on the sidewalk, and eating two purple Popsicles in a row. She greets a rain shower with the same enthusiasm, catching raindrops on her tongue and dancing in puddles. The rain lowers the temperature, and the sun reappears. "It's nice and cool. I run to the playground and I swing high," ends the straightforward, first-person narrative. Urban children will see their own world reflected in the lively illustrations, while those from outside cities will see a setting too rarely depicted in picture books.

Cummings, Pat. *My Aunt Came Back*. 1998. Board book: HarperCollins. Ages 18 months and up.

On the appealing cover of this board book, a young woman swings a child around with an air of free-spirited joy. That same African American woman, clad in different wonderful clothes on each page, radiates energy as she visits her niece and brings her presents after traveling around the world. The somewhat nonsensical rhyme explains, "My aunt came back from Bucharest / She brought me back a quilted vest," while the pictures show the girl in an embroidered vest. The illustrations, saturated with pastel hues, have a batiklike look that suits the subject. On the final double-page spread, the girl announces that this time she gets to travel with her aunt, a fitting end to an imaginative book.

Curtis, Jamie Lee. *Tell Me Again about the Night I Was Born*. Illustrated by Laura Cornell. 1996. Hardcover: HarperCollins. Ages 2½ years and up.

In the authentic voice of a child, the narrator asks to hear all the well-loved details about the night she was born and her parents came in great excitement to adopt her. Scratchy, humorous watercolors show them frantically packing, flying, arriving at the hospital, and then taking their adored baby home. Lighthearted but full of love and warmth, this is a celebration of family that children will enjoy whether or not they were adopted. Only older toddlers will sit through this story, but parents might want to tell it in their own words if it's an important topic in the family.

Dabcovich, Lydia. *Sleepy Bear*. 1982. Paperback: Dutton. Good for groups. Ages 15 months and up.

This time-tested book follows a large bear from fall to winter to spring, with a very brief text and likable pictures. First, the bear notices it is getting cold, leaves are falling, and birds are flying away. With a big yawn, he finds a cave and settles in. The rounded strokes in the illustrations and the soft-looking snow make his winter sleep appear cozy and comfortable. In fact, he looks a bit annoyed to be awakened by sun and birds but rejoices when he hears bees and remembers honey. The last full picture shows him loping across a flowery meadow after a swarm of bees. A simple story that holds children rapt.

Davis, Katie. *Who Hops?* 1998. Hardcover: Harcourt. Paperback: Harcourt. Good for groups. Ages 2 years and up.

Aimed perfectly at the humor of toddlers, this clever book asks a question, gives three right answers, and then gives an obviously wrong fourth answer. In response to "Who hops?" the vivid illustrations show a frog, a rabbit, and a kangaroo. Then, in a deadpan manner, with a picture of a cow's head, the words say, "Cows hop." No doubt children will correct that outrageous notion before turning the page, where the text concedes, "No they don't! Cows moo and give milk, but they don't hop!" A speculative-looking cow has a thought balloon coming out of its head, with a silly picture of a cow hopping in it. The same pattern continues for flying, swimming, and crawling. The final pages depict children trying out each of the movements themselves. Enjoy this as a guessing game, a humorous read-aloud, a prelude to imitating the animals' actions, or all three.

Day, Alexandra. *Good Dog, Carl*. 1985. Paperback: Aladdin. Board book: Simon & Schuster. Ages 15 months and up.

In this nearly wordless book, a huge black dog is left in

charge of a baby one day, and they proceed to create delightful messes together. They bounce on the bed, try on jewelry in front of the mirror, get into the fish tank, and more. But before the mother comes home, the dog, Carl, cleans up all traces of the mischief, with no harm done. You can make up words as you go along or just enjoy the pictures together. Even very young children are attracted to this and the other books in the series.

Degen, Bruce. *Jamberry*. 1983. Hardcover: HarperCollins. Paperback: HarperCollins. Board book: HarperCollins. Good for groups. Ages newborn and up.

Give yourself a treat and start reading this to your newborn. Few rhyming books for children are as much fun as this rollicking tribute to berries. Long before your child understands the words, he or she will love the sounds. The loose premise is that a boy and a bear are picking all different kinds of berries, but that's really just an excuse to play with language. The pictures match the text in exuberance, showing the boy and bear buried neck-high in berries, dancing in them, playing with them, and eating them, with great lines like, "Raspberry / Jazzberry / Razzamatazzberry. Berryband / Merryband / Jamming in Berryland." Enjoy with berries, real or imaginary, but be sure not to miss this "jam jamboree."

Demarest, Chris. *The Cowboy ABC*. 1999. Hardcover: DK. Ages 2 years and up.

Watercolors with an old-fashioned flair show an object or a word associated with cowboy life for each letter of the alphabet. "A is for Appaloosa, a trusty steed. B is for Buckaroo, who rides at top speed." The rhymes are easy and natural, and the pictures will be of great interest to cowboy fans, who get to see cowboys—a few of whom seem to be female—at their work.

While toddlers have no need to learn the alphabet yet, this is an entertaining excursion to the Old West for young cowboy fans. If the text gets too long, just study the pictures together.

Demarest, Chris L. *Honk!* **1998. Hardcover: Boyds Mills. Good for groups. Ages 12 months and up.**

Flaps in books don't always last long, but that's because children enjoy them so much. Flaps are used to good effect on each page of this barnyard tale, which opens with a little goose who is lost. Every time it sees an object, starting with a laundry basket, the goose asks, "Honk?" By opening a flap, you can see the animal behind the object. The dog behind the laundry basket barks, "Woof." The cat under the pillow meows. The horse behind the stack of hay says, "Neigh." But when the goose nears the road, a car races by. The goose hears, "Honk! Honk!" and from behind the car emerges its mother, at last. Light entertainment, with flaps to lift and animals to name and imitate.

dePaola, Tomie. *Pancakes for Breakfast.* **1978. Hardcover: Harcourt. Paperback: Harcourt. Ages 2 years and up.**

This wordless book tells a story that is easy to follow with pictures full of comical expressions. A woman thinks of pancakes when she awakes one morning, so she starts to make them with her cat and dog looking on. In assembling the ingredients, she has to go to fetch an egg from her henhouse and to milk her cow. She churns butter and, last of all, visits a neighbor to buy maple syrup. But alas, when she gets home, the cat and dog have broken the eggs and spilled the milk. What will she do? Resourceful as always, she comes up with a way to have the breakfast she wants. You can "read" this a little differently every time, and maybe occasionally in conjunction with cooking—and eating—pancakes.

Dijs, Carla. *Are You My Mommy?* 1990. Hardcover: Simon & Schuster. Good for groups. Ages 18 months and up.

In a familiar story line, a young animal goes looking for its mother, asking a series of other animals, "Are you my mommy?" The baby chick has just hatched when it sets off, encountering a cat, rabbit, goose, and sheep, before finding Mrs. Hen. Of course, young listeners know perfectly well that the cat and others aren't the chick's mother, which makes the questions amusing. The illustrations have clean lines and only a few colors, set against a white background. In each picture, the head of the adult animal pops up nicely above the top of the book. While breaking no new ground, this basic book with its predictable, satisfying ending, will appeal to very young children. A companion book, now out of print, *Are You My Daddy?* uses the same format.

Dodds, Dayle Ann. *Sing, Sophie!* Illustrated by Rosanne Litzinger. 1997. Paperback: Candlewick. Ages 2¹/₂ years and up.

"I bumped my knee, I scratched my nose, / I lost my shoe, I tore my clothes. / Whenever trouble passes by, / I don't worry, I don't cry. / 'Cause I'm a cowgirl, don't you see? / Yippee-ky-yuu! Yippee-ky-yee!" Sophie loves to sing the crazy songs she makes up, while strumming her guitar. But one day, no matter where she goes to sing, a family member asks her to sing somewhere else. With a huge cowboy hat and red cowboy boots, she keeps moving around the farm, singing a different, funny song at each stop. Only when Sophie quiets the screaming baby with a catchy song does her family come to see her talent. The song lyrics read like crazy poems, which toddlers will love.

Dotlich, Rebecca Kai. *Away We Go!* **Illustrated by Dan Yaccarino. 2000. Hardcover: HarperCollins. Ages 12 months and up.**

Sparkling colors and stylized shapes introduce many ways to get from one place to another. Some are commonplace—such as a wagon, bike, sled, and skateboard—while others are as unusual as a hot air balloon and a cable car. The clean design varies page arrangement, while the text consists mainly of the vehicle names. Amusing touches, such as a dog in an open-cockpit airplane, and thoughtful ones, such as including a wheelchair, characterize this fine book, which has unusually sturdy pages to stand up to multiple readings.

Dotlich, Rebecca Kai. *What Is Round?* **Photographs by Maria Ferrari. 1999. Hardcover: HarperCollins. Ages 2 years and up.**

The appealing cover of this book gives a taste of what is to come, showing a crisp photograph of a multicolored lollipop and posing the title question, "What Is Round?" Each page follows suit, with clear color photographs and round objects to identify. The text simply names the objects, such as "A bubble, a bead, a bagel, a ball." Then on the final double-page spread, which offers an assortment of objects, not all of them round, comes the challenge, "What else is round? Your turn to try!" The pages present a good combination of familiar and slightly less familiar objects, arranged gracefully together. Heavy pages make this gamelike book, which may get a lot of use, unusually durable.

Downey, Lynn. *The Flea's Sneeze.* **Illustrated by Karla Firehammer. 2000. Hardcover: Henry Holt. Ages 2 years and up.**

In this lighthearted tale about a disastrous sneeze, all the barn animals, except for a flea, are sleeping peacefully: "A rat, a cat, / A black-eyed bat; / A cow, an owl, / A feathered fowl; / A dog, a hog, / An old barn frog." Witty acrylic paintings show them spread out in a spacious barn, with zs coming out of their mouths. But the flea, perched on the slumbering mouse's back, is coughing and sniffling, and feels a sneeze coming on. Although no one hears him, he does ask, "Does eddybody hab a tissue for be?" before his sneeze explodes in huge black letters. With a domino effect, the rat is blown awake and scares the cat, and so on, until everyone is awake. The rhyming verses are uneven, but the artwork will undoubtedly amuse children.

Doyle, Charlotte. *You Can't Catch Me.* Illustrated by Rosanne Litzinger. 1998. Hardcover: HarperCollins. Good for groups. Ages 2 years and up.

A round-faced child running excitedly from an unknown pursuer smiles and calls, "You can't catch me." Meanwhile, three animals are each chasing another: a dog chases a cat, a bug chases a bee, and a squirrel chases another squirrel. The lilting text describes the chased animals getting away, pauses on a page to ask where they are (so children can point them out behind bushes), and then relates that the animals are caught. That leaves the child still running—or does it? Laughing, the child ends up in a warm hug from the chasing adult: "You caught me! Whee!" Big expressive faces and lush colors characterize the pictures in this lap-size book.

Eastman, P. D. *Go, Dog. Go!* 1961. Paperback: Random House. Board book: Random House. Ages 15 months and up.

Parents may remember this popular book from their own childhood. With an upbeat text of basic words, it explores different concepts using dogs. The opposites "in" and "out" take the form of dazed-looking dogs entering and leaving a maze. For colors, the cartoonlike illustrations show a red dog perched on a small blue tree, and more. Some of the book's ample humor emerges from mismatched sizes. Two huge dogs in roller-coaster cars far too small for them are going up, while a little dog in a car too big for it is going down, demonstrating another pair of opposites. Although the text jumps around a lot, the illustrations unify the book, as does a running gag about a dog and a hat. As fast-moving as the roller coaster and full of fun.

Ehlert, Lois. *Color Farm*. 1990. Hardcover: HarperCollins. Board book: HarperCollins. Good for groups. Ages 18 months and up.

Brilliant colors and clever die-cut shapes create the faces of farm animals in this striking book. Geometric cutouts form the animals' heads. When the page is turned, the cutouts show the geometric shape against a black background. The text consists of the animal and shape names. Young children may find it difficult to discern some of the animals, but after hearing the words, they will start to see the shapes, and they are certain to enjoy the cut-out sections. The board book is slightly smaller than the original and leaves out some wonderful pictures at the end, although as board books go, this is unusually attractive. If you start with the board book for your young child, be sure to check out the longer version later.

Ehlert, Lois. *Color Zoo*. 1989. Hardcover: HarperCollins. Board book: HarperCollins. Good for groups. Ages 18 months and up.

Like its companion book, *Color Farm*, this stunning book combines bold colors and clever die-cut shapes to form animal faces out of geometric shapes. The shapes—which include star, circle, heart, diamond, hexagon, and more—are reviewed every few pages and again at the end. Another page at the end lists the colors used, while the final page shows all the animal faces again. Because the pictures rely so heavily on geometric shapes, children may initially have trouble identifying some of the animals but can still enjoy the artwork. As with *Color Farm*, the board book is slightly smaller than the original and leaves out some pictures at the end. However, it is still unusually beautiful, so if you start with this less destructible version, be sure to check out the longer version, which is a Caldecott Honor Book, when your child gets older.

Ehlert, Lois. *Feathers for Lunch*. 1990. Hardcover: Harcourt. Paperback: Harcourt. Good for groups. Ages 12 months and up.

This tall, thin book brims with color and creativity as it introduces twelve common North American birds. Bright collage illustrations show a cat prowling a yard with a bell around its neck to warn the birds of its presence. Small labels identify the life-size birds and the many colorful plants near them, while large typeface conveys the main text. You can either read the main story line or stop and read the labels, too. When your child is older, add in the information at the book's end, which gives more details about each bird, its size, food, and home range. A visual feast to connect with the real birds in your neighborhood.

Ehlert, Lois. *Fish Eyes*. 1990. Hardcover: Harcourt. Paperback: Harcourt. Board book: Harcourt. Good for groups. Ages 6 months and up.

Pure pleasure to look at, this long, narrow book swims with colorful fish on every page. Yes, it's a counting book, but babies don't need to know that. They will simply be entranced by the neon colors and strikingly gorgeous fish: big fish, small fish, fish swirling around, and fish with cut-out holes in their eyes that show through to the next page. Toddlers may get into the counting as well as comparing and contrasting the different fish on each page, which have common features like stripes but different colors and shapes. The minimal text serves mainly to tie together the extraordinary illustrations. A prize-winning catch.

Ehlert, Lois. *Growing Vegetable Soup*. 1987. Hardcover: Harcourt. Paperback: Harcourt. Good for groups. Ages 18 months and up.

This striking book uses large print, a brief text, and graphically stunning illustrations to introduce gardening to very young children. It opens with a brightly colored rake, shovel, and hoe, then goes on to planting seeds. Large hands place seeds in little holes in the soil and, on the next page, transfer small green shoots from pots into the ground. The cut-paper collages show rows of garden plants getting larger and producing buds. The background colors grow brighter, moving from blues and greens into reds, pinks, and purples. On every page, labels identify the tools, plants, and vegetables by name. You can stop and read these or stick with the simple story in the large typeface. A recipe for vegetable soup completes this outstanding book. Another wonderful Ehlert book about food is *Eating the Alphabet*, which is slightly more advanced and equally beautiful.

Ehlert, Lois. *Planting a Rainbow*. 1988. Hardcover: Harcourt. Paperback: Harcourt. Good for groups. Ages 18 months and up.

Bold colors leap off the page in this tribute to flower gardens. Imaginative graphics show the beginnings of a flower garden and follow it as it grows. Greenery marked by labeled sticks soon turns into magnificent flowers. After the garden is blooming profusely, the book divides the flowers by color, with a series of pages that get progressively bigger. The clever aspect of this and many other Ehlert books is that you can read them to a very young child, following the large-print, brief text that tells the story, while also enjoying the unusually vibrant pictures. As your child gets older, you can add in the information given in smaller print, such as the flower names. A must for gardeners with young children.

Ehlert, Lois. *Snowballs*. 1995. Hardcover: Harcourt. Paperback: Harcourt. Board book: Harcourt. Ages 18 months and up.

If you live where it snows, be sure to share this book with your child—and get it in the larger versions rather than the board book to fully benefit from the gorgeous artwork. Ehlert, one of the great talents in children's book illustrating, creates a snow family using white paper decorated with colorful objects like knit hats, mittens, strawberries, corn kernels, buttons, and plastic forks. The snow dad, mom, boy, girl, baby, cat, and dog extend across the long pages, until the story reveals what happens when the sun comes out. Your child will insist on stopping to look at the decorative objects—and will undoubtedly want to build a similar snowman. A striking double-page spread shows all the decorative objects, which could prompt a game of finding them throughout the book. A total wintry delight.

Elgar, Rebecca. *Is That an Elephant over There?* 1998. Board book: Sterling. Good for groups. Ages 12 months and up.

Like the better-known *Where's Spot?* by Eric Hill, this board book conceals animals behind flaps on every other page.

The question is always the same: "Is that an elephant over there?" Four times, the answers are similar, depending on the animal. Behind the first flap hides a zebra, with the words "No! It's a zebra." Then, "No! It's a tiger," followed by a hippo and a lion. In the last picture, the answer changes to "Yes! Hooray! It's an elephant." Young children who have started speaking can quickly join in the repetitive text. Even the illustrations repeat themselves, with the same pictures of leaves and colorful flowers on the borders and flaps. With the fun of participating in the questions and answers, and the pleasure of opening the flaps, this small book will probably get a lot of wear.

Elgar, Rebecca. *Jack: It's Bathtime/Jack: It's Bedtime/Jack: It's Playtime.* **1998. Board book: Kingfisher. Ages: 12 months through 2 years.**

These original board books use large flaps to help tell stories about a dog named Jack. In *It's Bathtime*, Jack needs a number of things to get ready for his bath. He stands, smiling, on the left-hand page, while a flap labeled "yellow" opens to reveal his duck. " 'Quack, quack!' said Jack." Each page mentions a different color: red boat, green towel, and so on, until they all appear together in a pop-up picture on the final pages. The same format organizes the other two books, about getting ready for playtime, which shows patterns like stripes and checks, and bedtime, in which Jack counts slippers, toys, and more. The design works well, and the details are geared to babies and toddlers.

Ellwand, David. *The Big Book of Beautiful Babies.* **1995. Hardcover: Dutton. Board book: Dutton. Good for groups. Ages 3 months and up.**

Unusual as it is to see black-and-white photographs these days, this large book demonstrates how effective they can be.

Each page shows a baby, often in close-up, starting with a smiling infant. Opposite is a crying baby, with the text across the two pages reading, "Baby happy, / baby sad." To vary the rhythm after four pages of faces, a double-page spread shows a pair of hands in one photo and a pair of feet in the other. The multicultural cast of babies is seen laughing and crying, wet and dry, dressed and bare. A perfect book for the many babies and toddlers fascinated by looking at babies. The smaller board book may prove serviceable, but it doesn't do the photographs full justice.

Emberley, Ed. *Go Away, Big Green Monster!* 1992. Hardcover: Little, Brown. Good for groups. Ages 2 years and up.

This book is brilliant in its simplicity, design, and understanding of children. It begins, "Big Green Monster has two big yellow eyes," on a page that is black except for cut-out holes that show yellow eyes. Using cutouts, each page adds a feature to the monster: long nose, big red mouth, squiggly ears, and more. When the monster is complete, the words declare, "YOU DON'T SCARE ME!" and the book reverses direction, eliminating each feature page by page. The final page, which is black, declares that the monster won't come back, "Until I say so." A young child has the pleasure of being frightened while having control over the monster's appearance. A highly satisfying picture book.

Emberley, Rebecca. *My Colors/Mis colores. My Numbers/Mis números. My Opposites/Mis opuestos. My Shapes/Mis formas.* 2000. Board book: Little, Brown. Ages 18 months and up.

Boldly colored cut-paper illustrations make these little books a visual delight. At the same time, they introduce concepts in simple ways, using English and Spanish on each page.

The one about colors is the most basic, with a page of the color on one side and an object that illustrates it on the other. For example, a slightly textured red page contains the words *red* and *rojo*, while the facing page has a red apple with the words *apple* and *la manzana* on it. *My Numbers* also keeps to a basic level, counting objects from one to ten in English and Spanish, with exquisite pictures. The books on shapes and opposites present harder concepts but can be enjoyed for the artwork and the fun of identifying objects. These small gems were created for this size and format with great success.

Ernst, Lisa Campbell. *Bear's Day/Cat's Play*. 2000. Board book: Viking. Ages 6 months through 2 years.

Gentle colors and rounded figures characterize these original board books about a child playing. In *Cat's Play*, the child's companion is a fat gray-and-white cat. Short phrases describe their time together: "Hello, cat / Gentle pat / Time to eat / Clean and neat." Each page has a phrase and a centered picture in pastel hues, with just enough variety in design to stay interesting. With a similar format, color scheme, and rhyming text, *Bear's Day* pairs the same child, who could be male or female, with a toy bear. They have tea together, play with blocks, clap hands, read, draw with crayons, and take a nap. Both sweet board books are fun to read aloud.

Falconer, Ian. *Olivia Counts/Olivia's Opposites*. 2002. Board book: Atheneum. Ages 2 years and up.

The young pig Olivia has star quality and embraces life with aplomb. She first appeared in the longer books *Olivia* and *Olivia Saves the Circus*, which you will want to read when your child is a bit older. In these elegantly designed board books, illustrations that rely on blacks, whites, and grays highlighted with red convey Olivia's energy and personality as she counts through familiar items—"one ball, two bows"—and demonstrates opposites—"up, down, long short." While you may laugh even more than your children do at the wonderfully funny pictures, everyone will love meeting this unforgettable pig.

Falwell, Cathryn. *Feast for 10.* 1993. Hardcover: Clarion. Ages 18 months and up.

Crisp cut-paper illustrations that stand out against a clean background show an African American mother and her five children shopping for, preparing, and enjoying a large meal. While numbers are one aspect of the story, counting from one to ten twice, the story and pictures offer plenty to children not yet ready to count. Pushing their cart in the grocery store, the family gathers a rhyming list of items: pumpkins for pie, chicken to fry, beans, greens, tomatoes, and potatoes. The rhymes come naturally, with just a few words on each page, and humor emerges in details like the five kinds of beans, which include jelly beans. After loading the car, this middle-class family heads home to start cooking together with the father's help. In the final, warm picture, ten people gather to share the feast.

Falwell, Cathryn. *Nicky & Grandpa.* 1991. Hardcover: Clarion. Ages 12 months and up.

A red-haired baby stands in his crib, looking uncertain. "Where's Grandpa?" reads the large print on generous white space. "Here he is!" proclaims the next page, with a smiling, young-looking grandfather reaching for Nicky. The grandfather changes Nicky and then dresses him after a short search for Nicky's shoes. Every other page asks the question "Where?" about something: first Grandpa, then the shoes, then Bunny. The question draws in listeners, who can point out the answer in the picture on the following page. The two head outdoors, where Nicky plays in a sandbox and Grandpa reads the *New York Times*. After this plug for reading, Grandpa reads a picture book to Nicky. Uncluttered collage illustrations, small size, and sturdy pages suit this to its young audience. One in a series, some of which are out of print but may be available at your local library.

Falwell, Cathryn. *We Have a Baby*. 1993. Hardcover: Houghton. Paperback: Houghton. Ages 12 months and up.

Pastel illustrations full of comforting rounded shapes show loving parents and a little child welcoming a baby into their family. The short phrase on each page starts with the words "A baby," such as "A baby to carry," "A baby to kiss," and "A baby to rock." The pictures illustrate the action, with the older sibling—who could be a girl or boy—included in the actions. The father interacts with the children as much as the mother does. His skin color, which matches the little child's, is slightly darker than his wife's and baby's, a subtle touch not mentioned in the text. This gentle book lends itself to preparing a sibling for the arrival of a baby but will also entertain babies themselves, who will see their lives reflected in simple ways.

Faulkner, Keith. *The Wide-Mouthed Frog: A Pop-up Book*. Illustrated by Jonathan Lambert. 1996. Hardcover: Dial. Good for groups. Ages 6 months and up.

Many children are enchanted by this short pop-up with four animal faces that emerge from the pages. The story comes from a longer folktale about a bragging frog. Each of four animals—the frog, a bird, a mouse, and finally an alligator—announces what it eats. The pop-ups feature the frog's tongue coming out, the bird's beak, and the mouse's whiskers. When the alligator says that it eats frogs, the wide-mouthed frog makes its getaway in a big splash. Bright watercolor illustrations combine with clever paper engineering to make this a favorite for one-on-one reading and in groups.

Feiffer, Jules. *Bark, George*. 1999. Hardcover: Harper-Collins. Good for groups. Ages 2 years and up.

When his mother tells George, a lanky puppy, to bark, he answers with a "meow" and then a series of other animal noises. So his mother takes him to a vet, and the man pulls animal after animal out of George's throat. The problem seems to be solved until a surprising twist at the end reveals that George has a new but similar problem. On clean, wide pages, the cartoonlike illustrations show funny facial expressions and brilliant body language. A clever, catchy story from a master cartoonist.

Flack, Marjorie. *Ask Mr. Bear*. 1932. Hardcover: Simon & Schuster. Paperback: Aladdin. Good for groups. Ages 18 months and up.

Charming old-fashioned pictures show a towheaded boy named Danny contemplating what to get his mother for her birthday. He starts out to see what he can find and meets Mrs. Hen. When she offers an egg for his mother, he replies, "Thank you, but she has an egg." Goose, Goat, Sheep, and Cow make similar suggestions, which he politely declines. Although the animals won't accompany him there, Danny goes off to the woods to ask Mr. Bear, who has a splendid idea. The text is longer than in many books for this age group, but the repetition makes it possible for toddlers to follow, and they will enjoy the increasing group of animals. Parents will especially appreciate the sweet end.

Fleming, Denise. *Barnyard Banter*. 1997. Hardcover: Henry Holt. Paperback: Henry Holt. Board book: Henry Holt. Good for groups. Ages 12 months and up.

Distinctive illustrations replete with color and texture raise this barnyard book above many others. Its rhyming text works unusually well, too, inviting children to imitate the animals and soon join in the entire text. "Cows in the pasture, *moo, moo, moo*. / Roosters in the barnyard, *cock-a-doodle-doo*." After several animals make their noises, the same question occurs, "But where's Goose?" Children will notice and start looking for the goose that appears somewhere in every picture. The illustrations, created from paper pulp in delicious hues, exude energy, culminating in two large pictures, drenched in sunny yellow, of the goose honking and the words "There's Goose!" An outstandingly beautiful book matched by an appealing text.

Fleming, Denise. *The Everything Book*. 2000. Hardcover: Henry Holt. Ages 2 years and up.

This aptly named book has a little of everything in it: rhymes, counting, colors, and more. It's a book to dip into rather than read from beginning to end. More important, the artwork makes it rewarding to open to any page. Fleming creates vibrant textured illustrations from colored paper pulp, giving her books a unique and striking appearance. Each double-page spread touches on a new topic, usually one related to the page before. A rhyme about chickens feeding is followed by a baby at mealtime. Then a gorgeous page highlights fruits and their colors, followed by kitchen utensils that make good toys. Your child may favor certain pages or just enjoy the range of familiar topics and bouncing verses. You could collect similar objects from around your house to add a play activity to the reading.

Fleming, Denise. *In the Small, Small Pond*. 1993. Hardcover: Henry Holt. Paperback: Henry Holt. Good for groups. Ages 15 months and up.

The highly talented Fleming followed up her outstanding book *In the Tall, Tall Grass* with this companion volume, which was named a Caldecott Honor Book. With a similar glorious palette and well-crafted text, this takes a child to a pond, where blues, greens, and yellows blend in stunning combinations. Fleming creates her unique artwork from colored paper pulp, adding a rich texture to the illustrations. The child first sees a frog, which observant children will notice on almost every page, though it isn't mentioned. The engaging rhymes describe action in the pond: "Wiggle, jiggle, tadpoles wriggle," followed by "Waddle, wade, geese parade." The book moves subtly from morning to night and spring to winter, forming a perfect whole that's pure pleasure to look at.

Fleming, Denise. *In the Tall, Tall Grass*. 1991. Hardcover: Henry Holt. Paperback: Henry Holt. Good for groups. Ages 15 months and up.

"In the tall, tall grass, / crunch, munch, caterpillars lunch," opens this superb book. A child watches the progress of a caterpillar through the grass, where it passes hummingbirds that dart, dip, and sip; bees that strum, drum, and hum; and other small animals described in the brief, rhyming words, which are cleverly incorporated into the pictures. For example, when the bats "swoop," the word itself is shaped like a wing. The innovative art technique employs colored paper pulp in a gorgeous palette with an appealing texture. A joy to look at and read aloud.

Fleming, Denise. *Lunch*. 1992. Hardcover: Henry Holt. Paperback: Henry Holt. Board book: Henry Holt. Good for groups. Ages 18 months and up.

A cheeky little mouse is sniffing as he emerges from his mousehole, very hungry indeed. In oversize, vibrant illustrations, he makes his way onto a table and starts to eat. The book's design lends itself to a guessing game in which the color of a food is given and a partial glimpse of it, such as the end of an ear of corn with the words above it, "sweet yellow." On the next page, the phrase is completed with "corn," with the rest of the ear showing, now partially eaten by the mouse. With each food, the mouse acquires a new color on his fur, until by the end, it is splotched with all different hues. Well satisfied, he makes his way back to his mousehole with color trailing behind him. Gorgeous, textured illustrations combine with well-paced words to make a real crowd pleaser.

Fleming, Denise. *Mama Cat Has Three Kittens*. 1998. Hardcover: Henry Holt. Good for groups. Ages 15 months and up.

Another gorgeous book by Fleming, this one tells the simple story of a mother cat and her three kittens, Fluffy, Skinny, and Boris. Whatever Mama Cat does, Fluffy and Skinny imitate her like good kittens. They wash their paws and sharpen their claws when she washes and sharpens hers. They walk as she does on a stone wall and chase leaves as she does. Where's Boris? He's napping, at least until the other three start napping. Then Boris has a few things to do on his own until he joins them. Words with an easy rhythm and rich, textured pictures of cunning kittens combine to make another winner from a major talent in the field. A must for cat lovers.

Fleming, Denise. *Time to Sleep*. 1997. Hardcover: Henry Holt. Paperback: Henry Holt. Ages 15 months and up.

Striking illustrations in glorious autumn colors fill the large pages of this engaging book. As it opens, Bear sniffs the air and realizes that it is time to crawl into her cave and sleep, but first, she must tell Snail. Huge Bear finds tiny Snail and says, "It is time to seal your shell and sleep." But first Snail must tell Skunk, who tells Turtle, who tells Woodchuck, who tells Ladybug. Ladybug then wakes up Bear to tell her to go to her cave to sleep, to which Bear grumbles, "I *am* in my cave. I *was* asleep." So Ladybug crawls under a nearby log and, on the final page, all the animals wish each other good-night. A wonderful combination of picture and text, this is perfect for bedtime or anytime you want to feast your eyes.

Ford, Miela. *Bear Play*. 1995. Hardcover: Greenwillow. Ages 12 months and up.

Expressive photographs of polar bears at the zoo turn into a story that children will identify with. The first photo focuses on the face of a polar bear, with simple text in large type that reads, "Let me think." Like many a bored child, the bear is wondering what to do and decides to call a friend. By "call," it means roar rather than use the telephone. They play in water and come across a ball to balance, throw, and catch. When the conversational text reads, "You have to go?" the two friends seem a bit sad and nuzzle noses as they agree to play tomorrow. If you are lucky enough to live near a zoo with polar bears, combine the book with a trip to see the real thing. Look for Ford's other animal photo books, such as *Follow the Leader* and *Little Elephant*.

Ford, Miela. *Sunflower.* **Illustrated by Sally Noll. 1995. Hardcover: HarperCollins. Good for groups. Ages 18 months and up.**

This appealing book illustrates the process and excitement of planting a sunflower seed and watching it grow. The words come from a little girl, and once the flower starts growing, the pictures show its progress measured against her body: "Up to my knees. Up to my nose. Over my head." Each short phrase appears on a different page, surrounded by white space and a yellow border, opposite a full-page, uncluttered painting in bright colors. Throughout, the girl's black cat appears as a silhouette somewhere in each picture, which children are sure to notice and enjoy. A pleasure to read whether you can plant a sunflower with your child or just experience the fun of gardening vicariously.

Fox, Christyan, and Diane Fox. *Fire Fighter Piggy Wiggy.* **2001. Hardcover: Handprint. Good for groups. Ages 2 years and up.**

A smiling, cartoonish pig is dashing across the cover of this book, wearing a uniform and carrying a ladder. On the endpapers, the pig appears in striped blue-and-white underwear, surrounded by pieces of a firefighter's uniform and equipment. A fire engine zips by as the story opens, prompting the little pig's dreams of "all the things that I would do if I were a fearless fire fighter." The dreams include wearing a big yellow hat, sliding down a pole, and riding around in a fire engine with "a flashing light and a screaming siren," conveyed in energetic pictures. Young children with the same dreams will love this book.

Fox, Mem. *Hattie and the Fox.* **Illustrated by Patricia Mullins. 1987. Hardcover: Simon & Schuster. Paperback: Simon & Schuster. Good for groups. Ages 12 months and up.**

In this fresh story with superb illustrations, a hen named Hattie notices a nose in the bushes one day. Her fellow farm animals respond in a jaded manner with comments repeated throughout the book. The sheep says, "Who cares?" The horse, "So what?" and the cow, "What next?" There always is something next, as Hattie sees more and more of the creature in the bush. Children will realize far before Hattie does that it's a fox and probably dangerous. The fuzzy collages created from torn tissue paper combine beauty and humor, giving the animals personality and adding to the action. The repeated refrain of animal comments invites older children to chant along with the book and makes the story more accessible to younger ones. Outstanding.

Fox, Mem. *Time for Bed.* Illustrated by Jane Dyer. 1993. Hardcover: Harcourt. Board book: Harcourt. Good for groups. Ages newborn and up.

A nearly perfect combination of words and text, this has become a favorite in many families. The hardcover version is unusually large, providing generous space for the lovely watercolors of animals at night. For the very young, the words will be the main attraction, so the board book will work until they are old enough to appreciate the larger illustrations. "It's time for bed, little mouse, little mouse / Darkness is falling all over the house," chants the opening line, setting the gentle pattern and rhythm for the whole book. A soft-furred mouse is curled over a baby mouse whose eyes are not yet open. Then comes a fluffy baby goose and graceful parent under a glorious, star-studded night sky. The final pictures show a curly-haired child tucked in and falling asleep. Lull your little one to sleep with this outstanding bedtime book, while you admire the exquisite artwork.

Frasier, Debra. *On the Day You Were Born.* 1991. Hardcover: Harcourt. Ages newborn and up.

While this stunning book does not fit the normal profile of

a book for babies, many parents love it so much that they pass on their enthusiasm even to infants. The text, which is fairly long, reads like a poem in which the whole world celebrates the birth of a child. At the same time, the words and pictures celebrate the natural world. Sun, moon, ocean, trees, and finally, people appear in the extraordinarily beautiful cut-paper illustrations to welcome the newborn baby. "We are so glad you've come!" reads the final line. Don't be surprised if tears fill your eyes reading this. Meanwhile, your child will enjoy the bright colors and the sound of your voice. If your young child finds the book too long and abstract, save it for later years, when you can also share the facts about nature given on the final pages.

Freedman, Claire. *Where's Your Smile, Crocodile?* Illustrated by Sean Julian. 2001. Hardcover: Peachtree. Ages 2 years and up.

Who won't recognize Kyle the Crocodile's feelings when he wakes up grumpy one morning? His mother observes that he's lost his smile. "Why don't you go out and play? You'll soon find it again." All the brightly colored animals that Kyle encounters ask, "Where's your smile, Crocodile?" When he explains that he lost it, they try to bring it back. The parrot makes silly noises and makes everyone laugh except Kyle. Orange Monkey makes funny faces and a huge pink elephant blows water, but Kyle doesn't smile. Adults will especially appreciate the solution to Kyle's problem. It is only when *he* tries to cheer up Little Lion Cub does Kyle forget his own problems and cheer up. Large paintings in thick, rich colors create a lush jungle and personable animal characters. Although the text may be long for some two-year-olds, others will be captivated by the humor and happy ending.

Freeman, Don. *Corduroy.* 1968. Hardcover: Viking. Paperback: Puffin. Ages 18 months and up.

The teddy bear Corduroy, who lives in a store's toy department, realizes one day that he is missing a button. He sets off after the store closes to find a replacement, leading to a series of funny adventures in the store. In the morning, Corduroy wakes up to the smiling face of a girl who has come to take him home. This simple story, with its apt scratchboard pictures, has captivated children for decades. Followed by the equally delightful A Pocket for Corduroy.

French, Vivian. Oh No, Anna! Illustrated by Alex Ayliffe. 1997. Hardcover: Peachtree. Good for groups. Ages 12 months and up.

As the title suggests, Anna gets into trouble throughout this amusing book. A toddler whose mother is carrying in boxes from the car, Anna first finds a red bucket. Turn a flap on the right-hand edge of the page to see red liquid spilling from the bucket and the refrain in large typeface, "Oh no, Anna!" Next, Anna finds some green yarn and, behind the flap, gets tangled in it, with the cat's help. Vibrant illustrations with flat colors depict Anna as a scruffy, happy toddler. By the time Anna's mother catches sight of the mess, Anna has also knocked over a vase of flowers, spilled the cat's milk, and scribbled on the carpet with black pen. The last page shows the mother, undaunted, about to transform cleaning up into a game. Well-designed flaps, bright pictures, and an appealing refrain make this a winner. Also meet Anna in Not Again, Anna and Let's Go, Anna.

Galdone, Paul. The Three Billy Goats Gruff. 1973. Hardcover: Houghton. Paperback: Houghton. Good for groups. Ages 2¹/₂ years and up.

For children who can handle the ugly troll, this is a great version of the familiar Norwegian folktale. The language preserves the cadence of oral tradition, with phrases that echo long after the book is closed. The story grips toddlers, pre-schoolers, and early elementary school children so well, it will grab the attention even of a restless group of listeners. The tension builds as, first, the littlest billy goat gruff crosses the bridge and gets stopped by the troll; then the middle billy goat gruff; and finally, the largest one, who defeats the hideous, wild-haired troll. Perfect for young ones who crave excitement, this may be a bit too scary for those who don't. A shortened, milder version for the younger set goes by the same title but is illustrated by Stephen Carpenter. In either case, don't miss this traditional favorite.

Gardiner, Lindsey. *Here Come Poppy and Max*. 2000. Hardcover: Little, Brown. Good for groups. Ages 15 months and up.

Bright-faced Poppy loves to imitate animals, offering chances for children to participate in this book as well as listen to it. With her spotted dog, the mop-haired child "walks tall like a giraffe, splashes like a duck," and "waddles like a penguin." The droll illustrations in a fine variety of colors show Poppy, her dog Max, and the animal in question spread across the pages, demonstrating the movements. Poppy's clothes also echo the look and color of each animal, something that will intrigue many children. An appealing concept, well executed and likely to please its audience. Followed by *When Poppy and Max Grow Up*.

Gentieu, Penny. *Baby! Talk!/Wow! Babies!* 2000. Board book: Crown. Ages 3 months through 2 years.

Happy babies, hungry babies, busy babies, and more appear on the pages of these board books full of photographs. From the close-up on the covers to the sweet final pages, each book contains only color photos of babies showing different emotions and doing different activities. The multicultural cast smiles, claps hands, hides, cries, and yawns. *Wow! Babies!* shows more faces, while *Baby! Talk!* shows the bodies as well. At your library, you might find the non–board book, larger versions, now out of print, which work better for the photographs. The smaller versions, however, will still entrance babies who love to look at other babies.

George, Kristine O'Connell. *Book!* Illustrated by Maggie Smith. 2001. Hardcover: Clarion. Good for groups. Ages 2 years and up.

All parents who love books will want to read this to their child. It opens with a plump-faced, brown-skinned young child squatting down to open a present. The child, not identified as a boy or girl, is delighted, just as the nearby cat is delighted with the ribbon. "I like the way you open. I can turn your pages by myself," the child says to the book, later reading it to the cat and then reading it upside down. The book serves to amuse the child alone and then is shown to a baby sibling. Better yet, a mother with an empty lap is happy to take up the child and book, and spend some cozy time together. Acrylic paintings in delicious colors show the child and family celebrating the many wonderful aspects of a book. Sturdy pages add to the durability of this outstanding picture-story book. Don't miss it!

Geras, Adèle. *Sleep Tight, Ginger Kitten.* Illustrated by Catherine Walters. 2001. Hardcover: Dutton. Ages 2 years and up.

Kitten lovers will like this tale about Ginger Kitten looking for a napping place. He starts outdoors in a flowery springtime setting but finds the wooden chair too hard. Entering a house, he tries a variety of places that don't work out—behind a door, in a box, on the hall mat. The large-eyed, ginger-colored kitten innocently leaves a mess wherever he goes. Eventually, Ginger Kitten finds the perfect napping spot, where a smiling child nestled on a sofa near a glowing fire welcomes him wholeheartedly. The final picture is a close-up of the sleeping kitten, deeply content at last.

Gershator, Phillis and David. *Greetings, Sun.* **Illustrated by Synthia Saint James. 1998. Hardcover: DK. Paperback: DK. Good for groups. Ages 2 years and up.**

Striking illustrations with vivid, flat colors share the same elegant simplicity as the text in this celebration of the day. Two black children, almost abstract in their composition, greet the day and the objects around them. "Greetings, sun. Greetings, breeze. Greetings, toes. Greetings, knees." Listeners may even join in by touching the body parts named, then hopping and jumping as the two do on their way to school. A walk past palm trees and blue ocean leads to a bright red one-room school, where more objects are greeted. After school, the two end the day at home, saying good-night to the sun and greeting the moon. The brief phrases and familiar objects make this work well for the intended audience of young children.

Gerth, Melanie. *Ten Little Ladybugs.* **Illustrated by Laura Huliska-Beith. 2000. Hardcover: Piggy Toes Press. Ages 6 months and up.**

This wildly popular book uses die-cut holes and little three-dimensional ladybugs attached to the pages to charm very young viewers. The text follows a familiar rhyming pattern that moves from ten to one, starting with the verse "Ten little ladybugs sitting on a vine, along came a butterfly—then there were Nine." Although the implication is that the ladybugs are being eaten one by one, in fact they all show up happy and healthy on the last page with the other animals named. The illustrations, which have an airbrushed look, are not outstanding, but that won't keep many babies and toddlers from being mesmerized by the candy-colored ladybugs.

Gibbons, Gail. *My Baseball Book/My Basketball Book/My Football Book/My Soccer Book*. 2000. Hardcover: Harper-Collins. Ages 2¹/₂ years and up.

These small books explain soccer, baseball, basketball, and football through simple text and useful pictures. While you probably won't want to read them to a two-year-old from cover to cover, they will be useful for young children who are interested in a sport because a sibling plays or because they've seen it elsewhere. Using labeled illustrations, the books show the fields and their parts, equipment, and roles of specific players. They also discuss points, simple rules, and time segments. Cheerful pictures of boys and girls playing together add information and portray the games as fun. Fine basic introductions for young children.

Gibbons, Gail. *Playgrounds*. 1985. Hardcover: Holiday House. Ages 2¹/₂ years and up.

The many children who frequent playgrounds may enjoy seeing their familiar elements in this brightly colored book. It opens with a look at all sorts of swings. The main text, which runs across the top of the pictures in a blue border, is straightforward in its description of the playground equipment. Labels appear near different items in the somewhat static illustrations: baby swing, tire swing, rope swing, and more. Then it's on to seesaws, a sandbox, slides, and a simple merry-go-round. In each picture, smiling children with a variety of hair and skin colors play together, with watchful adults looking on. A large picture near the end enumerates things to bring to the playground, such as jump ropes, balls, and tricycles. While not outstanding, Gibbons's books explore a child's world and introduce new topics in simple, approachable terms that make them useful and comforting.

Ginsburg, Mirra. *Across the Stream.* **Illustrated by Nancy Tafuri. 1982. Hardcover: Greenwillow. Paperback: Mulberry. Good for groups. Ages 12 months and up.**

With only a brief, rhyming text, this story creates a strong plot accessible to young children. A hen and three chicks wake up, as if from a bad dream, when a fox peers in from the roof of their henhouse. The fox doesn't see them escape as they run to a stream. There they meet a duck and three ducklings, who are kind enough to carry them across the stream. Although all the illustrations are wonderful, the one of the hen riding on the duck's back, with her wings encircling the duck's neck, stands out. The spacious watercolors contain just enough detail to interest the audience, who will point out other animals in the pictures, including the fox on their trail. Once across the stream, they have left the forlorn-looking fox behind them, providing the reader with a welcome sense of relief.

Ginsburg, Mirra. *Good Morning, Chick.* **Illustrated by Byron Barton. 1980. Hardcover: Greenwillow. Paperback: Mulberry. Good for groups. Ages 12 months and up.**

This barnyard story creates exactly the right level of tension and drama for the very young to enjoy. In it, a chick is born from "a little house / White and smooth," shown cracking open and the chick hatching out. He meets his loving mother, Speckled Hen, who teaches him to eat and scares off a hissing cat. When the chick tries to imitate a crowing rooster, he gets into a bit of trouble and lands near a frog in a puddle, but all ends well. The well-crafted tale completes most sentences with the phrase "like this," offering a comforting rhythm throughout. Barton's uncluttered, childlike drawings bring the farm to life in bright colors and personable animals. A treat.

Ginsburg, Mirra. Translated from the Russian of V. Suteyev. *The Chick and the Duckling*. Illustrated by Jose Aruego and Ariane Dewey. 1972. Paperback: Aladdin. Good for groups. Ages 12 months and up.

Humor on a child's level infuses this book about a duckling and the chick that follows it. Amusing pen-and-ink illustrations, simply colored, show the duck emerging from its shell. " 'I am out!' he said." Turn the page and see a yellow chick emerge from its shell and announce, "Me, too!" So begins a series of actions that the duck takes with the chick following in kind. The duck takes a walk through a flower-filled meadow. "Me, too!" the chick says. They dig holes, find worms, and chase butterflies, with just a sentence or two per page. But when the duck decides to take a swim, and the chick jumps into the water after him, all is not well. The duck pulls out the chick, who can't swim and who finally starts to think for itself. A satisfying story with a plot just exciting enough for a young child.

Gliori, Debi. *Can I Have a Hug?/Tickly under There*. 2002. Board book: Orchard. Ages 3 months and up.

These unusually large board books will appeal to the very young with their short format, brief text, and on-target topics. In *Can I Have a Hug?*, a grown-up bear tries hugging an owl, a beehive, a bunny, and a spider before it hugs its own bear cub, who has been in all the pictures. "I love the hugs I share with you the very best of all," proclaims the parent as it hugs the cub, with the other animals snuggling in, too. *Tickly under*

There shows the bear parent admiring different parts of its cub: finger, toes, eyes, nose, legs, arms, and "very tickly tum." Parents reading this may want to incorporate actions that go with the words, admiring their own offspring. In both books, the gentle pen-and-watercolor illustrations are set against generous white space, giving them an open, appealing look.

Gomi, Taro. Translated by Amanda Mayer Stinchecum. *Everyone Poops*. 1993. Hardcover: Kane/Miller. Paperback: Kane/Miller. Ages 18 months and up.

In this refreshingly straightforward book, which opens with the words "An elephant makes a big poop. A mouse makes a tiny poop," simple watercolors on bright backgrounds show lots of animals and several humans. Popular with young children (and parents trying to toilet train their children), it asks questions such as "What does whale poop look like?" A clever design and touches of humor characterize this Japanese import, which has sold enormously well in the United States. Also look for the similar *The Gas We Pass*, by Shinta Cho.

Greenfield, Eloise. *Big Friend, Little Friend/My Daddy and I . . . /I Make Music/My Doll, Keshia*. Illustrated by Jan Spivey Gilchrist. 1991. Board book: Black Butterfly. Ages 9 months and up.

Poet Eloise Greenfield turns her talents to the everyday concerns of young children in these four board books. *Big Friend, Little Friend* contrasts the narrator's older friend, who teaches him things and takes him to the playground, with how he does the same for his younger friend. The text is short, with the pen-and-watercolor pictures of African American children conveying much of the story. In *My Daddy and I . . .*, a young boy and his father play, do household tasks, and read together. In the two books about girls, one shows a girl making music and dancing, encouraged by her parents, while in the other, she plays with, and cares for, her doll.

Greenfield, Eloise. *Water, Water*. Illustrated by Jan Spivey Gilchrist. 1999. Hardcover: HarperCollins. Good for groups. Ages 18 months and up.

Even young children encounter water all around them, as this gentle picture-story book illustrates. A young African American boy goes out in the rain, fishes from a grassy shore, walks a ship's deck, looks at a waterfall, takes a bath, and drinks a glass of water, all with adults nearby, taking care of him. Pen-and-watercolor pictures use lots of blues and greens, and flowing lines, to reflect the subject. The short sentences, which link the pages, rhyme as they describe the boy's small adventures. A simple story about a familiar aspect of everyday life.

Grossman, Bill. *My Little Sister Ate One Hare*. Illustrated by Kevin Hawkes. 1996. Hardcover: Crown. Paperback: Random House. Good for groups. Ages 2 years and up.

"My little sister ate one hare. We thought she'd throw up then and there," opens this riotously funny counting book. With a perfect match of writer and illustrator, it bounces the reader along from one to ten. Two through nine describe increasingly disgusting foods that the sister eats, mostly rodents, reptiles, and insects. The punch line is hilarious. Don't worry about the numbers, just revel in the kid humor.

Guarino, Deborah. *Is Your Mama a Llama?* Illustrated by Steven Kellogg. 1989. Hardcover: Scholastic. Paperback: Scholastic. Board book: Scholastic. Good for groups. Ages 18 months and up.

A young llama named Lloyd goes about asking his friends, "Is your mama a llama?" The different animals answer by giving clues about their mothers, such as, "She's got big hind legs and a pocket for me . . . So I don't think a llama is what she could be." The listener has a chance to guess what kind of animal is being described before turning the page to where the mother animal appears. Playful pictures show the animals in outdoor settings, ending with a nighttime picture of Lloyd and his mother together; the original edition displays the detailed pictures far better than the board book does. The rhyme bounces along, with answers easy enough for young listeners either to guess or to remember the next time.

Hague, Kathleen. *Ten Little Bears: A Counting Rhyme*. Illustrated by Michael Hague. 1999. Hardcover: Morrow. Ages 2 years and up.

For those who like their illustrations cute and ornate, Michael Hague's teddy bears fit the ticket. A counting rhyme from ten to one serves as the vehicle for paintings of detailed scenes, mostly outdoors, of teddy bears playing like children. On each page, another bear leaves the group, such as, "9 Little Bears, / Learning how to skate. / One slipped and fell— / Then there were eight." The format remains the same for each double-page spread, with the picture on the right and the verse on the left, circled by the appropriate number of teddy bears. Children will find plenty to look at while also searching for the bear described in the verse. See the same bears in *Alphabears* and *Numbears*.

Haines, Mike. *Countdown to Bedtime*. Illustrated by David Melling. 2001. Hardcover: Hyperion. Ages 2 years and up.

This "Lift-the-Flap" book follows the escapades of Bandit, a raccoon, and Spike, apparently a porcupine, in a countdown to bedtime. With ten minutes to go, are Bandit and Spike ready for bed? Lift the flap and open the door to see that they are busy playing with friends. The next page, with nine minutes left, shows the two still in their dress-up clothes, with little flaps concealing their faces. The countdown continues through saying good-bye to friends, having milk and cookies, taking a bath, and putting on the right pajamas after a little mix-up. The flaps are a bit haphazard, but the characters are affable and children will enjoy their bedtime antics. Although it ends on a sleepy note, this will probably work better when there's plenty of time to play with the flaps.

Hall, Zoe. *Fall Leaves Fall!* Illustrated by Shari Halpern. 2000. Hardcover: Scholastic. Good for groups. Ages 2 years and up.

The green leaves on the front endpapers become yellow, red, and brown on the back endpapers of this tribute to autumn. The cut-paper collage illustrations start off with two children lying on the grass under a tree. Two pages later, the leaves above them have changed colors, the signal for the children to catch the leaves, kick them, collect them, and observe their different shapes. Then it's time to rake and jump in the piles. Inside their house, the children make pictures by gluing the leaves to paper and adding touches with crayons. A page at the end supplies information for older children on how leaves grow. Sparkling pictures with clean lines and vivid colors work beautifully with the simple text. If you live where the leaves turn colors, incorporate this book and some of its activities into your autumn rituals. For a similar, seasonal book, see *It's Pumpkin Time*, by the same team.

Hargrove, Linda. *Wings Across the Moon.* Illustrated by Joung Un Kim. 2001. Hardcover: HarperCollins. Ages 2 years and up.

It's dusk and the moon is rising. A child and mother observe the natural world and wonder at the wings they see and the sounds the wings make. "Moth's wings, *Flutter, hum, and whir.* / Goose's wings, *Whistle, whoosh, and furl.*" Luminous illustrations show a small house in the country where the child sees birds and insects in the garden and sky. The well-crafted prose has a soothing beat that moves the action quietly toward bedtime and the final scene of the child asleep, with wings against the moon seen through the bedroom window.

Harper, Isabelle. *My Cats Nick and Nora.* Illustrated by Barry Moser. 1995. Paperback: Scholastic. Ages 2 years and up.

Barry Moser has directed his considerable talents as a watercolorist to a simple story written by his young granddaughter. She describes in simple words a visit from her cousin and how they play with her two cats. The highlight of the book is the artwork, with its large, wonderful illustrations of the two girls and the cats. For dog lovers, see *My Dog Rosie*, another eye-catching book by the same team.

Harris, Robie H. *Happy Birth Day!* Illustrated by Michael Emberley. 1996. Hardcover: Candlewick. Paperback: Candlewick. Ages 2 years and up.

Many children like to hear the story of their birth. This large book, which tells such a story in a mother's voice, starts, "I'll never ever forget the moment you were born." It continues through the baby's first day, with wonderful close-ups of the crying baby and the beaming parents. Friends and relatives come, and "Everyone was so happy and so excited to finally meet you!" Each small action of the new baby is noted with pleasure—yawns, burps, sneezes, hiccups. The baby nurses, has more visitors, and finally falls asleep. Bathed in an atmosphere of love, the story celebrates the birth of all babies through its warm illustrations and joyful text.

Harris, Trudy. *Up Bear, Down Bear.* **Illustrated by Ora Eitan. 2001. Board book: Houghton. Ages 12 months and up.**

This board book relies on only three words to tell its story, first used on the opening pages. A yellow-haired little girl lifts her teddy bear out of bed, saying, "Up, Bear!" Then, as she pulls him behind her on the way downstairs, it reads, "Down." The graceful watercolor pictures use only a few broad strokes of gentle reds, blues, greens, and yellows. Outside, the girl tosses her bear in the air—"Up"—and catches it as it arcs—"Down." Where is the dramatic tension? The bear flies up and lands in a tree: "Up?" The girl jumps, throws a ball, and tries to climb the tree, to no avail. Luckily, the wind helps her out: "Down!" She holds the bear close and, going up and down hills, takes it safely home. A small, appealing book, remarkable in its simplicity.

Hathon, Elizabeth. *Oh, Baby!: A Touch-and-Feel Book.* **1999. Board book: Grosset & Dunlap. Ages 9 months through 2 years.**

Although some of the features of this book won't last long, your child will certainly enjoy it until then. The cardboard cover starts off the fun, with a fuzzy, blue tassel attached to the hat of a smiling baby. The next texture is the soft surface of a teddy bear in the lap of a beaming, brown-skinned child. Then comes a mobile attached to a slender ribbon—fragile but fun. Your child can also look in a shiny surface like a mirror, scratch and sniff a patch on a daffodil, open a flap to see a puppy, and feel the ribbon edging on a blanket. The photographs are mundane, but the variety of toylike aspects is appealing.

Also see the author's other touch-and-feel book, *Night-Night, Baby!*

Hayes, Sarah. *Eat Up, Gemma.* Illustrated by Jan Ormerod. 1988. Hardcover: Lothrop. Paperback: Mulberry. Ages 18 months and up.

As her older brother explains, baby Gemma won't eat no matter how often family members say to her, "Eat up, Gemma." She throws her breakfast on the floor, bangs her spoon, feeds pizza to the dog, and more. All dressed up one morning, the family heads off to church, where Gemma finally sees food she wants: the artificial fruit on a woman's hat. Cleverly, the brother, who is fairly young himself, comes up with the idea of arranging fruit and a bowl to imitate the hat, and finally, Gemma eats. Delightful illustrations with warm tones show an extended black family caring for their littlest one. Also, look in your library for *Happy Christmas, Gemma*, now out of print.

Hayes, Sarah. *This Is the Bear.* Illustrated by Helen Craig. 1986. Paperback: Candlewick. Good for groups. Ages 18 months and up.

This delightful British import opens with a teddy bear falling into a garbage can, pushed by a dog: "This is the bear who fell in the bin. This is the dog who pushed him in." The first sentences set the pattern and rhythm for the book, introducing new characters, including the boy who owns the bear, and then returning to the bear and the dog. The bear goes on a journey to a dump, and the boy and dog follow to rescue him. After a few setbacks, they all return home safe and sound, and the bear takes a bath. To the boy's surprise, the bear enjoyed his day out and hopes for another one soon. Humorous details in the pictures and humorous aspects of the text will amuse adults while the story entrances young listeners. The first in a short series.

Hazen, Barbara Shook. *Where Do Bears Sleep?* Illustrated by Mary Morgan Van Royen. 1998. Hardcover: HarperCollins. Good for groups. Ages 18 months and up.

A soothing atmosphere prevails as animal after animal snuggles to sleep. Rounded pictures, surrounded by white, reveal bears in a den, a pig in a pen, horses in stables, and owls perched on gables. The pared-down rhyming text describes where they sleep, with enough variation in the rhythm to ward off monotony. Farm animals, pets, and wild animals bed down for the night, until the final picture, where a mother tucks her sleeping daughter into bed. Quiet watercolors capture the spirit of the bedtime verses.

Heap, Sue. *What Shall We Play?* 2002. Hardcover: Candlewick. Good for groups. Ages 2 years and up.

Three friends negotiate about what to play in this upbeat book. Lily May keeps saying, "Let's play fairies," but Matt and Martha overrule her several times before she has her way. The games lend themselves to imitation and will have your child joining in the play. First, the three are trees—one big, one shaky, and one quiet—reaching for the sky. Then they play cars—fast, bumpy, and new—beeping in a traffic jam. Then, cats, followed by "wibbly-wobbly Jell-O." Finally, Lily May prevails, and the other two succumb to the magic of being fairies. Vibrant pictures with a childlike look match the story beautifully.

Henkes, Kevin. *Owen's Marshmallow Chick.* 2002. Board book: HarperCollins. Ages 18 months and up.

This excellent little book was created for the board book

format, rather than reduced from a larger size, and it shows. Each picture of the young mouse Owen fits the page, while the text also corresponds to the size. "On Easter morning," it opens, "Owen's basket was full. In it were jelly beans and gumdrops and buttercream eggs and a big chocolate bunny and a little marshmallow chick." On the ensuing pages, Owen happily eats up one item at a time, each of them his "favorite." The uncluttered pictures show him expressing his delight in different ways, ending with the marshmallow chick, which he befriends instead of eating, and lovingly kisses good-night. Children who meet this personality-packed mouse toddler can look forward to reading about him again in the longer, also wonderful, book *Owen*.

Henkes, Kevin. *Sheila Rae's Peppermint Stick*. 2001. Board book: Greenwillow. Ages 18 months and up.

Oh, to have a peppermint stick like the one Sheila Rae has. She is dancing around, holding the sparkling stick: "It was long. And striped. And thin. And sweet." Needless to say, her younger sister Louise wants it, too. Dressed in human clothes, these mice act just like children. Sheila Rae can't resist teasing Louise, who guesses that the peppermint stick has "Thirteen-seven" stripes. But when Sheila Rae climbs on a stool to hold the stick out of reach, the result is a stick broken in half, perfect for sharing. Written and illustrated to suit the small format, this is another gem by Kevin Henkes, whose longer book *Sheila Rae the Brave* stars the same sisters.

Hest, Amy. *In the Rain with Baby Duck*. Illustrated by Jill Barton. 1995. Hardcover: Candlewick. Paperback: Candlewick. Good for groups. Ages 2 years and up.

Contrary to what you might expect, Baby Duck does not like the rain and doesn't want to walk in it, even to Grampa's house for pancakes. Her parents pay no attention to Baby Duck's complaints. "Don't dally, dear. Don't drag behind," calls her mother, "Don't dawdle, dear! Don't lag behind!" Expansive pen-and-watercolor illustrations, cleverly streaked with rain, show a disgruntled yellow duckling and her well-dressed parents. Luckily, Grampa understands Baby Duck perfectly and solves the problem when he produces dashing red boots and a red umbrella. The first in a series, this is a delightful story with equally delightful pictures.

Hest, Amy. *Kiss Good Night.* Illustrated by Anita Jeram. 2001. Hardcover: Candlewick. Good for groups. Ages 2 years and up.

Charming acrylic paintings show a row of houses on a windy night. The next illustration is a close-up of one of the house windows, with a little bear gazing out: "It was a dark and stormy night on Plum Street." Having established the cold outside, the house's glowing interior seems all the warmer and cozier. His mother tucks the little bear, named Sam, into bed and reads him his favorite book. Children will enjoy pointing out the little mouse and its mouseholes that appear in many of the pictures as Sam's mother goes through his nighttime ritual. But his mother has forgotten something. "Ready now, Sam?" she asks. "Oh, no," he replies. "I'm waiting." Children and parents will guess what he's waiting for long before he gets it, his good-night kiss. A comfy book likely to become a popular bedtime choice.

Hill, Eric. *Where's Spot?* 1980. Hardcover: Putnam. Paperback: Putnam. Board book: Putnam. Good for groups. Ages 12 months and up.

One of the most popular books for young children, this is the first in a long series about a curious puppy named Spot.

When Spot's mother finds his dinner bowl still full, she goes looking for him. On each double-page spread, she finds a place he might be hiding. "Is he behind the door?" The large blue door opens, and behind the flap is a bear eating honey, who answers, "No." Behind the door in the grandfather clock, a snake gives the same answer. A bright pink piano hides, surprisingly, a hippo, and a lion is lurking under the stairs. Simple, clean figures outlined in black are set against a white background, focusing attention on the mother dog and her ultimately satisfying search. The incongruity of the animals in their hiding places will amuse young children, who will love opening the flaps over and over again. Absolutely not to be missed.

Hill, Susan. *Backyard Bedtime*. Illustrated by Barry Root. 2001. Board book: HarperCollins. Ages 12 months and up.

This little board book combines soothing rhythms and entertaining pictures for bedtime. The verses, which name plants and animals that are falling asleep, end with musical phrases like the tree-song's "Whisper, whish sigh" and the friend-song's "You're safe, I'm here." In the backyard, a nearby pond, the neighborhood street, and finally the bedroom, everything is going to sleep. The soft-hued illustrations add a whimsical touch by giving faces to pumpkins, trees, flowers, and houses, all of them looking drowsy and content.

Hindley, Judy. *Eyes, Nose, Fingers, and Toes: A First Book All about You*. Illustrated by Brita Granström. 1999. Hardcover: Candlewick. Paperback: Candlewick. Good for groups. Ages 2 years and up.

Large illustrations, a playful spirit, and invitations to join in make this just right for toddlers. Eager young children from different ethnic groups demonstrate different parts of the body, starting with the eyes. Then on to the nose for blowing and sniffing, and ears "to hear a story with." Lots of animals, real and stuffed, join the children in the expansive pictures, giving listeners more to look at. Many of the pages encourage children to imitate the actions, with phrases like "Arms go up. Arms go down," and "Hands are to hold and pat and clap! Hands are to hide behind your back." Children will be stretching and clapping and jumping and smiling as you read through this upbeat book.

Hines, Anna Grossnickle. *My Own Big Bed*. Illustrated by Mary Watson. 1998. Hardcover: Greenwillow. Ages 2 years and up.

For children about to move from a crib to a bed, this book reassures them by addressing possible concerns. A little girl clad in pajamas and sticking close to her teddy bear announces that she will sleep tonight in "a brand new *big* bed just for me." Then she thinks of all the problems she might have and how to solve them, repeating the phrase "I can fix that." Worried about falling out, she piles cushions and pillows around the sides of the bed. Lonely? She gathers her stuffed animals to sleep with her. Scared? Her teddy bear and ferocious dragon will protect her. After a story from her father and a kiss from her mother, she settles in happily for the night.

Hines, Anna Grossnickle. *What Can You Do in the Rain?/What Can You Do in the Snow?/What Can You Do in the Sun?/What Can You Do in the Wind?* Illustrated by Thea Kliros. 1999. Board book: Greenwillow. Good for groups. Ages 12 months and up.

This outstanding quartet of board books explores different kinds of weather, so one of the four will suit any given day. Each features a multicultural array of children taking part in childlike activities that correspond to the weather. The brief text answers the title question again and again. "What can you do in the snow?" elicits the responses, "Watch it fall. Catch a snowflake. Stamp a trail," and more. The gentle watercolors play with the small format beautifully, putting the focus on the child, often with a cat or dog. Small touches of humor will make parent and child smile. Read one of these on an appropriate day—or anytime—and perhaps add some ideas of your own about what a child can do in certain weather.

Hines-Stephens, Sarah. *Bean Soup/Soup Too?/Soup's Oops!* **Illustrated by Anna Grossnickle Hines. 2000. Board book: Harcourt. Ages 12 months through 2 years.**

Soup is a little black-and-white dog who lives with a young child and a cat named Bean. In *Bean Soup*, Soup and Bean interact, demonstrating simple opposites. Bean is "up" on a bookshelf, while Soup is "down" below the cat, but the short book can also just be read as a story of friendship. *Soup Too?* pairs the toddler and the dog, with Soup jumping into the tub with the child and later snuggling with the child on an adult's lap. In the third book, the three characters play inside until Soup knocks over some flowers, and the child comes up with the solution of playing outside. Well-composed pictures use the unusually small format of these board books skillfully to convey the appealing stories.

Hoban, Tana. *Black on White/White on Black.* **1993. Board book: Greenwillow. Ages newborn through 2 years.**

Infants respond visually more to contrast and patterns than to colors, which makes these two small books perfect for them. Plus, the books are visually stunning in their own right. In *Black on White*, black silhouettes of familiar items stand out against a shiny white background, starting with a bib, then a fork and spoon. Most of the objects have simple contours, although the butterfly is intricate and lovely. *White on Black* reverses the process, with white objects against a shiny black background. It opens with a baby bottle and toy horse, and ends with striking white silhouettes of an apple and a banana. Talk with your baby about the pictures, trace the outlines with your fingers, even prop the books open while you are changing your child, as you start to make books part of your infant's daily life.

Hoban, Tana. A *Children's Zoo*. 1985. Hardcover: Greenwillow. Good for groups. Ages 12 months and up.

Although we know that young children like to look at photographs of animals, few books for them have the large photographs that work best. This is a time-tested exception by a photographer who has created many fine children's books. Set against a black background, a photograph of a zoo animal appears on the right-hand page, while the animal's name and three words about it appear in white typeface on the left. For polar bears, the words read, "white / big / growls" above "polar bear" in uppercase type. Two bears prowl in the photo. Penguin, seal, zebra, parrot, lion, and others make up the zoo portfolio. Adults and older siblings will be interested in the chart at the back, which recaps the animals, where they are from, their habitat, and their eating habits.

Hoban, Tana. *Is It Red? Is It Yellow? Is It Blue? An Adventure in Color*. 1978. Hardcover: Greenwillow. Paperback: Morrow. Good for groups. Ages 12 months and up.

In a well-designed exploration of colors, pages consist of color photographs with one or more colored dots under them. Even very young children will take pleasure in pointing out the corresponding color in the photos. The first, for example, has only a red dot, with a photo of a child in a red raincoat, carrying a red umbrella, set against a dark city street and sidewalk. While providing a guessing game, the photographs are also well composed and interesting in and of themselves. The game can be continued into real life or imitated by creating your own books from photos cut from magazines, with colored dots beneath. One of many fine concept books from photographer Tana Hoban.

Hoban, Tana. *Of Colors and Things*. 1989. Paperback: Morrow. Ages 15 months and up.

If you are looking for eye-catching photographs of familiar objects to show your child, this is a beautiful solution to your problem. This wordless book groups photographs of items by color, with four items on a page. Three illustrate the color, while the fourth combines the color in question with other colors. For example, the page for red, divided into four quarters by a cross of two thick red lines, shows a red box, leaf, and pair of mittens. The fourth square has plastic boxes stacked one on the next, in bright yellow, red, green, and blue. Thus, every page provides the game of naming the objects as well as finding the square with the different colors and naming those, too. Or you can just enjoy the crisp, satisfying photographs together.

Hoban, Tana. *Red, Blue, Yellow Shoe*. 1986. Board book: Greenwillow. Ages 3 months through 2 years.

Hoban uses crisp, color photographs to good effect for the very young in this small board book. On each of the ten pages, a photograph of a familiar object is set against a light background. Each object is a different color, and the only word on the page names the color. A companion book, *1, 2, 3*, has a similar format, with numbers as the only text and each page showing a different number of familiar objects. Two similar books, now out of print, are *What Is It?*, which has no text at all and just invites the child to name the object, and *Panda, Panda,* with photographs of a panda performing different actions described by single words. These excellent little books make unusually fine use of the small, cardboard format.

Hoban, Tana. *What Is That?/Who Are They?* 1994. Board book: Greenwillow. Ages newborn through 2 years.

Like Hoban's earlier *Black on White* and *White on Black,* these two use black-and-white pictures on glossy cardboard pages to satisfy an infant's attraction to patterns and high contrast. *What Is That?* has white silhouettes on black backgrounds, showing everyday objects, beginning with a pacifier. A fuzzy toy rabbit, a stroller, a balloon, and other items are arranged on the small pages. *Who Are They?* focuses on animals, presenting black silhouettes of parent and baby sheep, pigs, dogs, cats, and ducks. In both cases, the results are surprisingly elegant in their simplicity. Play around with these books, describing the pictures in words, making animal noises, tracing the outlines, or whatever appeals to you. The main goal is a positive interaction with your infant, initiating years of enjoying books together.

Horenstein, Henry. *Arf! Beg! Catch! Dogs from A to Z.* 1999. Hardcover: Scholastic. Ages 12 months and up.

Although this isn't aimed at babies and toddlers, those who love dogs will love this book. Disregard the alphabet aspect of it and delve into the photos. Even very young children will smile at the large photographs of many breeds of dog. The alphabet provides the organization of adjectives for the twenty-six color photos, which illustrate such words as *hairy*, *itchy*, and *jump*. The dogs jump through hoops, leap after Frisbees, roll over, scratch, and more. The dynamic photographs do justice to the popular subject.

Hubbell, Patricia. *Bouncing Time*. Illustrated by Melissa Sweet. 2000. Hardcover: HarperCollins. Good for groups. Ages 12 months and up.

"How will you bounce today, baby? Bounce, bounce, bounce," begins this rollicking rhyming text. Colorful, childlike paintings show a mother and young daughter, smiling together, joined by bouncing animals at home and then at the zoo. The little girl bounces in her backpack as she and her mother watch lions and tigers, monkeys and pandas, and even hippos and elephants bouncing joyfully. Then the two bounce their way home. The vibrant illustrations, with thick strokes of color against simple backgrounds, match the words. Enjoy pointing to and naming the animals, but even better, bouncing along with the story.

Hubbell, Patricia. *Pots and Pans*. Illustrated by Diane de Groat. 1998. Hardcover: HarperCollins. Good for groups. Ages 12 months through 2 years.

It would be impossible to read this book without getting out the pots and pans to join in. In true baby style, the child in the pictures—who could be a boy or girl—gets into the pan cupboard to have a good time. A cat and dog join in with equal excitement, then a pair of legs appear on the scene that turn out to be a frazzled but resigned father. The words clang along in fine imitation of the sounds of pots, pans, lids, cans, and the spoons that bang on them. The realistic watercolor illustrations, which stay close to the floor at baby's-eye level, get increasingly lively until they slow down toward the end, when father and child sit amid the chaos. A slice of life straight from the experience of most one-year-olds, this is exactly on target.

Hubbell, Patricia. *Sea, Sand, Me!* Illustrated by Lisa Campbell Ernst. 2001. Hardcover: HarperCollins. Ages 2 years and up.

On the cover of this cheerful book, a girl enthusiastically opens her arms as if to embrace her day at the beach. First, the girl and her mother squeeze their beach ball and other beach necessities into the trunk of their Beetle and head out. They set up their beach umbrella, then comes, "Flippy-floppy sun hat. Wiggly-waggly toes. Mommy rubbing lotion on my nose, nose, nose." The energetic verse blends with the buoyant pictures, which show the girl befriending a boy and building a sand castle with him. Splashing in the sea, exploring tide pools, and eating a picnic lunch round out the happy day. "Shadows on the sand now. Sun hanging low. We pack up our beach bags. Home we go," with hopes of returning another day. The perfect prelude to a trip to the beach or a wonderful vicarious excursion in winter.

Hubbell, Patricia. *Sidewalk Trip.* Illustrated by Mari Takabayashi. 1999. Hardcover: HarperCollins. Ages 2 years and up.

"I'm splashing through a puddle with a *splish, splish, splish.* / Ice cream! Ice cream! Ice cream! is my wish, wish, wish." This sentiment, which you may have heard from your own child, comes from a girl who hears the ice cream truck in her neighborhood. She radiates excitement as she and her mother walk on city streets, encountering friends, dogs, pigeons, babies, a policeman, and finally the longed-for ice cream cone. Bright paintings with a folk art feel create a friendly urban setting to go with the bouncing, energetic verses. You might well want some ice cream on hand for this rhyming story.

Hubbell, Patricia. *Wrapping Paper Romp*. Illustrated by Jennifer Plecas. 1998. Board book: HarperCollins. Ages 12 months to 2 years.

What adult won't recognize the topic of this board book: a baby who's more interested in the wrapping paper than the present. An adorable baby in a striped romper lifts its hands in joy at the sight of a large, beribboned present. Turn the page and find the baby happily flinging the wrapping paper around, while a spotted cat plays with the ribbon. "Crinkle it. Wrinkle it. Wear it for a crown. Listen to the paper snap. Flap it up and down," crows the clever text. But wait, there's more. Inside the box, the baby finds tissue paper, perfect for hiding in or tearing for peekaboo. Beneath the tissue paper are three teddy bears, which the baby carelessly throws aside in favor of more tissue paper. Finally, the toddler stands smiling, surrounded by a paper mess, with the cat hiding in the box. An excellent, original board book with sprightly pictures and unmistakable insight into young children.

Hudson, Cheryl Willis. *Animal Sounds for Baby/Good Morning, Baby/Good Night, Baby/Let's Count, Baby*. Illustrated by George Ford. 1995. Board book: Scholastic. Good for groups. Ages 3 months and up.

These large board books present young African American children enjoying their surroundings, families, and friends. *Animal Sounds for Baby* takes place at a petting zoo, where a boy and his mother watch the animals, and the text asks what each animal says. The counting book can be read for the sake of naming familiar objects and enjoying the realistic illustrations that characterize all the books. In *Good Morning, Baby*, a girl wakes up to a new day, gets dressed, and eats breakfast. In its companion book, a boy gets ready for bed with a bath and a book. With so few board books about African Americans, this quiet quartet is all the more welcome.

Hudson, Cheryl Willis, and Bernette G. Ford. *Bright Eyes, Brown Skin*. Illustrated by George Ford. 1990. Paperback: Just Us Books. Good for groups. Ages 18 months and up.

This large book celebrates African American children through its rhyming words and illustrations of two boys and two girls. The children arrive for nursery school, where they paint, dance, play clapping games, eat lunch, play dress-up, listen to music, read, and finally settle down for a nap. Their interactions are friendly and playful as the short phrases sing their praises: "Bright eyes, cheeks that glow / Chubby fingers, ticklish toes." Although the details of their facial expressions are awkward in places, the large, colorful illustrations, which work well for reading to a group, convey happiness and energy.

Hunter, Sally. *Humphrey's Corner*. 2001. Hardcover: Henry Holt. Ages 2 years and up.

Soft charcoal illustrations washed with strokes of watercolor invite children into this gentle book about Humphrey, a young elephant. In his light-filled room, cluttered with toys, Humphrey is looking for his rabbit, Mop, which he finds as well as his blanket, Mooey. He piles the two, and a small stool, into a box on a string and pulls it around the house in search of the perfect place to play. The bathroom has some advantages, but after he spills shampoo, it's too sticky. He dons red high heels and collects a sparkling necklace at his mother's dressing table. Humphrey tries the linen closet, too, before he finds just the right spot, with some help from his mother. A cozy story with pleasing pictures. Humphrey also appears, with his big sister, in *Humphrey's Bedtime*.

Hurd, Thacher. *Cat's Pajamas*. 2001. Board book: Harper-Collins. Ages 18 months and up.

Hip cats are on the prowl in this lively little board book. Collage illustrations show brightly painted cats under a photograph of a nighttime cityscape. Snappy nonsense words fill the short text—"Boom Bam Boom," "Rum Tum Tum," and "Doodley-doo"—making it a romp to read aloud. After eating a huge fish, the cats start making some music, playing drums, guitar, and trumpet, perched on a big, shiny car. But not everyone wants noise all night. A dog with a megaphone appears in the alley to quiet down the cats: "Stop that BOP! Cut that sound!" And so they do, all six cats snuggling into one large bed that floats among the stars. The high-energy pictures and words will grab those young children who have had more than their share of placid barnyard books.

Hurd, Thacher. *Mama Don't Allow*. 1984. Hardcover: Harper-Collins. Paperback: HarperCollins. Good for groups. Ages 2½ years and up.

Vivid colors and funny comments in cartoons fill this popular book about a swamp band that outwits some alligators. When the possum Miles gets a saxophone for his birthday, his parents want him to play outside. Walking through town making a racket, he finds three other musicians, and they head to the swamp to practice, calling themselves the Swamp Band. To their surprise, the "sharp-toothed, long-tailed, yellow-eyed alligators" like their music and invite them to play at the Alligator Ball on a riverboat. The elegantly dressed alligators dance all night, but afterward they plan to cook up some Swamp Band soup, until Miles outwits them. A crowd pleaser, this book includes the music and words to the folk song "Mama Don't Allow," so you can sing along to, and with, your child.

Hurd, Thacher. *Zoom City*. 1998. Board book: Harper-Collins. Ages 12 months and up.

Inventive illustrations and a slightly wild text separate this from the more traditional, sedate board books. Photographs of snazzy cars, made snazzier through the collage artwork, zoom around with dogs at the wheel. Like words out of a comic book come the phrases "Be-Bop, Ka-ZOOM!" and "BOOM! BANG! BOOM!" Although they stop at a red light, the cars pick up too much speed after it turns green. Going faster leads to disaster, a car crash in which no dogs are hurt but the front of the cars end up crumpled. In come the tow trucks to take them in for repair. All fixed up, the cars are whizzing around on the road again. While not all parents will like the car crash, the excitement and wonderful noises will appeal to many young children.

Hutchins, Pat. *The Doorbell Rang*. 1986. Hardcover: Green-willow. Paperback: Mulberry. Good for groups. Ages 18 months and up.

This is a cheerful picture-story book with a phrase that children will soon chime in on. Ma has made twelve cookies, six each for Victoria and Sam—until the doorbell rings and they have to share them with two friends. They are about to eat, when the doorbell rings again and more friends appear. With each ring, the total of twelve must be divided again. While this works with older children as a book about division, for younger children it serves as an amusing story with crisp, friendly pictures and a great rhythm. Read it with cookies!

Hutchins, Pat. *Good Night, Owl*. 1972. Hardcover: Simon & Schuster. Paperback: Aladdin. Good for groups. Ages 12 months and up.

"Owl tried to sleep," says the line next to an owl with its eyes shut, perched on a tree during the day. But sleeping during the day is hard: "The bees buzzed, / buzz buzz, / and Owl tried to sleep." As animal after animal finds a spot on or near the tree, owl hears more noises but still tries to sleep. The text and tidy pictures introduce each new animal and its sound without repeating all the previous ones until all ten, most of them birds, have had a page to themselves. With both of Owl's eyes finally wide open, the story repeats all the animals and noises in one long, noisy list. When night falls, and the other animals are ready to sleep, Owl has a little surprise for them that will amuse young listeners.

Hutchins, Pat. *My Best Friend*. 1993. Hardcover: Greenwillow. Good for groups. Ages 2 years and up.

Friendship becomes increasingly important in the lives of young children. In this realistic story, a child welcomes a slightly older friend who has come to spend the night. The older friend is better at nearly everything, which the younger one admires. "My best friend knows how to paint good pictures and doesn't get fingermarks on the paper," proclaims the narrator, whose face and hands are bright with paint. The older friend even knows how to read. Tidy, cheerful gouache illustrations show two dark-skinned children running, jumping, and eating, then settling in for the night, when the younger child turns out to be less afraid of the dark than the friend, a satisfying end to a fine story.

Hutchins, Pat. *Rosie's Walk.* **1968. Hardcover: Simon & Schuster. Paperback: Simon & Schuster. Board book: Simon & Schuster. Good for groups. Ages 15 months and up.**

This clever picture-story book has endured more than thirty years and still delights children with its slapstick humor. Rosie, a hen, leaves her henhouse to take a walk around the farmyard, never noticing that a fox is following her. With incredible good luck, she escapes him at every turn, stepping on a rake that hits the fox, walking by a pond that the fox falls into, and other episodes on her short journey. Children like the sensation of knowing something that Rosie doesn't know, watching her close brushes, and seeing the fox finally running away, pursued by a swarm of bees. Crisp pictures in patterned oranges, greens, and browns depict the oblivious hen and the thwarted fox.

Hutchins, Pat. *Titch.* **1971. Paperback: Aladdin. Good for groups. Ages 18 months and up.**

Sometimes it's hard being the youngest, as Titch well knows. See him on the opening page, a small figure against a large white background, with the straightforward words "Titch was little." He has two older siblings, Mary and Pete, who are, respectively, "bigger" and "a lot bigger." With a clever use of parallel sentences and pictures, Hutchins shows the advantages of being bigger. Pete has a great big bike and Mary, a slightly smaller bike. Turn the page and find Titch pedaling way behind them on his little tricycle. The other two have kites; Titch has a pinwheel. And so it continues, until the element of surprise at the end, when a small item Titch has turns out to be the biggest of all. Also enjoy the other excellent books in the series, *Tidy Titch, Titch and Daisy,* and *You'll Soon Grow into Them, Titch.*

Imershein, Betsy. *Trucks/Construction Trucks*. 2000. Board book: Simon & Schuster. Ages 15 months and up.

For the child whose eyes are drawn to every truck on the road, these two board books will be pure pleasure. The first features a variety of trucks you might see in your neighborhood or on a highway: fire truck, garbage truck, delivery truck, and so on. *Construction Trucks* would be perfect to take along to visit a building site, for identifying the trucks there. Each double-page spread shows one or two photographs of trucks against a bright background, with the name in large letters and a short paragraph of description. Followed by *Farm Trucks* and *Rescue Trucks*.

Inkpen, Mick. *Kipper*. 1992. Paperback: Harcourt. Ages 2 years and up.

This amusing tale introduces the lovable dog Kipper for the first time. Adults will appreciate his resolution, as the book opens, to clean out his basket. He tosses aside his tattered rabbit, smelly old blanket, soggy ball, and old bone. But now the basket is no longer comfortable. "He twisted and he turned. He wiggled and he waggled. But it was no good. He could not get comfortable." So the little brown-and-white dog goes outside, where he sees two ducks looking comfortable as they stand on one leg. But that doesn't work for him. Some wrens look cozy in a flowerpot, but when Kipper tries to climb in, he's too big. Droll pen-and-watercolor pictures show his quest for comfort, which takes him—not surprisingly—back to his good old blanket, bunny, ball, and bone. Kipper is well worth meeting, here and in the rest of the series.

Inkpen, Mick. *Kipper's Book of Colors/Kipper's Book of Numbers/Kipper's Book of Opposites/Kipper's Book of Weather.* **1995. Hardcover: Harcourt. Board book: Harcourt. Ages 12 months and up.**

Kipper, a brown-and-white dog with perky ears, goes through life with a slight smile, looking pleased about everything. In these four books, which come in hardcover or slightly smaller board book editions, the personable dog explores simple concepts. A well-designed layout with ample white space enhances the pictures, which combine humor and information. Kipper introduces colors through familiar objects such as a brown teddy bear and red strawberries. The number book starts with "One Kipper," then goes through the number ten with different animals on each page. The other two books do a similarly fine job of making young children giggle while they absorb simple information. Bravo for Kipper.

Inkpen, Mick. *Wibbly Pig Can Make a Tent/Wibbly Pig Is Happy/Wibbly Pig Likes Bananas/Wibbly Pig Opens His Presents.* **2000. Board book: Viking. Ages 12 months through 2 years.**

The most successful board books are designed for their small format, and these are no exception. The smiling, rosy-cheeked Wibbly Pig fits right in the pages with just a few other objects in the illustrations. When he opens his presents, he is set against a white background with a couple of gifts and, in the final picture, surrounded by wrapping paper, his favorite part. In *Wibbly Pig Likes Bananas*, each page shows him making a choice, such as choosing among red, yellow, and blue balloons. The text then invites the listener to choose, too. Clearly, this delightful quartet is written and illustrated by someone who understands very young children and what they like.

Intrater, Roberta Grobel. *Peek-a-Boo!/Smile!* **1997. Board book: Scholastic. Ages newborn to 2 years.**

Babies who love to look at the faces of other babies will find these two small books very satisfying. Each displays eleven color photographs of babies' faces plus a small one on the back cover. The children—who have different skin, eye, and hair colors—express a variety of emotions in *Peek-a-Boo!*, although only a few are playing peekaboo. In *Smile!*, the smiles range from tentative to highly amused. The short phrases of text don't add a lot, so feel free to make up your own or just enjoy the photographs. Sturdy cardboard pages make this a book you can give to your child to stare at and chew.

Intrater, Roberta Grobel. *Peek-a-Boo, You!* **2002. Hardcover: Scholastic. Good for groups. Ages 3 months through 2 years.**

Most books with photographs of babies' faces are fairly small, making this a real find for parents whose child loves pictures of babies. Eight darling babies are partially hidden behind large flaps, playing peekaboo with the reader. "Peek-a-boo! Where are you? I'm under my blanket, hiding from you," read the words on a page where a flap of a quilted blanket hides all but the baby's eyes and forehead, and folds down to show her smiling. The facial expressions vary, as do skin and hair color. The flaps, which are used more creatively than in many books, take the shape of a balloon, pinwheel, teddy bear, and cowboy hat. Sturdy pages and well-attached flaps will help extend the life of this nicely designed book.

Jam, Teddy. *Night Cars.* **Illustrated by Eric Beddows. 2000. 2d edition. Hardcover: Groundwood. Good for groups. Ages 2 years and up.**

A baby who has insomnia entertains himself by looking

out at the street below. Set in a busy city, the action continues all night with different people, cars, and trucks. Taxis, snowplows, a fire engine, a garbage truck, and ordinary cars stop and go as the wintry night continues. Sometimes the baby, who sits outside the main pictures, dozes off, but he wakes up again when he hears enticing noises. Tended by his father, the baby sings when morning comes, while the father yawns, and they go out to the café that they can see from the window. A loosely rhyming text and lively pictures make this an attractive book, especially for children who love cars and trucks.

Janovitz, Marilyn. *Look Out, Bird!* 1994. Paperback: North-South Books. Good for groups. Ages 2 years and up.

A circular story starts with a snail slipping, which in turn affects thirteen other animals, returning in the end to the snail. The yellow-and-pink snail slips off a leaf and hits a bird. The bird flies, and after turning the page, you see it frighten a frog. The frog jumps and topples a turtle. So it goes in a chain reaction, shown in humorous pen-and-watercolor illustrations. The verbs are crisp and the sentences, short. The animals have a lot of personality as they react to the intrusions in their lives. In the end, a fish spatters a moth, which frightens a snail, and the snail slips once more. Small voice balloons tell the snail's reaction, "Oh no! Not again!" And on the last page, the snail's voice warns, "Look out, bird!" Children will want to start the story again and possibly again, since it moves along with such verve and humor.

Jeram, Anita. *Daisy Dare.* 1995. Paperback: Candlewick. Ages 2 years and up.

The mouse Daisy can't resist a dare, and her three admiring friends—two boys and a girl—keep her trying new feats. She climbs trees that they are afraid to climb to get apples.

She walks high walls while they trail along below, and she even eats a worm. Agreeing to a truly dangerous dare, Daisy steals a bell from the collar of a gigantic cat and almost gets caught. But safe in a cozy house, Daisy basks in the admiration of her friends, who lift her on their shoulders, yet she also admits that she is scared—sometimes. A brief but exciting text and cheerful pictures make this a winner with young listeners. Also look in your library for the related *Contrary Mary*, now out of print.

Johnson, Crockett. *Harold and the Purple Crayon*. 1955. Hardcover: HarperCollins. Paperback: HarperCollins. Ages 2 years and up.

This brilliant little book has been entertaining parents and children for nearly fifty years with its creativity and excellent illustrations. A young boy named Harold decides to take a walk one evening and uses his purple crayon to draw the moon and a path. His magic crayon supplies him with everything he needs for an adventure: a tree, a dragon, a boat, a picnic, and much more. The memorable illustrations consist of simple black-and-white pictures of Harold plus the thick purple lines he draws with his crayon. After some fun and a bit of danger, Harold starts drawing windows in hopes of ending up back in his bedroom, which he eventually does. Not to be missed, this is a real gem.

Jonas, Ann. *Two Bear Cubs*. 1982. Hardcover: Greenwillow. Ages 12 months and up.

This clever, graphically elegant book tells of two bear cubs and their mother who begin their day emerging from a dark cave where only their eyes and outlines were visible. The mother is large and brown, the cubs smaller and brown, set against green grass and lighter green hills. The cubs spot something black-and-white walking by and follow it until it turns and chases them. When the chase is over, the bears are in an unfamiliar meadow. "And where is their mother?" Observant children will see the mother perched in a tree. As the bear cubs continue their simple adventures, told in short sentences, their mother watches, not seen by her offspring. A satisfying story with the additional fun of spotting the hidden bear.

Jones, Bill T., and Susan Kuklin. *Dance.* **1998. Hardcover: Hyperion. Good for groups. Ages 18 months and up.**

While very few books merit the designation "All Ages," this one comes as close as any to fitting that description. It is an exquisite photo-essay about modern dance, with pictures of dancer-choreographer Bill T. Jones. The simple words in conjunction with the terrific photographs convey a love for dance and movement that will get young children moving, too. The book inspires imitation, as Jones flexes his hands and fingers expressively, kicks, rolls, squats, curves, jumps, and lies on the floor. His graceful body, dressed only in black pants, is set on a white background, with the words well placed against the white. Children are natural dancers, which this glorious book will encourage.

Joosse, Barbara M. *Mama, Do You Love Me?* **Illustrated by Barbara Lavallee. 1991. Hardcover: Chronicle. Board book: Chronicle. Ages 15 months and up.**

A young girl asks how much her mother loves her, even when she is naughty, and receives warm, reassuring answers. The twist on this familiar theme is that the two are Inuits, and the text and pictures draw on their unique culture: "What if I put salmon in your parka, ermine in your mittens, and lemmings in your mukluks?" asks the girl, whose mother's answer affirms her love. Vibrant watercolor illustrations with gorgeous patterns expand the simple, rhythmic text, adding to the characters' personalities and to the setting. Ceremonial masks appear in the corner of several pages and on the endpapers, a nice detail in a well-designed book. The splendid illustrations deserve to be viewed in the large version, not the board book.

Jorgensen, Gail. *Crocodile Beat*. Illustrated by Patricia Mullins. 1988. Hardcover: Bradbury. Good for groups. Ages 2 years and up.

Soft-edged illustrations created from torn tissue paper are the highlight of this animal-filled story. It opens with a crocodile basking in the sun and water, waiting for prey. But not to worry—in the end, the other animals send him packing in a clever way. Meanwhile, each page introduces one wild animal after another in lovely pictures and a text that relies heavily on animal sounds. Monkeys chatter, snakes hiss, lions roar, and bears growl, all inviting children to join in. While parents may notice that the assorted animals are unlikely to live near one another, young children won't mind. A visual treat with an unexpected ending.

Kalan, Robert. *Jump, Frog, Jump!* Illustrated by Byron Barton. 1981. Hardcover: Greenwillow. Paperback: Morrow. Ages 2 years and up.

Life is dangerous in the pond, as a bright-eyed frog finds out one day. Using a familiar cadence, the story begins, "This is the fly that climbed out of the water." In the next round frame, the frog appears, with the words "This is the frog that was under the fly that climbed out of the water." The frog catches the fly. How? "Jump, frog, jump!" That refrain sounds throughout the book. From then on, though, the frog jumps to escape predators: a fish, snake, turtle, and some boys with a net.

Not for the fainthearted, this is a dramatic story with a strong rhythm and vibrant pictures.

Kalan, Robert. *Rain*. Illustrated by Donald Crews. 1978. Paperback: Morrow. Good for groups. Ages 12 months and up.

With only a few words on each page, this book takes a young child through a rainstorm in graphically impressive pictures. It opens with a double-page spread of bright blue, broken only by the relatively small words "Blue sky." A yellow sun and white clouds appear on the blue background, then change to gray clouds and no sun. Children won't be surprised to turn the page and find gray sky followed by rain. The rain slants down in lines made up of the word *rain* repeated again and again, a wonderful image. That image then comes down over green grass and a black road, a red car and orange flowers, a brown fence and purple flowers, with a rainbow to follow. A quiet but effective tribute to a rainy day.

Kasza, Keiko. *A Mother for Choco*. 1992. Hardcover: Putnam. Paperback: Putnam. Good for groups. Ages 18 months and up.

Shown in the amusing watercolors as a bright yellow bird with a blue beak and striped feet, Choco first appears looking forlorn. He lives alone and wishes he had a mother, so one day he sets off to find one. He encounters three animals and sees that each of them is like him somehow. But the adult animals regretfully point out their differences, too. The giraffe is yellow but doesn't have wings. The penguin has wings but not round cheeks. When the bird sees Mrs. Bear, he realizes that she looks nothing like him, but she overcomes the difference with her kindness. She offers to be his mother and takes him home, where her other children are also animals but not bears.

This can be read as a story about adoption or interracial families or just as a heartwarming tale with a happy ending.

Katz, Karen. *Counting Kisses*. 2001. Hardcover: McElderry Books. Ages 12 months and up.

"Ten little kisses on teeny tiny toes," says the line across from a mother kissing her baby's toes. Then, "Nine laughing kisses on busy, wriggly feet." Down through the numbers it goes, with each page suggesting another delightful way to bestow kisses on a well-loved baby. The round-faced child, clad in pink clothes with red hearts, revels in the affection from her parents, grandmother, sister, cat, and dog. Mixed-media illustrations meld small patterns and flat perspectives into unusual, appealing pictures that focus on the happy baby. This kissing countdown, which ends at bedtime, may inspire a similar, cozy ritual in your own family.

Katz, Karen. *Where Is Baby's Belly Button?* 2000. Board book: Simon & Schuster. Ages 3 months through 2 years.

Large flaps made of heavy paper and securely attached to the pages work best for the very young, as this book demonstrates. Use this with babies by moving the flaps yourself until they are old enough to help. Like a game of peekaboo, the flaps cover a body part. Each page asks a question, such as "Where are baby's eyes?" Moving the flap reveals the hidden part and answers the question, "Under her hat!" Rounded shapes with several colors and patterns characterize the inviting pictures in this successful board book.

Keats, Ezra Jack. *Peter's Chair*. 1967. Hardcover: Viking. Paperback: Puffin. Ages 18 months and up.

Things just haven't been the same for Peter since his baby sister appeared on the scene. His mother asks him to be quiet when his block tower falls over. Worse, his father is painting Peter's baby furniture pink. In protest, Peter decides to run away from home with his dog, Willie—all the way to the sidewalk in front of his house. He takes his little chair with him, to keep it from being painted, and finds to his surprise he's too big to sit in it. His loving parents figure out a way to make Peter feel welcome again in the family. This longtime favorite with outstanding collage illustrations makes a perfect readaloud. Other books about Peter include *Whistle for Willie* and *The Snowy Day*.

Keats, Ezra Jack. *The Snowy Day*. 1962. Hardcover: Viking. Paperback: Viking. Board book: Viking. Good for groups. Ages 12 months and up.

One of the best picture books ever published, *The Snowy Day* is a timeless story about a boy named Peter who wakes up one morning to find it has snowed during the night. He spends his day enjoying the snow, making tracks, a snowman, and snow angels. That night, Peter dreams that the snow melts, but he wakes up to enjoy another day of snow. The book has a memorable combination of a simple, lyrical story and exquisite illustrations. The bright collage pictures convey Peter's sheer happiness in the snow, the thrill of sliding down a steep hill, and the joy of waking up to a snowy day. Winner of the Caldecott Medal. Other wonderful books about Peter include *Whistle for Willie* and *Peter's Chair*.

Keller, Holly. *Geraldine's Blanket*. 1984. Hardcover: Greenwillow. Paperback: Mulberry. Ages 2 years and up.

Geraldine has no intention of giving up her blanket no matter what her parents want. When her exasperated mother tells her that the frayed blanket looks silly, Geraldine replies, "Then don't look at me." But when she receives a new doll meant to replace the blanket, Geraldine supplies her own solution: she makes the blanket into a dress for the doll. This very simple story creates a strong female character, a plot that engages young children, and a clever resolution. A gem, this is the first in a series about the strong-minded Geraldine.

Kitamura, Satoshi. *Cat Is Sleepy/Dog Is Thirsty/Duck Is Dirty/Squirrel Is Hungry.* 1996. Board book: Farrar, Straus & Giroux. Ages 9 months and up.

Life isn't always easy for animals, as the priceless facial expressions on these four creatures convey. Poor cat, whose eyelids are at half-mast, is sleepy but can't find a place to sleep. He tries the top of the piano—too noisy. The sink—too cold and slippery. His ideas and facial contortions will bring laughter and then relief when he finds a child's welcoming lap. Duck, who looks baffled, goes on a walk and runs into rain, mud, wind, and more mud until he happily rinses off in a pond. Dog and Squirrel also have problems to solve. Dog wants a drink, and Squirrel finds a walnut that takes so long to hide, he ends up eating it. These four books offer amusement to adults as well as children, always a welcome attribute.

Koide, Tan. *May We Sleep Here Tonight?* Illustrated by Yasuko Koide. 1982. Hardcover: McElderry Books. Good for groups. Ages 2 years and up.

Three charming gophers wearing daypacks and colorful hats are lost in the woods one evening when they spot a house with lighted windows. But when they reach the door and knock, no one answers. Timidly, they open the door and see a toasty, tidy house with a fire going in the woodstove. Although they worry it's rude to stay, they are so tired, they can't resist. After crawling into bed, they're startled to hear a knock and a request to come in. Two bunny rabbits, also lost on a hike, ask, "May we sleep here tonight?" Then three raccoons show up with the same question. When all eight are snug in bed, the door creaks open on its own, and for one moment, they are all petrified. Fortunately, it turns out very well indeed. For children who enjoy a little scare while safe at home, this hits just the right note.

Kopper, Lisa. *Good Dog, Daisy!* 2001. Hardcover: Dutton. Good for groups. Ages 18 months and up.

This charmer is the most recent in an amusing series about a bull terrier and a baby with lots of personality. Baby likes to play with Little Daisy, one of Daisy's puppies. Baby orders the puppy around with some success, until the mother dog appears on the scene. Then Baby finds that she's the one sitting, lying down, and speaking, the very commands she had given the puppy. When the human mother comes on the scene, she, too, ends up on the floor, with Daisy licking her face. It's hard to say who is cuddlier in the pastel pictures, Baby, Little Daisy, or Daisy herself. The first book, *Daisy Thinks She Is a Baby*, is out of print, but you might find it in your library, while *Daisy Is a Mommy*, *Daisy Knows Best*, and *Daisy's Babies* are still available.

Kraus, Robert. *Whose Mouse Are You?* Illustrated by Jose Aruego. 1970. Hardcover: Simon & Schuster. Paperback: Simon & Schuster. Good for groups. Ages 12 months and up.

A favorite for more than thirty years, this book skillfully combines words, pictures, and a theme that appeals to the young. It opens by asking a little, forlorn mouse, "Whose mouse are you?" Alas, his mother, father, and sister are all in peril, in a cat, a trap, and far from home. The illustrations use clean lines, only a few colors, and lots of white space, highlighting the facial expressions of the mice. In a plot that gives the power to the youngest, the little mouse rescues his mother and father and finds his sister. Their joy at being reunited is followed by a happy twist at the end. Not to be missed. Followed by *Where Are You Going, Little Mouse?* and *Come Out and Play, Little Mouse.*

Krauss, Ruth. *The Carrot Seed.* **Illustrated by Crockett Johnson. 1945. Hardcover: HarperCollins. Paperback: HarperCollins. Board book: HarperCollins. Ages 12 months and up.**

This classic picture-story book uses a short text and small pictures to tell the story of a young boy who plants a carrot seed, takes good care of it, then waits impatiently for it to grow. His parents and older brother tell him the carrot won't come up, but he persists, and in the end, a huge carrot proves he was right. The small format suits the story, as do the uncluttered pictures in browns and yellows. This deceptively simple book, which conveys an important message to young children about hope and persistence, has been a favorite for more than fifty years.

Kunhardt, Dorothy. *Pat the Bunny.* **1940. Hardcover: Golden. Ages 6 months through 2 years.**

One of the few baby books available sixty years ago, this small book pioneered the "touch-and-feel" genre in children's books. For some parents of young children, it remains a beloved, enduring classic, while others find it dated in look and content. Two characters, Paul and Judy, pat a bunny, play peekaboo, smell flowers, look in a mirror, and feel their father's scratchy beard. The book simulates the children's experiences with sandpaper for the beard, a patch of synthetic fur, a reflective piece of paper for the mirror, and so on. It is followed by a series of lesser-known touch-and-feel books, including *Pat the Christmas Bunny*, *Pat the Cat*, and more.

Kvasnosky, Laura McGee. *See You Later, Alligator.* **1995. Hardcover: Harcourt. Good for groups. Ages 2 years and up.**

Wordplay is at the heart of this jovial, slight book about different animal children whose teacher is saying good-bye at the end of the day. She starts with the familiar "See you later, alligator. After a while, crocodile," as those young animals leave the school. But that's just the beginning: "In a blizzard, little lizard. In a shake, garter snake." After a few rhyming lines describe an energetic day in the classroom, a couple of more creative good-byes take place before the book closes. Short and silly, this has heavy pages that will make it durable for young children captured by the book's sounds and bright pictures.

Lawrence, Michael. *Baby Loves.* **Illustrated by Adrian Reynolds. 1999. Hardcover: DK. Paperback: DK. Good for groups. Ages 12 months and up.**

"Baby loves Mommy and Daddy more than anything in the world. Except . . ." With these words swooping across the page, a plump baby with a lively air is pinching the father's nose in the first picture, with the mother in the background. Turn the page and find out that the baby loves breakfast more than anything in the world. But wait, it's Teddy that Baby loves best, except . . . The pattern goes on through familiar objects like a cat, slippers, flowers, and more. Large, humorous pictures show the baby, not identified as a girl or boy, reveling in noise and rain and bathtime. Exhausted parents tuck the baby into bed, reaffirming that they love Baby more than anything else in the world, even after a hectic day.

Lawston, Lisa. *Can You Hop?* Illustrated by Ed Vere. 1999. Board book: Orchard. Ages 12 months and up.

A bright green frog hops across the bright blue cover of this small book aimed at very young children. "I hop!" the frog proclaims on the next page, hopping out of a green puddle. Then, the frog asks a purple rhinoceros, "Can you hop?" to which the answer is "Stomp!" The question is repeated on every page to different creatures, who respond with their own motions. Bats flap, a monkey claps. Black lines trace the frog's soaring hop on every page and outline the animal forms, giving expressive round eyes to all the creatures. After several encounters, the frog happily finds another animal that hops, and they bounce off together. Created to fit the board book format, this succeeds wonderfully and will delight young animal lovers.

Leslie, Amanda. *Flappy Waggy Wiggly*. 1999. Hardcover: Dutton. Good for groups. Ages 12 months and up.

This satisfying book uses flaps far better than most movable books. Each page offers a guessing game for a child, asking a question that describes an animal and showing a bit of its head and tail. A word indicates the sound the animal makes. When the flap on the right-hand page is opened, the result is a full picture of the animal, plus its name. "Woof! Who has a waggy yellow tail and a sticky licky tongue? Dog." The vivid solid colors and large print add to the book's appeal. Sure to be popular.

Levine, Pamela. *One Sleepy Baby*. Illustrated by Stephanie Milanowski. 2001. Board book: HarperCollins. Ages newborn and up.

Read this charming book to newborns, who will enjoy the sounds while you put into motion some of the actions described. As your child gets older, share the illustrations with him or her. The baby in the pictures has a large, round face and one spiral curl of hair sticking up, lending a slightly humorous air. The baby's parents are counting through a bedtime procedure, starting with the number one and going through ten. The numbers include "5 Daddy hugs" and "7 Mama kisses," each of which could be acted out. The "2 tired eyes" and "10 tiny fingers" could be counted. Or the sweet, very brief verses could be read straight through as a prelude to bedtime.

Lewin, Hugh. *Jafta*. Illustrated by Lisa Kopper. 1983. Hardcover: Carolrhoda. Paperback: Carolrhoda. Good for groups. Ages 19 months and up.

Exquisite watercolor-and-ink drawings in shades of brown, set in generous white space, introduce a young African boy named Jafta. On each page, Jafta compares himself to an animal: "And sometimes I want to jump like an impala, and dance like a zebra, or just nuzzle like a rabbit." The illustrations vary between energetic and restful, depending on the animal and the boy's mood. Young children will join in by naming the animals and at the same time observe Jafta experiencing familiar feelings of happiness, strength, weariness, and crankiness. The story lends itself to imitating Jafta's movements of jumping, dancing, cuddling, stamping his feet, and running. A gem of a book featuring a child reveling in his surroundings and emotions.

Lewis, Kevin. *Chugga-Chugga Choo-Choo*. Illustrated by Daniel Kirk. 1999. Hardcover: Hyperion. Board book: Hyperion. Good for groups. Ages 12 months and up.

A catchy rhyme and attractive pictures make this a favorite, not just for children enchanted by trains. The wide pages follow the progress of a toy train as toy people load it with freight and guide it through a journey past stuffed animals. Every few pages the rhyming text moves into a refrain for children to join in, which uses variations on the words "chugga-chugga choo-choo" and "whoooooooo! whoooooooo!" The airbrushed illustrations with lots of glossy colors offer plenty of detail but still manage to look uncluttered. The final picture pulls back to reveal a boy in bed, surrounded by extensive toy train tracks and a host of stuffed animals, now all asleep. Try for the full-size edition, not the board book, to enjoy the pictures fully.

Lewis, Rose. *I Love You Like Crazy Cakes*. Illustrated by Jane Dyer. 2001. Hardcover: Little, Brown. Ages 2½ years and up.

"Once upon a time in China there was a baby girl," begins this glowing book about how a woman adopted her baby daughter. With unmistakable love, the narrator tells her story as if speaking to her daughter, telling of her longing for a child, her trip to China, and her meeting with her soon-to-be daughter: "I had been waiting for you my whole life." They return home to loving friends and family, and happy times together. Exquisite watercolors full of beautifully patterned fabrics enhance the warm feeling of the story. A delight for the eye and the heart, this will be accessible only to older toddlers, but parents may want to start reading it earlier for their own pleasure.

Lindgren, Barbro. *Sam's Cookie/Sam's Teddy Bear*. Illustrated by Eva Eriksson. 1982. Hardcover: Morrow. Ages 12 months and up.

These two small books, imported from Sweden, pack a lot of dramatic tension for the younger crowd. Sam is enjoying a cookie in the first book, when Doggie comes along and snatches it from him. Sam gets angry, then Doggie gets angry. What will happen? Mother saves the day, giving Sam another cookie and Doggie a bone. Each page carries a short sentence, with a small picture that illustrates the action. The same format holds for the story about Sam's teddy bear, whom he kisses, licks, bites, and throws. The crisis occurs when the teddy bear ends up in the potty. This time, Doggie saves the day by rescuing the toy bear. The expressive, scruffy-haired toddler experiences similar moments of drama in the other books in this series.

London, Jonathan. *Crunch Munch*. Illustrated by Michael Rex. 2001. Hardcover: Harcourt. Board book: Harcourt. Good for groups. Ages 12 months and up.

Young children who like to identify animals will enjoy the large pictures and creative sounds in this book, which asks the question "How do animals eat?" For example, on one page, a large cat has its pink tongue in a bowl of milk. The answer to "How does a cat eat?" is "Lippity-lap, lippity-lap." The pages all follow the same pattern, with a question, an answering sound, and a cartoonlike illustration. The last few pages recap all the questions and sounds. Then come the lines, "Now take a seat. How do you eat?" A child sits at a table, wearing a bib and playing with a box of animal crackers that correspond to the animals in the book. *Wiggle Waggle* and *Snuggle Wuggle* look similar and deal, respectively, with how animals walk and hug. The board book versions of all three cut several pages from the originals.

Losordo, Stephen. *Cow Moo Me*. Illustrated by Jane Conteh-Morgan. 1998. Board book: HarperCollins. Ages newborn through 2 years.

Sometimes a nonsense poem supplies just the right words

for talking to a baby and amusing a toddler. "Cow moo me /
cow moo you / cow moo milk / cow moo moo," opens this
small book. A similar rhyme about a different animal occurs
on each of the seven double-page spreads. The sunny collage
illustrations, heavy on pink and blue and yellow, have a humorous spirit, with a pig sprawling contentedly in mud and a
grinning frog splashing in a pond. The strong rhythm makes it
easy to read aloud.

**Maccarone, Grace. *A Child's Good Night Prayer*. Illustrated
by Sam Williams. 2001. Hardcover: Scholastic. Ages 6 months
and up.**

This gentle, nondenominational prayer reflects a child's
world and concerns. "Bless the moon / Bless the stars / Bless
my night-light / Bless my cars," begins the repetitive prose,
with illustrations of young children with different skin colors.
The charcoal-and-watercolor pictures have just the right feeling of softness for a bedtime book, creating a comfy setting.
The soothing words conclude with blessing water, earth, and
air, and "Bless the children everywhere." A thoughtful, appre-
ciative way to end a day.

**MacLeod, Elizabeth. *I Heard a Little Baa*. Illustrated by
Louise Phillips. 1998. Hardcover: Kids Can. Good for
groups. Ages 12 months and up.**

This small book puts flaps to very good use to create a
guessing game about animals. "I heard a little baa; / It woke
me from my sleep. / First I saw a woolly face," reads the left-
hand page, where a teddy bear is smiling. To complete the
rhyme, open the flap on the right, which looks like a door, and
see, of course, a sheep. Older children will notice that the
sheep's wool curls out under the flap, giving a clue to the hidden picture. The next animal, which growls and has a shaggy

paw visible, hides behind a chair. That sets the pace, with just enough visual and verbal information to make the guesses possible. The rhythm fits the tune of "Farmer in the Dell," if you want to sing this one.

Mahy, Margaret. *Boom, Baby, Boom, Boom!* Illustrated by Patricia MacCarthy. 1997. Hardcover: Viking. Good for groups. Ages 12 months and up.

In this cheerful story, Mama settles her baby in a high chair with lots of good food for lunch and turns her back to play her drums. Although Mama looks conventional, she declares, "Beating those drums makes me feel at ease with the world." What the baby and the reader know, and Mama doesn't, is that a group of animals has heard about the lunch and comes in the door. The baby obliges them by dropping her food bit by bit on the floor, to the cat, dog, chickens, sheep, and finally the cow: "Boom-biddy-boom-biddy MOO-MOO-MOO!" The mother sighs with happiness just as the cow races out, then turns to her happy child and gives her a banana, little knowing she hasn't eaten the rest. Large, rounded, colorful pictures suit the happy tone of this bouncing book about a drum-beating mother.

Mahy, Margaret. *17 Kings and 42 Elephants*. Illustrated by Patricia McCarthy. 1987. Hardcover: Dial. Good for groups. Ages 12 months and up.

Charm your child with the beauty of language in this unusual, rhyming book. The author revels in words and rhythms, matched by the illustrator's joy in color and shape. The beautifully executed artwork of batik paintings on silk glows with the same magical feeling as the verses. Close-ups zoom in on round-eyed elephants and grave tigers, elegant flamingos and dancing kings. On a large, double-page spread of colorful birds flying and perched in greenery, the words read, "Tinkling tunesters, twangling trillicans, / Butterflied and fluttered by the great green trees." No need to follow a story line here, just sink into the music of the writing and art.

Mallat, Kathy. *Brave Bear*. 1999. Hardcover: Walker. Paperback: Walker. Good for groups. Ages 2 years and up.

In this story about a bear and a bird, only the bear talks. It sees the bird, fallen on the ground from its nest, and asks, "Are you all right?" The bear, clad in a red-striped T-shirt, picks the bird up and offers to help. When the bear realizes that the bird's home is up a very tall tree, it worries but makes good on its offer by starting to climb with the bird perched on its shoulder. The generous size of the pages conveys how high the bear has climbed, while the brief text lets listeners know that the bear is scared. After a little setback, with a bit of help from the bird, the bear succeeds in returning the bird to its nest, where two other birds are waiting for its return. Although small, the adventure requires bravery and will grip young listeners, who will root for the brave bear.

Martin, Bill, Jr. *Brown Bear, Brown Bear, What Do You See?* Illustrated by Eric Carle. 1983. Hardcover: Henry Holt. Board book: Henry Holt. Good for groups. Ages 9 months and up.

"Brown bear, brown bear, what do you see? / I see a red bird, looking at me. / Red bird, red bird, what do you see?" sets the pattern and rhythm for this modern classic. Glorious collage pictures by Eric Carle fill the pages and delight the eye, as each animal in succession describes the next animal it sees. The story cumulates with a multiethnic group of children and a smiling teacher. Young children will quickly learn to anticipate the next animal and join in the chanting text. The book, which offers possibilities for talking about color and animals, is a nearly perfect combination of word and picture. Followed by the beautiful but not quite as rhythmic *Polar Bear, Polar Bear, What Do You Hear?*

Martin, Bill, Jr., and John Archambault. *Barn Dance!* Illustrated by Ted Rand. 1986. Hardcover: Henry Holt. Paperback: Henry Holt. Good for groups. Ages 2 years and up.

This toe-tapping rhyme starts off strong and keeps on going: "Full moon shinin', shinin' big an' bright, / Pushin' back the shadows, holdin' back the night." On the moonlit farm, rabbits jump over a sleeping dog on their way to the barn dance. A boy who spies them from his bedroom window follows in his pajamas to the barn, where all the animals are dancing to the scarecrow's fiddling. The boy joins them: "Out came the skinny kid, a-tickin' an' a-tockin'." Expansive watercolors show the antics of pigs, donkeys, chickens, and goats kicking up their heels until dawn. This book bounces along in a spirit of great fun like a rollicking square dance. Read it for the wonderful language and see if your child starts dancing along.

Martin, Bill, Jr., and John Archambault. *Chicka Chicka Boom Boom.* Illustrated by Lois Ehlert. 1989. Hardcover: Simon & Schuster. Paperback: Aladdin. Ages 9 months and up.

Not to be missed, this felicitous combination of rhyme and picture quickly becomes a favorite with young listeners. Letters of the alphabet are personified as children playing together and climbing a coconut tree. "Chicka chicka boom boom / Will there be enough room?" When all twenty-six letters have been named, and the last four are on their way up the tree, "BOOM! BOOM!" The tree bends and the brightly colored letters all fall out. Along come their adult, or uppercase, counterparts: "Mamas and papas / uncles and aunts / hug their little dears, / then dust their pants." Once the mess is straightened out, the little ones secretly begin to climb the tree again. The jubilant, candy-colored pictures pair perfectly with the wonderful words, which will quickly have children chanting along. A board book version, *Chicka Chicka ABC*, ends halfway through the story, which is disappointing if you know the original. In either case, don't think of this as an alphabet book—just have a great time with it.

Martin, Rafe. *Will's Mammoth*. Illustrated by Stephen Gammell. 1989. Hardcover: Putnam. Paperback: Putnam. Ages 2 years and up.

Mesmerizing illustrations celebrate a boy's fascination with woolly mammoths and his refusal to believe that mammoths have disappeared. Knowing better than his parents, he ventures out into a snowy day and finds one. With a cry of joy, he begins his journey on the mammoth's back. They encounter more mammoths as well as saber-toothed tigers, bears, wolves, and early human cave dwellers. The lovable mammoth picks a purple flower for Will, who treasures it as he falls asleep that night. Gammell's extraordinary illustrations sweep across the large pages, splashed with drops of paint. The short text is beautifully hand-printed in bright colors, a part of the book's elegant design. The appealing cover illustration of Will on his mammoth will attract young children to this prehistoric adventure.

Marzollo, Jean. *Do You Know New?* Illustrated by Mari Takabayashi. 1998. Board book: HarperCollins. Ages 6 months through 2 years.

What do babies know about? This small book uses simple rhyming verses to explore that question. "Do you know blue?" it asks on one blue page, answering on the opposing page,

"Why, yes, I do. Blue, blue, I do." The pattern continues with a shoe, a cow that goes "moo," peekaboo, and a mirror to show "you." Round-faced children with different skin colors provide a focus on pages that have pastel backgrounds. The final page, for "you," has a reflective piece of paper for a mirror, which gives a very wavy reflection. You might want to substitute a little hand mirror at this point as a surprise ending to this book, which intrigues babies.

Marzollo, Jean. *I Spy Little Animals/I Spy Little Wheels*. Photographs by Walter Wick. 1998. Board book: Scholastic. Ages 18 months and up.

Here are two of the seven board books in the I Spy Little series, a simplified variation on the popular I Spy books. In each of these small books, the right-hand page is a crisp, color photograph with a number of items in it, sometimes cluttered and sometimes with space between them. On the left-hand page, two or three items are shown and named for a child to locate in the photograph. In *I Spy Little Animals*, the list includes toy animals to find along with other familiar objects; in *I Spy Little Wheels*, a toy vehicle such as a truck or an airplane is included. At the end, two pages display more objects to go back and find. All the books in the series follow the same format, providing hours of entertainment for a child who enjoys the challenge.

Marzollo, Jean. *Mama Mama/Papa Papa*. Illustrated by Laura Regan. 1999. Hardcover: HarperCollins. Board book: HarperCollins. Ages 3 months through 2 years.

The relationship between baby and mother, and baby and father form the focus of these quiet board books. Animal parents and their offspring appear on every page with a gentle verse that emphasizes the parent's care for the young one. A mother koala with a baby on her back appears in *Mama Mama*, with the simple verse, "Mama, Mama, / Play with me, / Carry me / So I can see." The soft pictures in both books portray the animals realistically, set against uncluttered backgrounds. Seven animal fathers tend to their children in *Papa Papa*, including a sea horse, swan, and penguin. The soothing rhythm will appeal to babies, while the parents will appreciate the theme about parental love.

Mayer, Mercer. *A Boy, a Dog, and a Frog*. 1967. Paperback: Dial. Ages 2½ years and up.

What a wonderfully effective story this is, all without words. Small black-and-white pencil drawings show a boy in oversize boots carrying a bucket and net, accompanied by a small dog. The first thing they see at a pond in the woods is a frog with a smirk on its face, sitting on a lily pad near the water's edge. The boy rushes down with his net to capture the frog, only to trip and fall into the water. The boy pursues the frog, to no avail, then heads back home. A delightful, unexpected ending brings the three together again. Expressive body language and faces of all three characters make this enormous fun. One in a series, to which you and your child can supply the dialogue and motivations of the characters.

Mayer, Mercer. *There's an Alligator under My Bed*. 1987. Hardcover: Dial. Good for groups. Ages 2 years and up.

The narrator of this brief story believes that an alligator lives under his bed. "But whenever I looked, he hid . . . or something." Tired of being scared, the boy devises a clever plan to lay a trail of goodies from his bed, down the stairs, and into the garage. Sure enough, when he hides and watches, an alligator emerges, eats the food along the trail, and crawls into the garage. The boy slams the door, then remembers to leave a note for his dad with an explanation and the comment, "If you need help, wake me up." Large, colorful pictures depict a bright-eyed boy and a huge green alligator. A similar book by Mayer, *There's Something in My Attic*, features a girl dealing with her fears. Another, *There's a Nightmare in My Closet*, may be scary for some children under three and problematic for parents who object to toy guns.

Mayo, Margaret. *Dig Dig Digging*. Illustrated by Alex Ayliffe. 2001. Hardcover: Henry Holt. Good for groups. Ages 18 months and up.

This oversize book will be pure paradise for toddlers who can't get enough of large vehicles. The expansive illustrations in poster-bright colors focus on a different vehicle on each double-page spread, accompanied by energetic prose. Fire engines, garbage trucks, cranes, dump trucks, and tractors are among the fascinating topics, with prose such as, "Tractors are good at pull, pull, pulling, / plowing up the field with a squelch, squelch, squelching. / Round go the wheels. See the dirt flying! / They can work all day." With eleven vehicles in all, this should have strong appeal among a certain audience.

Mayo, Margaret, editor. *Wiggle Waggle Fun: Stories and Rhymes for the Very Very Young*. 2002. Hardcover: Knopf. Good for groups. Ages 18 months and up.

This oversize anthology introduces wonderful writers and illustrators for the very young, with brief poems and stories, and a variety of pictures. It's a book to read a bit at a time, with some entries for toddlers and others for slightly older preschoolers. For example, "Looking for Bugs and Creepy-Crawlies," with pictures by Lydia Monks, would make a fine fingerplay for a parent to amuse a toddler or even a baby by adding actions for each phrase, such as "One worm, wriggle-wriggling" and

"Two spiders, spinning-spinning." On the other hand, "Cheesy Macaroni," with funny, detailed pictures by Leonie Shearing, would work better for older children who know the tune to "Frère Jacques." If a writer or an illustrator appeals to you, look for other books by him or her as well.

McBratney, Sam. *Guess How Much I Love You.* **Illustrated by Anita Jeram. 1994. Hardcover: Candlewick. Board book: Candlewick. Ages 18 months and up.**

Delightful pen-and-watercolor illustrations bring to life the Little Nutbrown Hare and the Big Nutbrown Hare in this bedtime story about parental love. Gentle browns and greens dominate as the little hare challenges the big one to guess how much the little one loves him. First, Little Nutbrown Hare stretches out his arms to show how much, but the big hare answers by stretching out his much longer arms and says, "But I love *you* this much." The comparisons escalate until the little hare proclaims he loves the big one "right up to the moon," after which the hare child falls asleep. The big hare gets in the last word in a way that some parents find more competitive than reassuring. But for those who warm to this father and child hare, this may become a childhood favorite, for reading to infants as well as toddlers. Avoid the board book version, though, which is missing some pictures.

McDonnell, Flora. *I Love Animals.* **1994. Paperback: Candlewick. Board book: Candlewick. Good for groups. Ages 15 months and up.**

A simple, brief text takes second place to the lushly colored acrylic and gouache illustrations in this celebration of animals. A rosy-cheeked farm girl, introduced on the cover, is proclaiming her feelings about animals on every page, starting, "I love Jock, my dog. / I love the ducks waddling to the water."

In the original, expansive pictures of the animals dominate large pages, making this an effective book to use with groups. The board version, though much smaller and lacking a few pictures from the endpapers and title page, still works quite well. The final pages in both declare, "I love all the animals. I hope they love me." McDonnell fans will want to read *I Love Boats*, which is out of print, and *Flora McDonnell's ABC*, which also features many animals for children to name.

McDonnell, Flora. *Splash!* 1999. Hardcover: Candlewick. Good for groups. Ages 12 months and up.

It's a sultry day in the jungle, "Hot, hot, hot! The elephants are hot." In oversize illustrations, a huge elephant and a baby one are set against a golden yellow background. On the next page, a huge tiger with its tongue hanging out appears with the sentence "Tiger is hot." And so is rhinoceros. But the baby elephant has an idea. The other three animals follow it down to the water, where the little one squirts the others. Anyone looking at the paintings will feel a palpable sense of relief as the cool blues of the water compete with the hot yellows. Making splashes and splooshes, the grown-up animals join in the fun. The expansive, uncluttered pictures and watery sounds will beguile the youngest children, while toddlers will appreciate the fact that the littlest animal came up with such a great idea.

McFarland, Lyn Rossiter. *Widget*. Illustrated by Jim McFarland. 2001. Hardcover: Farrar, Straus & Giroux. Ages 2½ years and up.

An endearing little white dog named Widget needs a home, a fact that will immediately tug at young (and older) listeners' hearts. In the lovely pen-and-watercolor pictures, he spots a house with a "door just his size." No wonder, for Mrs.

Diggs, who lives there, has six cats, whom she cherishes and caters to. Although Mrs. Diggs feels sorry for Widget, she explains that the cats, "the girls," can't stand dogs. But Widget is determined and wins them over by making himself as catlike as possible. Confused, the girls accept him and he settles into their comfy life, fitting right in. Yet it turns out his dog traits prove helpful when something happens to Mrs. Diggs. Adults reading this the first time may well laugh out loud at the turn of events, so beautifully conveyed by the pictures. An amusing, unpredictable story, this is a real winner.

McGee, Marni. *Wake Up, Me!* Illustrated by Sam Williams. 2002. Hardcover: Simon & Schuster. Good for groups. Ages 15 months and up.

Large pictures show a toddler welcoming a new day, starting with the words, "Wake up, ears. Wake up, eyes." The child, not identified as a girl or boy, hugs a teddy bear, a constant companion during the morning to come. Sleepy father and mother greet the child, hugging and tickling, and preparing breakfast. "Wake up, legs. Wake up, feet. Tummy says it's time to eat." Soft-edged watercolors match the mood, supplying details not mentioned in the story, including a huge yard for playing in. After breakfast, it's time to go out—with both parents—to enjoy the day. The same warm spirit comes across in the companion book, *Sleepy Me*.

McKee, David. *Elmer's Colors/Elmer's Friends/Elmer's Weather*. 1994. Board book: Lothrop. Ages 15 months through 2 years.

Elmer is a patchwork elephant, bright with colored squares in a world of gray elephants. In these three board books, the cheerful Elmer enjoys the world around him. He explores colors, mostly in nature but including a pink strawberry ice cream treat. Birds pop up in the book about Elmer's many animal friends and again in *Elmer's Weather*, in which he delights in all sorts of weather, from lightning storms to sunshine.

McPhail, David. *Emma's Pet*. 1985. Paperback: Dutton. Ages 2 years and up.

In this small book about a bear child looking for a pet, Emma tries out a variety of possibilities. She feels that her own cat, which dislikes being dragged around, isn't cuddly enough. The first possibility is a bug, but "Even Emma couldn't say that it was cuddly." The mouse she picks up is cuddly but not big enough. The bird is soft but too busy. Emma's expressive face reacts to each animal she comes across in the engaging watercolors. Children will laugh as Emma is encircled by a snake and overwhelmed by a fish as big as she is. In the end, the surprising choice she makes turns out to be "the biggest, softest, cuddliest thing she had ever seen." A small gem with lots to look at and giggle over. If you like this, try *Fix-It* and check your library for the out-of-print, also entertaining, *Emma's Vacation*.

McPhail, David. *First Flight*. 1987. Hardcover: Little, Brown. Ages 18 months and up.

The young narrator, holding a toy airplane and teddy bear, announces that he is about to take his first flight. Pen-and-watercolor illustrations show him arriving at the airport, going through security, and boarding the plane, while a large picture shows workers readying his plane. His teddy bear, grown magically huge, sits with the boy and provides comic relief throughout the flight. A meal, a movie, some turbulence, and a nap round out the trip. A perfect introduction to air travel for young children.

McPhail, David. *Pigs Aplenty, Pigs Galore.* **1993. Hardcover: Dutton. Paperback: Puffin. Ages 12 months and up.**

Absolutely not to be missed, this is a treat for parent and child alike. Read it to babies for the irresistible language and later share the hilarious pictures. The narrator is a man who hears a noise one night and, after tripping on a banana peel, finds his kitchen full of pigs. The lively, rhyming text describes them in funny detail: "Pigs in tutus / Pigs in kilts / Pigs on skateboards / Pigs on stilts." They've made a mess, and it just gets worse when they send out for pizza. The wonderfully comic pictures show the pizza flying through the air, with all kinds of pigs having a great time, including one dressed like Elvis. Finally, the narrator has had enough and makes the pigs clean up and get ready for bed, not realizing that they will have the last laugh. Followed by *Pigs Ahoy!* and *Those Can-Do Pigs*, which are amusing but not as good as the first one.

Meddaugh, Susan. *Beast.* **1981. Paperback: Houghton. Ages 2 years and up.**

Anna is the youngest in her family and the bravest. When she spots a big, furry beast coming out of the forest, the rest of the family immediately declares it a dangerous, bad beast. Her father tries to shoot it unsuccessfully and decides it must be tricky as well as dangerous. Anna, however, wants to know more before she makes up her mind. Like a scientist, she tries to learn about it and discovers that the beast is far from dangerous. It cries and Anna comforts it, then sends it off home. Anna is a girl who promises to go far thanks to her inquiring spirit. Simple drawings of the small, determined girl and the huge, furry beast will charm readers.

Melmed, Laura Krauss. *I Love You as Much . . .* **Illustrated by Henri Sorensen. 1993. Hardcover: HarperCollins. Board book: HarperCollins. Ages 6 months and up.**

Parents will get caught up in the emotions expressed in this book about different animal mothers—and one human—and how much they love their offspring. Light-filled paintings with an impressionistic touch show a mother and child pair on each wide spread, with a sentence that keeps to the same pattern. "Said the mother horse to her child, 'I love you as much as a warm summer breeze,'" followed by, "Said the mother bear to her child, 'I love you as much as the forest has trees.'" The comparisons are drawn from the animals' environments and work well to convey a sense of warmth and love, ending with a mother soothing her sleeping baby.

Meyers, Susan. *Everywhere Babies.* **Illustrated by Marla Frazee. 2001. Hardcover: Harcourt. Good for groups. Ages 2 years and up.**

Babies show every emotion and facial expression in this wonderful book. "Every day, everywhere, babies are born," reads the large, hand-lettered text across the top of the first two pages. Below come smaller words above the babies they describe: "fat babies, thin babies, small babies, tall babies, winter and spring babies, summer and fall babies." Ten yawning, sleeping, squirming, and gazing babies are lined up side by side in captivating pen-and-watercolor illustrations. The verses describe how babies are kissed, dressed, fed, rocked, and more, showing babies with different color hair and skin, different families and settings. The adorable babies grow a bit older in each picture, starting with infants and ending at a first birthday party. Give this as a gift or keep it to share with your child, especially if a new baby is coming into your life.

Miller, Margaret. *Baby Faces/What's on My Head?* 1998. Board book: Simon & Schuster. Ages 3 months through 2 years.

Here are two in a series of board books that feature close-ups of babies' faces as they express emotions and try on an assortment of hats. Both have a very brief text on the left-hand page and a color photo on the right. In *Baby Faces*, the words describe a reaction to something we can't see: "yum-yum!," "yucky!," "uh-oh!," and more. The babies scrunch their faces, wrinkle their noses, lick their lips, and smile. *What's on My Head?* shows more smiling faces as a red fire hat, a green velvet frog, and a toy puppy, as well as more ordinary hats, adorn the children's heads. Although the photography could be crisper, the images will captivate many babies and toddlers.

Miller, Margaret. *Now I'm Big.* 1996. Hardcover: Greenwillow. Good for groups. Ages 18 months and up.

Although the "big" children in this photo-essay appear to be four or five, toddlers are drawn to the pictures of what the big kids can do. A recurring photograph shows six children in a group; opposite them on the first page are little photos of each as a baby. The straightforward text compares the two: "When we were born, we were very small. Now we're big!" In the following pages, each big child is singled out in the large picture. We see more photographs of that child as a baby, then contrasting shots of what the child can do now: dress himself or herself, clean up, ride a bicycle with training wheels, climb, and jump. The clear, well-composed photos of babies and older kids will fascinate toddlers. Also check out Miller's *Big and Little*, another effective photo-essay.

Miller, Margaret. *Where Does It Go?* 1992. Hardcover: Greenwillow. Paperback: Mulberry. Good for groups. Ages 2 years and up.

Two-year-olds will giggle with superiority as they look at the photographs in this guessing book. On the left-hand page, a child holds up a familiar item, with a question that asks where the item goes. For example, "Where does Tavo put his socks?" The opposite page gives four silly possible answers with accompanying photographs. "On his nose?" is one suggestion, with a photo of the boy putting a red sock on his nose. "On the dog's paw?" is another. Turn the page for the right answer, "On his feet!" and a joyful photograph of Tavo with the socks in the right place. The rest of the book follows in kind, with guaranteed laughs.

Miller, Margaret. *Whose Shoe?* 1991. Hardcover: Greenwillow. Good for groups. Ages 2 years and up.

Children who like guessing will love this book. Each sequence of pages shows a photograph of a shoe with the question "Whose shoe?" followed on the next page by the answer and two more photographs. The answer for jogging shoe is "Runner," with photographs of a woman running on one page and a young boy running on another. The clear, colorful photographs show a diversity of age, race, and gender, with touches of humor, such as huge clown shoes and a young girl in waders fishing for plastic fish. Another outstanding concept book that is fun to read. Also look for *Guess Who?* and check your library for *Whose Hat?*, now out of print.

Miller, Virginia. *I Love You Just the Way You Are.* 1998. Hardcover: Candlewick. Board book: Candlewick. Ages 18 months and up.

"One day Bartholomew was grumpy . . ." begins this realistic book about a little bear having a hard day. George, the adult bear who takes care of Bartholomew, gently helps, carrying the tired youngster on his back through the snow. At home, the cranky mood continues, getting worse at bathtime. With the room splashed with water, George looks as if he might get grumpy, too, but ends up saying to a surprised Bartholomew, "I love you just the way you are." Then off to a more cheerful bedtime scene. As in the other books in this series, "Nah" is Bartholomew's most frequently uttered comment, not unlike some human toddlers. Pencil-and-watercolor illustrations create an appealing duo in a homey setting.

Minters, Frances. *Too Big, Too Small, Just Right.* Illustrated by Janie Bynum. 2001. Hardcover: Harcourt. Good for groups. Ages 2 years and up.

Two rabbit friends lightheartedly explore opposites in this cheerful book. A yellow male rabbit and a pink female one start out looking for a bike. First, they peer up at an enormously tall bike: "Too big." Then, one rabbit perches on a tiny bike: "Too small." Then, turn the page and they are smiling as they set out on a tandem bicycle: "Just right." The pen-and-watercolor illustrations use vivid colors and cartoonlike characters, with comic touches for children to laugh at, such as the pictures of one rabbit dancing with a mouse, who is too short, and the other with a giraffe, who is too tall. Children will also like looking for the purple mouse that pops up on every page. Toddlers won't grasp all the concepts, but they will enjoy the rabbits' adventures and join in the refrain, "Just right."

Morgan, Mary. *Gentle Rosie/Wild Rosie.* 1999. Hardcover: Hyperion. Ages 18 months and up.

Read both of these books at the same time to make the most of them. Like many children, the small mouse Rosie has a gentle side and a wild one. *Gentle Rosie* shows her in her calmer moments, cuddling her doll, softly kissing her baby brother, and turning pages in a book. Pastel colors dominate the cute illustrations. Brighter colors characterize *Wild Rosie*, in which the mouse bounces her baby brother on the bed, and sings and dances instead of taking her nap. The upshot of her harmless fun is one very tired mouse as the book ends. Two more books in the series are *Patient Rosie* and *Curious Rosie*.

Most, Bernard. *Cock-a-Doodle-Moo!* 1996. Hardcover: Harcourt. Good for groups. Ages 2 years and up.

The rooster apparently has laryngitis, for when he tries to crow, "Only a whisper came out." Meanwhile, in the cartoonlike pictures, all the animals who should be waking up are still snoring in their voice balloons: z-z-zcluck, z-z-zoink, and z-z-zmoo. Rooster tries to wake different animals and the farmer with no luck but finally succeeds with one cow. The cow is willing to help but has a hard time learning to crow properly, with attempts like "Mock-a-Moodle-Moo." They finally settle for "Cock-a-Doodle-Moo," which succeeds in waking everyone up. Have fun with the snoring animals and the cow's funny variations on crowing, and you'll be sure to have your child giggling—and crowing around the house.

Murphy, Jill. *Peace at Last.* 1980. Paperback: Puffin. Good for groups. Ages 2 years and up.

The whole bear family goes to bed in their snug house, but Mr. Bear can't fall asleep. When Mrs. Bear starts to snore, he leaves to sleep in his son's room. When his wide-awake son makes airplane noises, Mr. Bear tries the living room, then the kitchen, yard, and car. Young children will laugh to see all the places he chooses to sleep, while adults may sympathize with his insomnia. The words offer many noises to make, such as the clock tick-tocking and the birds tweeting and, finally, the alarm going off just as Mr. Bear has fallen asleep. Fun to read aloud.

Murphy, Mary. *Some Things Change.* **2001. Hardcover: Houghton. Good for groups. Ages 12 months and up.**

Pitched at a perfect level for young children, this upbeat book explores the idea of change. It opens with a penguin sitting on a box, then using it as a cave and a boat, showing that the box can change. Then an adult and younger penguin join the first penguin and fly a kite together. "Cloudy days change to sunny," reads the typeface, which imitates a child's printing. Sure enough, clouds are scooting away as the sun shines from a bright blue sky. Later, the words say, "I change," showing the penguin getting measured, with the adult penguin commenting, "You're getting bigger." The perceptive prose reassures children that change can be enjoyable, that moods can change, that a child can change his or her mind, and that some things, like being loved, don't change. A delightful book with an important theme. Another wonderful, related book is *I Like It When . . .*

Narahashi, Keiko. *Is That Josie?* **1994. Hardcover: McElderry Books. Ages 2 years and up.**

This well-designed book asks questions about a little girl named Josie and answers by comparing her to an animal. "Is that Josie running fast through the grass?" "No, it's a cheetah. There she goes—wait for us." In the watercolor picture, the girl is running, with a somewhat transparent cheetah beside her. As the story progresses, the animals named become larger and more powerful, from a fox and a turtle to a hippopotamus and a crocodile, strong images for a young child to identify with. Take note of the wonderful endpapers, with Josie on one side in various positions and different animals on the other side imitating her.

Narahashi, Keiko. *Two Girls Can*. 2000. Hardcover: McElderry Books. Good for groups. Ages 2 years and up.
Using simple words and well-designed watercolor illustrations, this book describes lots of different things that two girls can do together, many of which go beyond stereotypes of young girls as friends. For example, they can dig a hole, make a tunnel, and fly a kite. Pictures show them playing leapfrog, seesaw, and tug-of-war. On one page, one of them declares, "Two girls can get really, really mad, then make up and be brave together." They climb walls and trees, dance and sing, and enjoy each other's company throughout. A tribute to girls' friendships and the range of the activities and emotions they share.

Newcome, Zita. *Toddlerobics*. 1996. Hardcover: Candlewick. Paperback: Candlewick. Ages 18 months and up.
Eight toddlers wait in line with their parents, grandparents, or caretakers on the title page of this book. Then, "Hats off, coats off, all rush in—everybody ready for toddler gym!" Get ready to have your child leave your lap and start joining in the fun. First, the smiling children touch their "Heads and shoulders, knees and toes. Eyes and ears, mouth and nose." Then the multiethnic group in their colorful playtime clothes flap their arms, jump, stretch, and bend down to touch their toes. Sometimes touching one another, sometimes spread against the white background, these toddlers will inspire listeners to try out the exercises. Like real children, the characters don't always get it right—they can't quite form a choo-choo train—but they have a great time trying. Just the book when you want to get your young one moving.

Newcome, Zita. *Toddlerobics: Animal Fun.* **1999. Hardcover: Candlewick. Good for groups. Ages 18 months and up.**

The adorable toddlers from the first *Toddlerobics* are back, this time imitating animals. Labeled by their names on the endpapers, the eight children start by waddling like penguins, then flipping their fins and swimming like fish. In a more complicated movement, which they can't all do, it's time to scuttle sideways like a crab. But most of the instructions are easier, such as "Quack like a duck" and "Go hop, hop, hop!" like a kangaroo. Certainly, the smiling children in the pencil-and-watercolor illustrations are having a great time together. The final movements lead them down to the ground, where they take deep breaths and don't make a sound. Enjoy this as a book to read and look at, or use it to prompt some imaginative animal imitations in your own home.

Numeroff, Laura. *What Mommies Do Best/What Daddies Do Best.* **Illustrated by Lynn Munsinger. 1998. Hardcover: Simon & Schuster. Ages 2 years and up.**

Here are two books in one. After starting at one cover and reading to the middle of the book, you turn the book upside down and start reading at the other cover. Each offers an uncomplicated text, with either "mommies" or "daddies" at the opening of each sentence. "Mommies can teach you how to ride a bicycle," begins one half of the book, showing a mother bear and little bear both riding bikes. The other half opens, "Daddies can teach you how to ride a bicycle," with a father hippo on foot lunging after a child on a bike. Both parents appear with their children making a snowman, baking, sewing, giving piggyback rides, gardening, playing in the park, and reading a bedtime story. The message that mothers and fathers can do the same parenting tasks comes across gently through the lighthearted illustrations of happy animal families. This contrast is lost in the newest publication format, in which each half is available as a separate, smaller book, but single parents may appreciate the abbreviated versions. Also packaged as one book are two stories in *What Grandmas Do Best/What Grandpas Do Best.*

Numeroff, Laura Joffe. *If You Give a Mouse a Cookie.* **Illustrated by Felicia Bond. 1985. Hardcover: HarperCollins. Paperback: HarperCollins. Good for groups. Ages 18 months and up.**

"If you give a mouse a cookie, he's going to ask for a glass of milk. When you give him the milk, he'll probably ask you for a straw." This sets the pattern of the book, with a charming little mouse clad in overalls making request after request of a good-natured boy. The boy, bemused by his parentlike role of looking after his enthusiastic new friend, fulfills each request. Unexpectedly, the mouse ends up cleaning the house before settling in for a story and drawing a picture. The picture leads to the cycle's starting over with another cookie and glass of milk. An irresistible combination of story and picture, not to be missed. A companion book is *If You Take a Mouse to the Movies,* while similar books are *If You Give a Pig a Pancake* and *If You Give a Moose a Muffin.*

O'Book, Irene. *Maybe My Baby.* **Photographs by Paula Hible. 1998. Board book: HarperCollins. Ages 3 months and up.**

For the many babies who love to look at photographs of other babies, this is an appealing little book. On each left-hand page, a baby smiles out, set against a white background. The first wears a cap and holds a medal; the second holds a cloth globe of the world and a plastic rocket ship. The rhyming text suggests a possible future for the babies—in this case, winning a race or rocketing into space. But then the prose quickly draws back to say, "It's surely too early to tell." Since all the babies wear diapers, it's not clear which are girls and which are boys, opening up the possible futures to both. While not an outstanding board book, this has an attractive design and eight lovable babies to admire.

O'Brien, Patrick. *Gigantic! How Big Were the Dinosaurs?* **1999. Hardcover: Henry Holt. Paperback: Henry Holt. Good for groups. Ages 2 years and up.**

Although this book was written for older children, brave young dinosaur fans will love it. On each oversize set of pages, a dinosaur appears near an object or a person that emphasizes the dinosaur's size. The seismosaurus towers above a backhoe, the triceratops confronts a mounted knight in armor, and the phobosuchus stretches out along the side of a fire engine. Some of the dinosaurs look fierce indeed, so this isn't for the fainthearted. The lurid paintings and well-chosen comparisons make it a winner for those who love the subject.

Ochiltree, Dianne. *Pillow Pup.* **Illustrated by Mireille D'Allancé. 2002. Hardcover: McElderry Books. Good for groups. Ages 2 years and up.**

Watch out for Maggie, a "pillow-pulling pup." The narrator, a golden-haired girl, is asleep when Maggie pulls away her pillow and starts to chew it. The furry little puppy shakes it and drags it and takes it for a "tail-wagging, floor-dragging, zig-zagging ride." Then the chase begins. In oversize pictures, the girl pursues the naughty pup, capturing the pillow only to find herself in a tug-of-war over it. Engaging, energetic illustrations convey the playful spirit of the game, which starts over again on the last page.

Ormerod, Jan. *Miss Mouse's Day/Miss Mouse Takes Off.* **2001. Hardcover: HarperCollins. Ages 2 years and up.**

A warm welcome to newcomer Miss Mouse, the beloved

stuffed animal of a rambunctious girl. Miss Mouse tells both of these stories from her point of view, with delightful illustrations that fill in the details. In *Miss Mouse's Day*, she relates a fun-filled day with the young girl, starting off with a cuddle and a look through a book. Pages with several framed panels show all their activities, from eating to artwork to dress-up to outdoors play. Both the mouse and the girl get progressively dirtier until they land in a mud puddle, with mud splattering everywhere. *Miss Mouse Takes Off* relates an airplane trip they take with the girl's mother, in which Miss Mouse manages to fall in food and pick up some colorful spots, but most of the time, they enjoy their journey. It's great to see the two friends throw themselves so enthusiastically into adventures.

Ormerod, Jan. *Peek-a-Boo!* 1998. Board book: Dutton. Ages 3 months and up.

Knowing how much the very young like to play peekaboo, Ormerod has crafted a book that acts like the game itself. Even the cover of this unusually tall board book has a flap that shows a child hiding behind mittened hands, and then the whole, smiling face when the flap is pulled down. Throughout the book, babies hide behind toys, clothes, and bibs and emerge smiling under the sturdy, large flaps. The question is always the same, "Where's the baby?" while the answer varies a little, such as "Bib-a-boo" and "I see you." The last of the six babies smiles on the flap and, when it is opened, has snuggled down to sleep. An on-target creation in a fairly durable format. Look in your library for the companion book, *Rock-a-Baby*, now out of print.

Oxenbury, Helen. *All Fall Down/Clap Hands/Say Goodnight/Tickle, Tickle*. 1999. Board book: Simon & Schuster. Good for groups. Ages 6 months through 2 years.

Four of the best board books ever published, these first

came out in 1987 and then with new, brighter covers in 1999. They were created as board books, larger than most, and they suit the format perfectly. They also beautifully convey topics of interest to babies in very brief texts and utterly irresistible pictures. Fat little babies with different skin colors and amounts of hair tumble around together in *All Fall Down*, singing and bouncing with joy. *Clap Hands* features the same cuddly children, clapping, eating, banging pots, and waving. *Say Goodnight* moves from swinging to sleeping, while *Tickle, Tickle* will delight children with its pictures of babies in mud, then in the tub, and finally being gently tickled. The set of four, or any one of these, makes a terrific baby gift.

Oxenbury, Helen. *I Can/I Hear/I See/I Touch*. 1986. Board book: Random House. Ages 3 months through 2 years.

These classic little books helped set the standard for outstanding board books. Each of them shows a roly-poly toddler exploring the world, with only one or two words on each page, which continue the sentence begun in the title. In *I Touch*, a ball and the word *ball* are on the left side of the first page and the child sprawls on a colorful beach ball on the right side: "I touch a ball." Later, a worm appears with the word on the left, and on the right, the child squats down, holding it up. The simple pen-and-watercolor pictures are uncluttered, with objects drawn from the everyday world of many children. Highly recommended.

Oxenbury, Helen. *Pippo Gets Lost /Tom and Pippo Go for a Walk/Tom and Pippo Read a Story/Tom and Pippo's Day*. 1998. Board book: Simon & Schuster. Ages 18 months and up.

Tom and his cloth monkey, Pippo, experience small crises together, but everything always comes out fine. Tom, a personable toddler, can't find Pippo one day but finds the monkey's scarf and hat before his mother spots the lost toy. "Tom tells Pippo to let him know before he goes away next time." The way Tom's words in these short books echo the sound of parents will amuse adults, while his problems will engage children's feelings. While occasionally the boy blames Pippo for making him run too fast or spill his food, the two have a warm friendship overall. The pictures were originally created for a larger format, now out of print, and feel a bit cramped, but Oxenbury's work is still a pleasure, as always. Look for other books about Tom and Pippo, too.

Pandell, Karen. *I Love You, Sun, I Love You, Moon.* Illustrated by Tomie dePaola. 1994. Board book: Putnam. Ages 6 months and up.

With a spirit many parents will appreciate, this small book celebrates nature in simple terms. On each double-page spread, a girl and a boy proclaim their love for the world around them. "I love you, flower. / I love you, rabbit." The clean, appealing pictures illustrate the familiar objects the children praise: rock, bug, bird, fish, and more, showing children of different ethnicities. The book opens with the sun and closes with the moon, followed by a group of children who are holding hands and saying, "I love you, earth. / And you love me."

Parr, Todd. *Big & Little/Black & White.* 2001. Board book: Little, Brown. Ages 3 months through 2 years.

Only four and a half inches on each side, these little books fit little hands. Their sturdy cardboard pages, which will endure a lot of chewing, also make them good for the very young. Each features vividly colored pictures outlined in black, centered on the small page. In *Big & Little*, the big item is on the left, starting with a simplified truck, across from a tiny tricycle on the right-hand side. The familiar objects include a big cake and a little cookie, a big tree and a little leaf, a big mommy and a little baby. *Black & White* pairs black things on the left and white on the right, starting with a black cat and white mouse and ending with two animals that combine black and white, a zebra and a penguin. With only two words per page, these appealing books suit their young audience.

Paul, Ann Whitford. *Hello Toes! Hello Feet!* Illustrated by Nadine Bernard Westcott. 1998. Hardcover: DK. Ages 12 months and up.

In sprightly illustrations, a girl wakes up one morning and greets her toes and feet, telling them, "Be the first to touch the floor, hop me to the closet door." In the closet, shelves display all kinds of shoes and slippers, including cowboy boots, skates, and sandals decorated with fruit. The girl, now dressed, opts for glittery red high heels. But, as older children will note, her faithful little dog follows behind her with flat green shoes. These come in handy for kicking the table at breakfast, then heading outside to leap, skip, slide, and swing. Vibrant colors and lots of humor in the pictures suit the spirit of the bouncing words. Switching to red cowboy boots, the girl trots like a horse, then discards the boots in favor of bare feet to squish through mud. With a focus on feet and a child's-eye view of the world, this records a lighthearted romp through a girl's active day.

Pilkey, Dav. *Big Dog and Little Dog/Big Dog and Little Dog Getting in Trouble/Big Dog and Little Dog Going for a Walk.* 1997. Board book: Harcourt. Ages 15 months and up.

In the first of these three board books, a tiny dog and a large one each are hungry and eat from their own bowls. Then they each get into their own beds, Big Dog into the big one and Little Dog into the little one. When they get lonely, the solution is unexpected and charming. In the sequel, the two friends get into trouble by tearing up a couch cushion, meaning no harm but making a mess. They also make a mess when they go for a walk, splashing in puddles and mud. Their owner, a woman whose full face never appears, hovers in the background, but the focus is on the pair of engaging, messy dogs.

Pinkney, Andrea, and Brian Pinkney. *Pretty Brown Face/ Shake Shake Shake/Watch Me Dance.* **1997. Board book: Harcourt. Ages 6 months and up.**

With a limited number of board books about African Americans, this trio is a welcome sight. They are about a black family enjoying music, dance, and one another in simple text and pictures. In *Pretty Brown Face*, a father is admiring his little son, pointing out his curly hair, wide-open eyes, proud nose, and strong chin. It ends with a page of silvery reflecting material, in which a child can see his or her "pretty brown face." *Shake Shake Shake* shows a mother, daughter, and perhaps the same little boy making music with a shekere, an African percussion instrument. In *Watch Me Dance*, a girl entertains her little brother, who is in a playpen, by dancing, jumping, and twisting to music as the little boy imitates her. Although Brian Pinkney's artwork is better in his larger books, these will please those looking for dance, music, or a celebration of African Americans in board book format.

Pluckrose, Henry. *Building a Road.* **Illustrated by Teri Gower. 1998. Hardcover: Watts. Paperback: Watts. Ages 2 years and up.**

Simple text and color photographs explain the process of building a road. The book describes in broad terms each step in preparing the road and the equipment that accomplishes it.

The photographs show how excavators dig and move the soil, spreaders level it, and dump trucks carry the soil away. Then the addition of asphalt requires a dump truck and road roller. Children fascinated by machinery will enjoy this introduction to road building.

Pomerantz, Charlotte. *The Piggy in the Puddle*. Illustrated by James Marshall. 1974. Hardcover: Simon & Schuster. Paperback: Aladdin. Ages 2 years and up.

"Mud is squishy, mud is squashy / Mud is oh so squishy squashy," reads one of the rollicking rhymes in this terrific story. A pig has jumped into the middle of a mud puddle, to the distress of her family. She defies their orders to get out, telling her father, "Squishy-squashy, squishy-squashy-NOPE!" Wonderfully amusing pictures show the well-dressed pig family finally giving in to the inevitable. When they can't get her out of the mud, they jump in to join her. A romp of a book, full of wordplay and inviting rhythms, this may well become a family favorite.

Prater, John. *Again!* 2000. Hardcover: Barron's. Good for groups. Ages 2 years and up.

Parents and grandparents will relate to the Grandbear in this perceptive book about children's persistence. Baby Bear rouses Grandbear from the hammock to play blocks. Well-composed watercolors show them building a tower of colored blocks, which Baby Bear happily pushes over—then wants to build again and again. Finally, Grandbear persuades Baby Bear to try something else, building sandcastles. They build them, Baby Bear stomps on them, and then wants to start over. So, too, with watering flowers and reading a favorite book, until they both fall asleep. A realistic, good-natured portrayal of grandparent and child.

Prater, John. *The Bear Went over the Mountain/Number One, Tickle Your Tum.* **1999. Board book: Barron's. Good for groups. Ages 12 months and up.**

These wonderful board books show warm interactions between a little bear and a big bear. *The Bear Went over the Mountain* takes place on a bed covered with pillows, some of which are on top of the big bear. The little bear is crawling around, over the big one, ticking its feet, sprawling all over. The big bear endures it with patience and pleasure. "Number one, tickle your tum" is the first move in a counting game between the same two bears. This game lends itself to imitation, since "number two" is to say "boo!" Other directions are to "touch your knee," "touch the floor," and more along the same lines. Appealing pencil-and-watercolor pictures use the large board book format very well. Read these and act them out when you are in the mood.

Priddy, Roger. *My Big Book of Everything.* **1996. Hardcover: DK. Ages 2 years and up.**

If you are looking for a book with many bright, small photographs of different items, this will fill your need. Each large double-page spread covers one or two of thirty categories, showing several dozen items that loosely fit the topic. Some will be more relevant to young children than others, such as the topics of clothes, toys and games, fruit, me and my body, baby animals, noises, and more. The photographs are set against white space, with thin lines forming frames for some of the smaller pictures. The items or animals are identified with their name in readable, black typeface. Some parents and children will find this too cluttered and overwhelming, but others will enjoy the variety.

Raschka, Chris. *Can't Sleep*. 1995. Hardcover: Orchard. Board book: Orchard. Ages 2 years and up.

A large, yellow moon is rising as this soothing bedtime book opens. The moon, which has a face, gazes down on a dog family getting ready for bed, where the youngest can't sleep. "When you can't sleep / the moon will keep / you safe. / The moon will stay awake." This and similar comforting sentiments recur as the dog listens to the family fall asleep, and the moon travels across the top of the page and down the right-hand side. When the little dog has finally dozed off, the moon gently kisses the dog. In the morning, in a lovely reversal, the moon goes to sleep and the little dog stays awake to keep her safe. A brilliant combination of poetic words and watercolors, this lullaby may well become a family favorite.

Raschka, Chris. *Charlie Parker Played Be Bop*. 1992. Hardcover: Orchard. Paperback: Orchard. Good for groups. Ages 6 months and up.

Jazz lovers will not want to miss this terrific book, which reads like an enchanting nonsense rhyme and so works as a book for the very young. Inventive pictures combine with a brilliant rhythmic text to echo Parker's recording of "A Night in Tunisia." "Boomba, boomba . . . Boppity, bibbitty, bop. BANG!" In an allusion to "Bird," Parker's nickname, various objects on bird's feet dance through the pages. Large, smoky illustrations of Parker and his sax seen from various angles provide a balance to the more whimsical creatures who fill the other pages. Unusual as it is, this creative book appeals enormously to children, who end up chanting the words just for fun. Give it a try, even if you don't know Charlie Parker's music. Also for preschoolers, see Raschka's *Mysterious Thelonious*.

Raschka, Chris. *Moosey Moose/Snaily Snail/Whaley Whale/ Wormy Worm*. 2000. Hardcover: Hyperion. Ages 2 years and up.

When so many children's books rely on either clothed, talking animals or realistic pictures, Raschka's slightly abstract paintings come as a pleasant surprise. He has created a series called Thingy Things, of which these four represent half. The texts are short and repetitive; the pictures consist of slashes and dots of paint that form animals. In *Moosey Moose*, a moose refuses his short pants and is happy only when he gets long pants—which he wears on his horns. *Whaley Whale* also uses gentle humor, with the whale hiding under a chair in a house, an unlikely event. *Wormy Worm* is exuberant, while *Snaily Snail* is reassuring. Unusual, small books that break the mold.

Rathmann, Peggy. *Good Night, Gorilla*. 1994. Hardcover: Putnam. Paperback: Puffin. Board book: Putnam. Good for groups. Ages 15 months and up.

This nearly wordless picture book will charm children right away when a gorilla steals the keys from a zookeeper, follows him, and lets the other animals out of their cages one by one. The gorilla, elephant, lion, hyena, giraffe, and armadillo, plus a little mouse carrying a banana, follow the zookeeper to his house and into his bedroom. But when the zookeeper's wife turns out the light, to her surprise, all the animals say, "Good night," and she leads them back to the zoo. Little does she know that the gorilla and mouse follow her back to the bedroom again. The clever pictures, which have the timing of a comical silent movie, intensify the joke. (The board book loses some wonderful touches on the endpapers and even in a few pictures.)

Rathmann, Peggy. *10 Minutes till Bedtime.* **1998. Hardcover: Putnam. Board book: Putnam. Ages 2 years and up.**

In this engaging book, a young boy watches in delight as hamsters tour his house in the ten minutes before his bedtime. Although his newspaper-reading father doesn't notice, ten hamster tourists—and then truckloads more—sightsee in the boy's bathroom and bedroom, play with his toys, and join him in his bath. With few words except the father's announcements, starting with "Ten minutes till bedtime," the countdown continues until the tired boy's final "BEDTIME!" The book relies on pictures full of clever, funny details, which will have children studying the pages with pleasure. (Don't miss the hamster family photos on the endpapers.)

Ray, Mary Lyn. *Red Rubber Boot Day.* **Illustrated by Lauren Stringer. 2000. Hardcover: Harcourt. Good for groups. Ages 2 years and up.**

It's raining, and a child presses against the screen door, smelling and listening and watching. Nothing identifies the child's gender as he or she colors with crayons, builds a block city, looks at a book, plays with toy cars, and has a party with dishes and dolls. It all leads up to a romp outside in the rain. Clad in a yellow slicker and shiny red rubber boots, the child stomps joyfully in puddles. Splashing, the child celebrates the boots, "Red boots. My boots. Red rubber made-for-rain boots." But the boots work just as well in puddles when the sun comes out. Lush acrylic paintings show the child having a splendid time. A perfect book to bring out on a rainy day, followed by a romp in the rain.

Rice, Eve. *Benny Bakes a Cake.* **1981. Hardcover: Greenwillow. Good for groups. Ages 18 months and up.**

In this brief, engaging story, preschooler Benny is having a birthday. Simple, colored-pencil pictures show him helping his mother mix up a cake, all the while making sure that the family dog, Ralph, is good. They read a book while the cake bakes, ice it, and then get ready to go on a walk, only to discover that Ralph has knocked the cake onto the floor and started eating it. Poor Benny cries while his mother calls his father and they solve the problem. Listeners will smile when the still teary Benny hears a knock at the door and opens it to find his father carrying a big cake. Eve Rice, who has a gift for writing and illustrating stories for very young children, knows just what will hold their attention. A charming book for parent and child.

Rice, Eve. *Sam Who Never Forgets*. 1977. Paperback: Morrow. Good for groups. Ages 18 months and up.

In this surefire hit for young children, the main character is Sam, a zookeeper clad in a blue uniform and jaunty cap. Every day at precisely the same time, Sam feeds the animals. "Sam never forgets," and the animals count on him. Bright, tidy pictures show him collecting the food and feeding animals one by one. They all thank him, starting with the giraffe and going on to the monkeys, seals, crocodiles, and others. Sam knows exactly what each of them likes best. But wait! Sam's cart of food is empty, and Elephant hasn't been fed. Has Sam forgotten? Just the right note of anxiety is sounded, with the animals and listener beginning to be worried, when Sam shows up with a big load of hay for Elephant. A flawless combination of appealing pictures and a story perfect for its audience. Not to be missed.

Richards, Laura E. *Jiggle Joggle Jee!* Illustrated by Sam Williams. 2001. Hardcover: Greenwillow. Good for groups. Ages 12 months and up.

Nonsense rhymes are great fun to read to babies and toddlers. This one relies on a bouncing rhythm, linked together by the refrain "What does the train say? Jiggle joggle jiggle joggle. / What does the train say? Jiggle joggle jee!" Soft pencil-and-watercolor pictures start with a sleeping baby who is drawn into a dreamland trip with a toy train and stuffed animals. While the youngest will enjoy the words more than the pictures, toddlers will point out familiar items in the dream landscape and join in the repeated phrases, which trip off the tongue.

Riley, Linnea. *Mouse Mess.* **1997. Paperback: Scholastic. Good for groups. Ages 15 months and up.**

This witty book creates a cocky little mouse who raids a kitchen one night. Superb cut-paper illustrations show him eating cookies and crackers, then raking cornflakes and jumping exuberantly into the pile. He goes on to sample lots of food, never putting anything away. "Splish-splash, the milk spills out. Food is scattered all about." Finally, he steps back and, in a droll twist, doesn't recognize his own work: " 'Who made this awful mess?' asks Mouse. 'These people need to clean their house!' " After a restful plunge in a cup of hot, soapy water, the mouse feels clean and well fed. He heads for his mousehole, leaving the mess for someone else to clean up. Parents will love the tongue-in-cheek humor, while young children will love the colorful mess and the bouncing text.

Robbins, Ken. *Trucks: Giants of the Highway.* **1999. Hardcover: Atheneum. Ages 2 years and up.**

Toddlers who love trucks will find plenty to look at in these stunning photographs. The brief text describes different aspects of tractor-trailers, their purpose, size, details about the cab and tractor, and more. The wide format gives room for many full-page photographs, which add information and beauty. The composition and color raise these photos far above those usually found in transportation books. Highly recommended.

PICTURE-STORY BOOKS FOR THE VERY YOUNG

Rockwell, Anne. *Fire Engines.* **1986. Hardcover: Dutton. Paperback: Puffin. Ages 15 months and up.**

With Mom and Dad reading nearby, a young dalmatian rides in a large toy fire engine, declaring, "I like fire engines." Children who feel the same way will want to study the details in this straightforward book about firefighters and their trucks. Uncluttered pictures in bright colors fill the wide pages with ladder trucks and pumper trucks, an ambulance, and the fire chief's car. Firefighters, also dalmatians, put out a fire in an apartment and on a dock, spraying water from a boat. The last page returns to the same picture as the first page, rounding out the story with the popular sentiment, "I want to be a fire fighter and drive a real fire engine when I grow up."

Rockwell, Anne. *Growing Like Me.* **Illustrated by Holly Keller. 2001. Hardcover: Harcourt. Good for groups. Ages 2 years and up.**

A happy boy enjoying a day outdoors muses on how different things in nature grow and change over time, including children. He sees white blossoms that, when you turn the page, have grown into plump blackberries. Blue eggs hatch into robins, caterpillars become butterflies. Nicely composed pictures in appealing colors illustrate the transformations. For the change from acorn to oak tree, the reader must turn the book to see the tree stretching the width of a double-page spread, which will intrigue young listeners. The boy ends by looking at his brother, proclaiming proudly, "One day you'll be a big boy—just like me."

Rockwell, Anne. *Things That Go.* **1986. Paperback: Dutton. Ages 18 months and up.**

With her usual clean illustrations, Rockwell brings together dozens of different vehicles and other "things that go."

Each double-page spread consists of squares and rectangles that hold vehicles, starting with "Things That Go on the Road." The ten pictures show trucks, cars, a camper, and a motorcycle, with brightly colored animals at the wheel, dressed as people. "Things That Go on the Water" reaches past standard vehicles to include a surfboard, inner tubes, sailboards, and water skis, along with various boats. Other categories show things that go in the air, on snow and ice, in the city, in the country, and more. While similar to Richard Scarry's books, this has a calmer, crisper feel to it but will similarly provide hours of browsing and lots to talk about.

Rockwell, Anne and Harlow. *At the Beach*. 1987. Paperback: Simon & Schuster. Ages 2 years and up.

A small girl in a red bathing suit goes to the beach with her mother one day. Her childlike voice describes the beach accoutrements and lunch they pack. A sturdy, smiling child, the narrator follows little sandpipers down the beach, declaring, "My feet make footprints in the wet sand. The sandpipers make footprints, too." She finds seaweed and seashells and wades among little fishes. Most of the pen-and-watercolor illustrations show her actively enjoying her surroundings, building sandcastles and swimming with her mother. Geared skillfully to the level of a young child, this is a good book to read before a trip to the beach or for an imaginary trip there.

Roddie, Shen. *Good-bye, Hello!* Illustrated by Carol Thompson. 2001. Hardcover: DK. Ages 12 months and up.

A toddler starts moving into new territory in this optimistic book, saying good-bye to diapers, high chair, and stroller and saying hello to potty, low chair, and feet. Color-saturated pictures show a pink-cheeked toddler, not identified by gender, happily leaving old habits and embracing new ones—

except when it comes to naptime, when a well-loved teddy bear is still a necessity. Large, sturdy pages showcase the exuberant illustrations. You can read this book as a subtle way to introduce your child to future changes or reinforce ones in progress, like changing from a crib to a bed. Or read it just for fun, which it is.

Root, Phyllis. *The Hungry Monster*. **Illustrated by Sue Heap. 1997. Paperback: Candlewick. Good for groups. Ages 18 months and up.**

A goofy-looking monster descends to earth in a rocket and goes looking for something to eat. Each thing that it sees looks good at first: "YUM!" But the daisy, rock, and tree prove to be inedible: "YUCK!" Children will feel the tension when the monster sees a girl eating a banana and yells, of course, "YUM!" "YIKES!" she replies, and quickly hands him the banana, providing a happy conclusion. This offers just the right amount of drama and scariness tempered with enough silliness to make it all a lot of fun. If you don't mind your child's acquiring the word *yuck*, have fun with this sunny, short book.

Root, Phyllis. *One Duck Stuck*. **Illustrated by Jane Chapman. 1998. Hardcover: Candlewick. Board book: Candlewick. Good for groups. Ages 15 months and up.**

A duck who gets stuck in the muck cries on every other page, "Help! Help! Who can help?" Animals come to try to rescue the duck—first two fish, then three moose, and so on up to ten dragonflies. Each animal makes a distinctive sound, which adds to the fun. Four crickets "pleep," while five frogs "plop." But the duck is still stuck. Even at the end, when all the animals gather to help and make their sounds, nothing happens. Then, for no clear reason, the duck rescues itself: "Spluck!" The richly colored paintings depict an expressive duck and a wonderful array of animals. The text, which is a bit cumbersome in the original version, actually works better in the abridged board book, but the pictures lose their impact. In either version, this will appeal to many young children.

Rose, Deborah Lee. *Into the A, B, Sea.* **Illustrated by Steve Jenkins. 2000. Hardcover: Scholastic. Ages 2 years and up.**

In this celebration of the ocean, cut-paper collages fill the pages with rich textures and colors. For each letter of the alphabet, a different sea creature appears, from stinging anemones through zillions of zooplankton. Rhyming phrases describe the animals' actions, such as "Where Eels explore and Flying Fish soar" and "Where Queen Angels glow and Rays swoop low." The book is not so much a vehicle for learning the alphabet as an introduction to sea creatures and a showcase for outstanding artwork. Young children will enjoy the sounds of the words, which read like poetry, the subject, and the beauty of the pictures. Three pages at the end supply a few facts about each creature. A book to enjoy and, later, learn from.

Rosen, Michael. *We're Going on a Bear Hunt!* **Illustrated by Helen Oxenbury. 1989. Hardcover: McElderry Books. Board book: Simon & Schuster. Good for groups. Ages 12 months and up.**

A must-read, this is a wonderful adventure that moves along as smoothly as a jump rope rhyme. A family on a bear hunt meets obstacles along the way but never really expects to meet a bear. The first challenge is "long, wavy grass," prompting the refrain that sounds throughout the book: "We can't go over it. We can't go under it. Oh, no! We've got to go through it!" You may want to add your own movements, which children who are old enough will imitate. Wade through the grass, parting it with your hands, as you read, "Swishy swashy! Swishy swashy! Swishy swashy!" Each new obstacle is met with similar sounds that trip off the tongue. When the family does encounter a bear, the series of panels shows them scurrying backward through all the earlier obstacles, to hide safely at home. While the board book certainly does not do justice to the pictures, you might want it to read to a baby—the sounds alone are a pleasure. But get the larger version for toddlers and to enjoy yourself.

Roth, Susan L. *My Love for You*. 1997. Hardcover: Dial. Board book: Dial. Ages 18 months and up.

Although this is a counting book, it can be read as a reassuring story that will please parent and child. It opens with a white mouse telling its young, brown child, "My love for you is bigger than 1 bear." Textured collage illustrations set a brown bear opposite two giraffes. The text for the giraffes continues the counting with "Taller than 2 giraffes." Each appealing picture shows more animals, with a comparison about the parent mouse's love. After the number ten, all the animals fill one double-page spread, where the parent declares its love "Greater than all of these together, forever." A sweet book, well designed and beautifully illustrated, that will strike a comforting note at bedtime or during the day. Avoid the board book version, in which the mice nearly disappear, they are so small.

Rounds, Glen. *Cowboys*. 1991. Hardcover: Holiday House. Paperback: Holiday House. Good for groups. Ages 2 years and up.

Rough, energetic drawings and a handful of sentences create an intriguing picture of a cowboy's life. A newly hired cowboy is shown trying to catch and saddle a horse, "but sometimes that's easier said than done." After the bucking horse throws him, the cowboy climbs back on and rides out onto the range with others, where they look for stray cattle and deal with a wild stampede. After rounding up the cattle and driving them into the corral, his day ends with supper. The wide format of the book suits the expansive lines of the treeless, dusty country. The hand-lettered text is nicely integrated into the pictures, which are sure to appeal to cowboy and horse fans.

Rowe, Jeannette. *Whose Ears?/Whose Feet?/Whose Nose?* 1998. Hardcover: Little, Brown. Good for groups. Ages 6 months and up.

This trio of complementary books will provide hours of entertainment, first for parents to read to infants and delight them by opening the flaps, then for toddlers to enjoy the guessing games. In each book, the title question is repeated on the left-hand page, while a flap hides most of an animal on the right-hand side, in bold, simple paintings. *Whose Ears?* has flaps that fold down the page, revealing the whole animal, such as a rabbit and the phrase "rabbit's ears" to answer the question. The pages fold up to show more than the feet in *Whose Feet?*, while a vertical half page covers the animal, except its nose, in *Whose Nose?* A perfect use of flaps to entertain the very young and invite interaction from the slightly older.

Russo, Marisabina. *Come Back, Hannah!* 2001. Hardcover: Greenwillow. Ages 2 years and up.

Young Hannah, clad in bright red overalls, loves to crawl. No matter what her mother is doing—writing a letter or making a phone call—Hannah can't sit still, even when she has a hammer and pegs or a cupboard of pans to play with. She crawls away, with her mother calling, "Come back, Hannah!" She crawls after balls and toward the sound of their dog's jingling collar. No wonder her mother chooses to read her a book about a race. But even then, Hannah races away until naptime finally arrives and she lies contentedly, at least for a moment. Her understanding mother seems to enjoy her child's energy. Vibrant colors characterize the gouache paintings, which enhance the story. Also look for *Waiting for Hannah*, now out of print, and *Hannah's Baby Sister*.

Ryder, Joanna. *Each Living Thing*. Illustrated by Ashley Wolff. 2000. Hardcover: Harcourt. Ages 2 years and up.

An ecological message that even young children can understand comes across in this beautiful book. As it says about the earth's creatures near the end, "Be aware of them. Take care of them. Be watchful. Let them be." Children of different ethnic groups appear throughout, starting with a girl who is carrying a recycling box down a driveway, past a dew-drenched spiderweb and a robin's nest. Then, on her way to the school bus, she sees a snake, a mouse, and a chickadee. Luminous paintings celebrate the natural world, showing a variety of terrain and animals as the day moves from morning to night. "Watch out for every living thing, for all beasts fine and free, who grace the earth and ride the skies and glide within the sea" expresses the book's theme perfectly. Young children will search for, and name, the animals, while absorbing the importance of treating the earth well.

Rylant, Cynthia. *Bunny Bungalow*. Illustrated by Nancy Hayashi. 1999. Hardcover: Harcourt. Paperback: Harcourt. Ages 2 years and up.

Oh, to live the life of these happy bunnies in their snug bunny bungalow. Rhyming couplets explain that the bunny family found a bungalow, painted it, and added a weather vane shaped like a carrot. Inside, Mother knits bunny quilts and sews white pillows, and tucks her five little bunnies into bed. Sweet pen-and-watercolor illustrations show her cuddling her littlest one, reading to all of her children, and giving them slightly riotous baths. Everything about this family is cozy as can be, with many details in the pictures not mentioned in the text. A satisfying visit to an idyllic life.

Saul, Carol P. *Barn Cat*. Illustrated by Mary Azarian. 1998. Hardcover: Little, Brown. Paperback: Little, Brown. Good for groups. Ages 2 years and up.

Exquisite hand-colored woodcut prints follow the adventures of a barn cat that is looking for something. Using numbers as a structure, the book shows the cat walking around the farm encountering different animals. "Barn cat at the red barn door. / Barn cat, what are you looking for?" Is it looking for one green grasshopper, two brown crickets, three black-and-orange butterflies? Each animal is identified by number and color, illustrated in large, lovely pictures. After reaching the number ten, a flock of sparrows, the listener finds out what the cat really wants. An attractive book with a rhythmic sound and lots to look at.

Scarry, Richard. *Richard Scarry's Best Word Book Ever*. 1980 revised edition. Hardcover: Western. Ages 12 months and up.

Here is a popular book to dip into again and again rather than read from cover to cover. Richard Scarry fans, of which there are many, love his tidy animals dressed in human clothes and his large pages packed with information. The seventy pages of this oversize volume offer hours of poring over labeled pictures that parents can identify to their young child and then, as the child grows, have the child say the words. Kenny Bear and his sister Kathy provide recurring characters, shown in their home, at mealtime, doing farm chores, and getting dressed, among other daily actions. Some pages simply illustrate items of interest: work machines, an airport, the zoo, firefighters, the beach, and much, much more. The cheerful drawings are bright and easy to recognize, in Scarry's characteristic style.

Schindel, John. *Busy Penguins*. Photographs by Jonathan Chester. 2000. Board book: Tricycle. Ages 15 months and up.

Many toddlers are attracted to penguins and love to look at photographs of them. This board book capitalizes on that by showing penguins on every page, demonstrating an action. "Penguins bumping" shows two with their chests together, while the following "Penguin jumping" shows one jumping into the water. Some of the phrases rhyme exactly; others have similar sounds. Parents may be taken aback by the picture of "Penguins pooping," but chances are, children will be fascinated. The pages are nicely designed with color frames around the delightful photographs.

Schwartz, Amy. *A Teeny Tiny Baby*. 1994. Hardcover: Orchard. Paperback: Scholastic. Ages 2 years and up.

Parents will adore this narrative told from the viewpoint of a tiny baby who knows the world revolves around him, while children will find a lot to look at in the excellent illustrations. "I'm a teeny tiny baby," it says on the first page, where a baby is sleeping on a huge bed with doting parents and grandmother looking on. But on the next page, the baby's mouth has opened in a huge circle and the adults are rushing toward him. The words read, ". . . and I know how to get anything I want." What does he want? To be "jiggled or tickled or patted or burped or rocked or carried or held close." He likes to go on rides and be taken through his urban neighborhood. He has a lot of interests and wishes, shown in wonderfully detailed pictures on large pages. Although the text runs long for some two-year-olds, it rings many familiar bells. A delightful book with an imaginative premise, followed by the companion book, *Some Babies*.

Schwartz, Roslyn. *The Mole Sisters and the Piece of Moss/The Mole Sisters and the Rainy Day.* **1999. Hardcover: Annick. Ages 2 years and up.**

Partway through, one of these enchanting stories proclaims, "The mole sisters are never dull." That's true, because these little moles embrace life so completely in this fresh series, which continues with more books. When the sisters emerge from their underground home to have a good time, they find a piece of moss that needs some adventure. They perk up its spirit and take it on a journey to the top of the hill, after which the sisters roll on home, have a few laughs, and go to bed. In another episode, they make the most of a rainy day, turning rain and sunshine to their advantage. Soft colored-pencil illustrations show round little moles with expressive faces in these endearing books from Canada.

Scott, Ann Herbert. *On Mother's Lap.* **Illustrated by Glo Coalson. 1992 revised edition. Hardcover: Clarion. Paperback: Clarion. Board book: Clarion. Good for groups. Ages 18 months and up.**

A comforting glow infuses this old favorite about a mother who makes room on her lap for both of her children. The cozy illustrations, revised from the 1972 edition, show an Inuit mother and her son, whose name is Michael. Michael, thrilled to have his mother's lap to himself at first, adds his toys, puppy, and blanket to the mix. When the baby cries, though, Michael protests that there's no room for her. His mother gently convinces him otherwise, and the three of them end up snuggling happily together. A reassuring book to those who have or are expecting new babies in the family.

Sendak, Maurice. *Alligators All Around: An Alphabet/ Chicken Soup with Rice: A Book of Months/One Was Johnny: A Counting Book/Pierre: A Cautionary Tale in Five Chapters and a Prologue.* **1962. Hardcover: HarperCollins. Paperback: HarperCollins. Ages 2 years and up.**

These four small books, known collectively as the Nutshell Library, have worn well for the past forty years. Although they all have a stated purpose—teaching the alphabet, months, counting, and a moral message—they can all be read for the pure pleasure of the words and pictures. The well-crafted texts will probably have your toddler repeating phrases like "Sipping once / sipping twice / sipping chicken soup / with rice." They will laugh as Johnny's room fills up with animals and as the alligators burst balloons and ride reindeer. *Pierre* is the most challenging of the four, with its stubborn hero taught a lesson by a lion. Carole King's musical version of these songs on the sound track from *Really Rosie* is a treat and adds another dimension to already wonderful books.

Sendak, Maurice. *In the Night Kitchen.* **1970. Hardcover: HarperCollins. Ages 2 years and up.**

This original work practically sings in words and pictures. A boy named Mickey falls out of his bed and down through the night into "the light of the night kitchen," a campy place where three bakers who look like Oliver Hardy are baking for the morning. The action is set against a background of starlight, with a skyline of buildings made from kitchen items—jam jars, salt shakers, eggbeaters, and more. The bakers mix Mickey into the batter, but he pops out, fashions himself a plane out of dough, and fetches milk for them by diving into a huge bottle. "Milk in the batter! Milk in the batter! We bake cake! And nothing's the matter!" The pictures are irresistible, and the rhythmic words will echo in your child's head, and yours, long after the book is closed. A Caldecott Honor Book.

Sendak, Maurice. *Where the Wild Things Are.* 1963. Hardcover: HarperCollins. Paperback: HarperCollins. Good for groups. Ages 2 years and up.

"The night Max wore his wolf suit and made mischief of one kind and another . . . ," begins this tour de force among picture-story books. After the incorrigible Max is sent to bed without his supper, a forest grows in his room, an ocean tumbles by, and Max takes off in a boat to where the wild things are. Max tames these huge, cuddly creatures, immortalized in brilliant illustrations. But once he is king, Max longs "to be where someone loved him best of all," so he sails back home. The combination of honed text and extraordinary pictures has made this book into a modern classic. Although some children and parents find the wild things too scary, most embrace Max's imaginative voyage and his happy return. Expect some Wild Thing imitations as children show their claws and roll their eyes like the creatures in the story. Winner of the Caldecott Medal.

Serfozo, Mary. *Who Said Red?* Illustrated by Keiko Narahashi. 1988. Paperback: Aladdin. Ages 18 months and up.

Delectable watercolors framed in soft-edged washes of color make this a joy to behold. A girl and boy in an idyllic country setting are arguing about colors in a typical childlike way. The boy keeps saying "red," while the girl teases him by misunderstanding and naming other colors. "You don't mean green? Look, here is green . . . ," and a frog leaps across the page, upsetting a barrel of green pickles, followed by a beautiful page of delicate green leaves. While this will re-enforce a child's knowledge of basic colors, its strength is in its outstanding illustrations and the on-target behavior of the children.

Seuss, Dr. *The Foot Book: Dr. Seuss's Wacky Book of Opposites.* **1968. Hardcover: Random House. Board book: Random House. Ages 3 months and up.**

One of Dr. Seuss's typical furry creatures prances proudly through this book about feet and opposites. While you won't be teaching your child the concepts of "left" and "right" for a while, the book's rhyme works so well, you can entertain a baby by reading it aloud. A slightly older child will enjoy the pictures, too, of different, zany creatures. Feet are, of course, one of the first things babies encounter, so it's fitting to begin what may be years of reading Dr. Seuss with this zippy intro-duction. Note that the board book is considerably shorter than the original, and the board book version with flaps slows down the rhyme and eliminates many of the pictures.

Seuss, Dr. *Green Eggs and Ham.* **1960. Hardcover: Random House. Board book: Random House. Ages 12 months and up.**

Even once you are grown, you may have the addictive rhymes from this book echoing in your head. "I do not like them, Sam-I-Am. I do not like green eggs and ham," protests the older, furry creature when Sam-I-Am tries to persuade him to eat green eggs and ham. No matter what Sam-I-Am suggests—in a house, with a mouse, on a boat, with a goat—the answer is "No." In classic Seussian pictures, the two travel up mountains and across sky-high tracks, on zooming cars and trains and boats. In the end, the protester tries the dish just to quiet down Sam-I-Am and finds that he does like green eggs and ham, a lesson parents will appreciate planting early. Read this to a baby and keep reading it for years to come, and your child will probably read it to his or her children, too.

Seuss, Dr. *Hop on Pop.* **1963. Hardcover: Random House. Ages 18 months and up.**

Although this book is aimed at beginning readers, parents find it entertains young children, too. The text hops energetically along, full of rhymes and wordplay. No story line ties it all together, and different Seussian characters take the stage every few pages, so you can pick this up and put it down at any point. The words are short and rhyming, such as "Where is Brown? There is Brown. Mr. Brown is out of town," accompanied by a bewildered figure flying over the rooftops. As a parent, you don't want to give your child a steady diet of Dr. Seuss's I Can Read books because they contain such limited vocabulary. But they work well as excursions into silliness that are easy to read with expression.

Seuss, Dr. *Mr. Brown Can Moo! Can You?: Dr. Seuss's Book of Wonderful Noises.* **1970. Hardcover: Random House. Board book: Random House. Good for groups. Ages 6 months and up.**

Although six-month-olds will probably not appreciate the pictures, they may be captivated by the nonstop wordplay in this Dr. Seuss favorite. It's one sound after another as you turn the pages: buzz, pop, klopp, eek, hoo, dibble dibble dibble dopp. Familiar animals and events make noises that the mustachioed Mr. Brown, who looks a bit like a human Cat in the Hat, imitates. Soon your child will be imitating them, too.

Not everyone is a Dr. Seuss fan, but if you are, try this one early on and see if it intrigues your child. The board book is an abridgment and loses some of the fun of the language.

Shannon, David. *No, David!* 1998. Hardcover: Scholastic. Paperback: Scholastic. Ages 2 years and up.

David is a handful, to say the least, so his mother's most frequent words to him are, "No, David!" In fact, the words appear on almost every page of this rowdy book as young David does something else annoying. Toddlers will recognize the actions that prompt the many *nos*. David draws on the wall, tracks in mud, runs down the street without his clothes on, plays with his food, and more. He doesn't mean any harm, but he finally gets a time-out. Luckily, he also gets a hug from his mother and some new words, "Yes, David . . . I love you!" *No, David!* was named a Caldecott Honor Book for the childlike pictures, which flawlessly convey David's rambunctious spirit. While not to everyone's taste, this delights many children, who find it funny and, perhaps, familiar. Followed by *David Goes to School*.

Shapiro, Arnold L. *Mice Squeak, We Speak.* Illustrated by Tomie dePaola. 1997. Hardcover: Putnam. Paperback: Penguin. Board book: Penguin. Good for groups. Ages 15 months and up.

Tomie dePaola's pleasing illustrations bring alive a simple poem about the sounds that animals and humans make. A black boy, white boy, and girl with Asian features cluster together, looking at a purring cat. "Cats purr" are the only words on the page. The next page says, "Lions roar. Owls hoot." Different background colors distinguish the two illustrations, each surrounded by a tidy frame. The noise each animal makes appears in printed letters in the picture. After seven animals, including "Mice squeak," one of the children declares, "But I speak!" The rhyming scheme is aptly simple and easy to read. The illustrations, which are uncluttered, use color to a wonderful effect. A delightful book to read again and again.

Shaw, Charles G. *It Looked Like Spilt Milk*. 1947. Paperback: HarperCollins. Board Book: HarperCollins. Good for groups. Ages 2 years and up.

This beautifully designed book sets white shapes against a dark blue background. Children will easily identify many of the shapes, such as a rabbit, bird, and tree. They will also chime in with the text, which repeats the same pattern on every page until the very end. "Sometimes it looked like Spilt Milk. But it wasn't Spilt Milk," read the first and last page. Then the last page says what the white pictures were all along—a cloud. A remarkably elegant book tested by time, this is a favorite to use with groups as well as at home. It also works adequately in the smaller board book format.

Shaw, Nancy. *Sheep in a Jeep*. Illustrated by Margot Apple. 1986. Hardcover: Houghton. Paperback: Houghton. Board book: Houghton. Good for groups. Ages 6 months and up.

"Beep! Beep! / Sheep in a jeep on a hill that's steep," opens this short romp about some silly sheep piled into a red jeep. Relying on words that rhyme with *sheep*, the well-crafted text tells its story in a way that children can soon repeat themselves. The sprightly colored-pencil illustrations give the sheep personalities and introduce other animals not mentioned in the text. Some hefty pigs, complete with tattoos, save the yelping sheep when their jeep gets stuck in mud, but more foolishness leads to another mishap. No matter—nothing can discourage the sheep for long. An absolute must for young children, this is the first in a series.

Shea, Pegi Deitz. *I See Me*. Illustrated by Lucia Washburn. 2000. Board book: HarperCollins. Ages 12 months through 2 years.

Here is a baby delighted with her own face, as many young children are. On the cover and first page, she is smiling at her own image in the mirror. The words ask, "Baby, can you find yourself in any other place?" The rest of the book explores other reflections in everyday life. She sees herself in her metal spoon and a blank television screen, where she's reflected holding the remote: "Baby in the silver spoon / lick,lick,lick. / Baby in the TV screen / click, click, click." Realistic pictures in gentle textures and pastel colors are clearly created for the small format and use the space well. A clever exploration of places a baby might catch a glimpse of herself.

Siddals, Mary McKenna. *I'll Play with You*. Illustrated by David Wisniewski. 2000. Hardcover: Clarion. Ages 2 years and up.

Sun, wind, clouds, rain, stars, and moon beckon to a multicultural cast of five in this small book. Each child, looking out the window, sees a wonderful chance to play. Says one, "I'll play with you, Wind. Just give me a whistle. / I'll come running, and you whoosh right through me." The accompanying picture shows a girl running through windswept leaves. Caldecott Medal–winning illustrator Wisniewski works in his usual cut-paper medium, scaled down to suit the audience well. The other children splash in puddles, see pictures in the clouds, and then all reappear again when it's time to go to bed.

Siddals, Mary McKenna. *Morning Song*. Illustrated by Elizabeth Sayles. 2001. Hardcover: Henry Holt. Ages 2 years and up.

Geared exactly toward young children who wake before

the sun rises, this opens with a boy peeking out from under his covers, saying, "Good morning, blankie." In the shadowy predawn, he continues to greet his surroundings, including his stuffed bear and bunny, and his own fingers and toes. Venturing out of bed, he picks up his baby doll and pretends to read it a book. Hints of morning sunshine brighten the illustrations and more color emerges as the morning arrives and the clock points to 6:30. The boy's exuberance and increasing energy, which reflect the morning spirits of many small children, culminate in a big hug with his father, who is dressed for work.

Siebert, Diane. *Train Song*. Illustrated by Mike Wimmer. 1990. Hardcover: HarperCollins. Ages 18 months and up.

Expansive paintings of railroad cars from the past are paired with a brief text that echoes the sounds of a train chugging along. "Creaking / clanking / air brakes squeal / moaning / groaning / steel on steel." Train lovers will be fascinated with the different cars and the workers, such as engineer and conductor. The essence of the book is the beauty of the countryside and the train, captured in lush illustrations and heard in the musical words. Those who enjoy this will also like *Plane Song*, *Truck Song*, and *Motorcycle Song*, by the same author.

Simmons, Jane. *Come Along, Daisy*. 1997. Hardcover: Little, Brown. Board book: Little, Brown. Good for groups. Ages 18 months and up.

Meet Daisy, a curious little duck who wants to explore the pond. Ignoring her mother's gentle comment, "Come along, Daisy," Daisy watches fish, chases dragonflies, meets a frog, and jumps from lily pad to lily pad. When the frog leaves, Daisy suddenly wants her mother, who is nowhere in sight. The pond now seems a bit ominous, and the sound of something coming closer creates dramatic tension. The relief is palpable when it turns out to be Daisy's mother. Radiant, oversize paintings show Daisy as a slightly clumsy, very lovable young duck. An excellent start to a series of books about Daisy. Skip the board book edition of this, which omits parts of the story.

Singer, Marilyn. *Boo Hoo Boo-Boo*. Illustrated by Elivia Savadier. 2002. Hardcover: HarperCollins. Good for groups. Ages 18 months and up.

Boo-boos are a topic of vital concern to little children but seldom addressed in books. This energetic story fills that gap, describing three children who fall and get hurt a little. First Lulu, who is twirling in her tutu. All roundness and enthusiasm, she jumps too high and lands on her bottom. "Oh, no! Boo hoo! / Lulu's got a boo-boo." So, too, with Andrew, who tumbles while acting like a choo-choo, and Zuzu, who trips while wearing Mama's muumuu. After some understandable crying, each gets fixed up and cuddled by a caring adult. Soon, they are good as new. Vigorous pictures capture the children's ups and downs while wonderful wordplay supplies the story.

Singer, Marilyn. *Fred's Bed*. Illustrated by JoAnn Adinolfi. 2001. Hardcover: HarperCollins. Ages 2 years and up.

The droll, star-studded illustrations open on the title page with young Fred drooping over the edge of his crib, looking dissatisfied. Wearing blue pajamas with star buttons and a sleeping cap, Fred proclaims, "I need a new bed." His mother playfully suggests he might like an eagle's nest, but Fred answers, "Too high." In a catchy pattern with a simple refrain, the story continues with Mama offering a rabbit's hole, a monkey's lap, a porpoise pod, and other imaginative beds. Finally, she describes just the big-boy bed that Fred needs, to his immense satisfaction. The perfect book for introducing a move from crib to bed, but also great for reading and enjoying the pictures at other times.

Sís, Peter. *Fire Truck*. 1998. Hardcover: Greenwillow. Ages 18 months and up.

Using mostly red and white, with thick black lines, the artwork reflects its subject in this short book with only a brief text. A boy named Matt, who loves fire trucks, sits surrounded by toy fire engines, cars, helmets, and even a hose. He also reads books about fire engines. Then, amazingly, one morning he wakes up as a fire truck. His upper body still looks like a boy, but from the waist down, he's a fire truck, complete with supplies. A page folds out to show him in his full glory, with a text that counts from one to ten, naming his gear. He drives around with the siren blowing, rescues a cat, and puts out a fire, clearly beside himself with happiness. Only the smell of pancakes transforms him back into a little boy, ready for breakfast. Vehicle fans will also enjoy *Trucks, Trucks, Trucks*, by the same author.

Slobodkina, Esphyr. *Caps for Sale: A Tale of a Peddler, Some Monkeys and Their Monkey Business*. Good for groups. 1940. Hardcover: HarperCollins. Paperback: HarperCollins. Ages 18 months and up.

This time-tested picture-story book about a man and some mischievous monkeys is a delight to read aloud, with refrains that inspire children to join in. "You monkeys, you," the peddler says, shaking his finger at some monkeys who have taken the caps he sells. "You give me back my caps." In response, "The monkeys only shook their fingers back at him and said, 'Tsz, tsz, tsz.' " The peddler finally gets his caps back when he throws down his own cap in disgust, and the monkeys in the tree, each wearing one of the caps, imitate him. Expect the phrase "you monkeys, you" and the finger-shaking response to become part of your family folklore from this irresistible tale.

Smith, Charles R., Jr. *Brown Sugar Babies*. 2000. Hardcover: Hyperion. Ages 15 months and up.

The eight adorable babies in these photographs glow with pleasure and personality. Each baby appears on four consecutive pages, with a different-color border for each child. The four pages combine close-ups and smaller photographs, one with a loving adult and the others just of the baby. The photos are so crisp, clear, and well composed, you feel you can almost touch the plump, smiling infants. The book celebrates the many shades of brown skin a child may have, while the text compares the colors to sweets: caramel-apple cheeks, little carob cherub, bubbling brown sugar, and more. A delicious photo album.

Spagnoli, Cathy, adapter. From a tale told by Blia Xiong. *Nine-in-One, Grr! Grr!* Illustrated by Nancy Hom. 1989. Hardcover: Children's Book Press. Paperback: Children's Book Press. Ages 2¹/₂ years and up.

In this entertaining Hmong tale from Laos, a tiger goes to a male god and asks how many cubs she will have. Rather carelessly, the god replies, "Nine each year," but tells the tiger that she must remember that number for it to happen. So the tiger makes up a rhyme and recites it: "Nine-in-one, Grr! Grr!" She is overheard by the clever Eu bird, who asks the tiger what her rhyme means. The answer dismays the bird, who realizes the island will soon be overrun with dangerous tigers. She goes to the god, but he admits that fate cannot be changed as long as the tiger remembers. So the bird distracts the tiger, who forgets her rhyme. The bird teaches it back to her as "One-in-nine, Grr! Grr!" thus saving the island's animals from being crowded out by tigers. Colorful silk-screened artwork that draws from Hmong stitchery enhances the tale.

Spinelli, Eileen. *In My New Yellow Shirt*. Illustrated by Hideko Takahashi. 2001. Hardcover: Henry Holt. Good for groups. Ages 2 years and up.

Instead of simply asking, "What is yellow?" this sunny book transforms a boy in a yellow shirt into different yellow objects. When the young narrator receives a yellow shirt for his birthday, his friend Sam deems it boring. But the narrator imagines things he could be that are yellow, starting with a duck, "quacking, splashing through a big puddle of sun." In one amusing picture, he has become a yellow taxi—"HONK! HONK!"—with headlights for eyes and a smile on the bumper, observed by an astonished Sam from a passing car. The flat acrylic paintings of round-faced children extend the story beyond the text, with Sam expressing surprise in many of the pictures. Use this as a springboard for a game of identifying colors, starting with yellow, in your child's world.

Spinelli, Eileen. *When Mama Comes Home Tonight*. Illustrated by Jane Dyer. 1998. Hardcover: Simon & Schuster. Paperback: Simon & Schuster. Board book: Simon & Schuster. Ages 2 years and up.

"When Mama comes home from work" is still a surprisingly rare concept in children's stories, making this beautiful book all the more welcome. Watercolors full of lovely details show a mother greeting her young daughter and spending relaxed time with her after work. Together, they eat and play, count cars out the window, and wish on stars. The mother bathes her child and reads to her, sings a lullaby, and tucks her in. Old-fashioned patterns on clothing and furniture combine with an unusually attractive palette to paint scenes you'd like to step into with your child. Not every day after work can be so idyllic, but this peaceful evening of mother and child together is a pleasure to share. Note that the large size of this book is more satisfying than the too-small board book.

Spowart, Robin. *Ten Little Bunnies*. 2001. Hardcover: Scholastic. Good for groups. Ages 18 months and up.

Pastel colors and a soft texture lend an air of sweetness to this simple counting book about bunnies. In its progression up to ten, the book starts out, "One little bunny drumming . . . Boom! Boom! / Two little bunnies flying . . . Zoom! Zoom!" Almost every action the bunnies take can be imitated by a child, making this a book for participation as well as for reading. The bunnies giggle, rake, sing, hug, and more, with smiles on their faces and energy in their movements. As with other counting books, assume your child is absorbing the numbers and concentrate instead on sharing the words and pictures.

Stadler, John. *Hooray for Snail!* 1984. Paperback: Harper-Collins. Ages 2 years and up.

Very simple language recounts a ball game in which Snail plays unexpectedly well. Snail gets up to the plate with a bat considerably bigger than he is and, to everyone's shock, slams the ball. Snail makes his slow way around the bases while the ball flies far out of the stadium and into outer space. Tension mounts as the ball zooms back and, after a nap, Snail heads for home. Hilarious pictures add to the appeal of this baseball story for the young. Also see *Snail Saves the Day*, now out of print, and *The Adventures of Snail at School*.

Steen, Sandra, and Susan Steen. *Car Wash*. Illustrated by G. Brian Karas. 2001. Hardcover: Putnam. Good for groups. Ages 2 years and up.

This ingenious book will change the way you and your child look at going through a car wash. With their father at the wheel, two children in the backseat find themselves surrounded by sea creatures with swishy arms, then a hurricane and tidal wave as water hits the car. Luckily, they survive the trip and emerge like a submarine: "Honk honk! Spit us out. Going up. All clear!" The rhythmic text uses short phrases, with the words integrated into the clever collage illustrations. An outstanding blend of word and picture about an experience many kids enjoy.

Steig, William. *Toby, Where Are You?* Illustrated by Teryl Euvremer. 1997. Hardcover: HarperCollins. Ages 18 months and up.

This vicarious game of hide-and-seek will have young children searching the pictures for Toby, a small, furry animal who is hiding from his parents. We first see him under a bed, looking out from under the fringed bedspread at his unsuspecting father's shoes. "Where on earth is that little rascal?" his parents ask each other. The uncomplicated text offers a sentence or two per page, along the lines of, "Is he up on the shelf? No. Of course not." Because children love knowing something that adults don't, they will be pleased to see more than Toby's parents, who finally give up. Although the soft-edged illustrations have more detail than most books for the very young, it simply makes the challenge of finding the hidden Toby more fun. Followed by *Toby, What Are You?*, more suitable for preschoolers.

Steptoe, John. *Baby Says*. 1988. Hardcover: HarperCollins. Ages 6 months and up.

A smiling baby graces the cover of this little book about young siblings. It opens with the baby sitting in a playpen while an older brother plays with blocks nearby. The baby, who could be a boy or girl, gently tosses a teddy bear out of the playpen and says, "Uh, oh." The older child gives it back. But guess what? The baby sends it over again. This time the older brother returns the bear with the words "No, no," but then relents and lifts the baby out of the playpen. The boy's patience is tried again, but his kindness overcomes his annoyance, and the two end up playing together. The soft colored-pencil pictures, which show the children as African American, are expressive but simple enough for the very young.

Stickland, Paul. *Dinosaur Stomp! A Monster Pop-Up*. 1996. Hardcover: Dutton. Good for groups. Ages 15 months and up.

"Jump and prance, it's a dinosaur dance!" If you want to grab and hold the attention of a toddler or a group of toddlers, reach for *Dinosaur Stomp!* While it doesn't have much text, it has the biggest, boldest pop-up pages around, all of colorful dinosaurs. Each page pops up in a different way: above the book, below the book, or straight out at you. Some young children may be momentarily scared by the emergence of one green dinosaur that seems about to take a bite out of the audience, but most toddlers will delight in the action. The pages are likely to be worse for the wear fairly soon, but this dinosaur extravaganza will be great fun while it lasts. Very popular for group storytimes in libraries and schools.

Stickland, Paul. *Ten Terrible Dinosaurs.* **1997. Hardcover: Dutton. Paperback: Puffin. Good for groups. Ages 15 months and up.**

Young children will fall in love with this dinosaur-laden counting book. Stretched across the first double-page spread stand ten colorful dinosaurs of different shapes and colors: "10 terrible dinosaurs standing in a line—soon began to push and shove until there were . . ." They act like a group of rowdy preschoolers all through the bouncing book. They dance, play tricks, throw things, bang their noses, and stomp around. One by one they disappear, until a mother dinosaur drags off a tired dinosaur, leaving one who starts to snore. The cleverly crafted text, which echoes the rhythm of "Five Little Monkeys Jumping on the Bed," invites the listener to join in. As with many early counting books, this can be read quite enjoyably without worrying about counting. Expect to read it many times!

Stickland, Paul, and Henrietta Stickland. *Dinosaur Roar!* **1994. Hardcover: Dutton. Good for groups. Ages 15 months and up.**

The wide format of this book allows huge dinosaurs to sprawl across its pages in vibrant glory. Although the text is built around opposites, children will be far more interested in the sound of the words and the excitement of the pictures. "Dinosaur roar, dinosaur squeak, / dinosaur fierce, dinosaur meek," opens the jaunty rhyme. Each page has at least two dinosaurs and often more, including a personable tiny one that reappears. The dinosaurs have funny facial expressions and body language and appear in vivid colors. This isn't a scientific introduction; it's a romp through a world of not-too-scary creatures.

Stoeke, Janet Morgan. *A Hat for Minerva Louise.* **1994. Hardcover: Dutton. Paperback: Puffin. Ages 18 months and up.**

The hen Minerva Louise has her own way of looking at the world. While the other hens in the henhouse don't like snow, Minerva Louise does and goes out exploring. But she is cold and realizes that if she had clothes like the scarecrow's, she could stay out longer. As she looks for clothes, she makes wonderfully silly mistakes that will have children giggling. She tries on work gloves, thinking they are shoes, and a clay pot that looks like a hat. The neatly drawn yet funny pictures add to her personality, especially when she struts back to the henhouse wearing the hat she has so cleverly improvised. One in a delightful series.

Stoeke, Janet Morgan. *Hide and Seek/Rainy Day.* **1999. Board book: Dutton. Ages 18 months and up.**

Oh, the pleasures of knowing more than someone else, even a plump hen like Minerva Louise. Children can't help but laugh because they see what she doesn't. In *Hide and Seek*, Minerva Louise proclaims her surprise when she can't see any of her farm animal friends. The child looking at the book, though, will see they are hiding, point them out, and maybe name them. On a day when it's raining, Minerva Louise thinks she has found shelter under a sheep, but children will realize that the sheep could move at any moment, and does. Her next solution for avoiding the rain is equally funny: she decides to go swimming. The illustrations suit the small format well, revealing a lovable, silly main character.

Sturges, Philemon. *I Love Trains!* **Illustrated by Shari Halpern. 2001. Hardcover: HarperCollins. Good for groups. Ages 12 months and up.**

Childlike pictures with black outlines and bright, flat colors start on the endpapers with three rows of tracks and labeled train cars. The story, told in the voice of a young boy, uses large print and only a brief text, with the focus on the illustrations. The rhyme scheme is simple and effective: "I like trains that hoot and roar / as they rumble by my door." Close-ups of various cars, starting with the engine, paint them in unlikely but attractive colors: purple for the engine, pink for a flatbed. Two cows and three pigs, who appear to be talking, stick their heads out of their boxcars. In a little surprise near the end, the boy sees his father waving from the caboose. An appealing combination of train facts and eye-catching pictures, this will entrance train lovers.

Suen, Anastasia. *Toddler Two.* **Illustrated by Winnie Cheon. 2000. Board book: Lee & Low. Ages 12 months and up.**

Two young Asian American children romp on the cover of this appealing little book. Delightful fabric illustrations with sewn and painted details lend it an unusual look, while the skillful use of flaps makes it all the more appealing to a young audience. Two children walk outside, with a flap as the door, where a tricycle, dog, swing, ball, drum, and sandbox await them. Each page plays with the number two, starting with two wings on a butterfly that open like a small pop-up. In other pictures, the flaps uncover two hands, eyes, ears, legs, and arms. You can use this to launch a game of finding things in pairs or just have fun with the pictures and words.

Suen, Anastasia. *Window Music.* **Illustrated by Wade Zahares. 1996. Hardcover: Viking. Paperback: Puffin. Ages 18 months and up.**

Stylized paintings saturated with color portray a girl's train journey with her mother. The minimal text, which never mentions the girl, echoes the sound of an old-fashioned train: "train

on the track / *clickety clack* / *wooo! wooo!* / passing through."
The short passenger train travels through the countryside past
horses, orange groves, shoreline, banana trees, and grapevines,
until it starts entering a more populated area. As night falls, it
pulls into a big city and "into the station, / our destination,"
where the girl's father awaits them. The striking illustrations
give children a lot to look at, while the sounds in the text
practically chant themselves.

Taback, Simms. *Joseph Had a Little Overcoat.* **1999. Hardcover: Viking. Ages 2 years and up.**

The playful spirit of this Caldecott Medal winner begins
with the dust jacket, on which a figure wears a raggedy coat
with die-cut holes that show through to the book's cover. In
the simple tale based on a Yiddish folk song, Joseph uses his
worn coat to make a jacket, the jacket to make a vest, the vest
to make a scarf, and so on. Each brightly colored double-page
spread has a garment-shaped hole that children will love peeking through. The clever collage illustrations, which echo primi-
tive folk paintings, brim over with funny details to delight
children and adults.

Tafuri, Nancy. *Have You Seen My Duckling?* **1984. Hardcover: Morrow. Paperback: Morrow. Board book: Greenwillow. Good for groups. Ages 12 months and up.**

This nearly wordless book draws in young children with its
search for a straying duckling. A mother duck who has eight
little ones returns to the nest to find only seven still with her.
The eighth duckling is hidden in every picture, while the
mother goes around the pond asking various animals, "Have
you seen my duckling?" The search gives artist Tafuri the opportunity to show lots of pond wildlife and plants in her graceful illustrations, for which this was named a Caldecott Honor

Book. A happy ending ensues as the family is united for the night and nestles down together under a darkening sky. An outstanding choice for the very young, best read in the large size rather than the board book.

Tafuri, Nancy. *Silly Little Goose!* 2001. Hardcover: Scholastic. Good for groups. Ages 12 months and up.

This oversize book starts with an overview of a farmyard, its sheds, and garden patches, all the places that Goose will try to visit. "One windy morning, Goose sets out to make a nest." Those who study the picture will notice a farmer's hat blowing off his head, although the largest object is the big white goose, saying "Honk!" The goose tries spot after spot on the farm, starting with the pig yard. But the pigs object, and the phrase sounds, "Silly little goose!" That refrain recurs each time the goose tries out a new spot. After disturbing cats, sheep, and chickens, the goose makes her nest successfully in the farmer's hat: "Hooray for little goose!" With wonderfully large animals, all making noises, and a zippy rhythm, this will delight young children.

Tafuri, Nancy. *Spots, Feathers, and Curly Tails*. 1988. Hardcover: Greenwillow. Good for groups. Ages 18 months and up.

In this creative book aimed at just the right level for young children, Tafuri makes a guessing game out of animals' features. She supplies enough clues to make the answer possible, starting with the question "What has spots?" accompanied by a picture showing only the back and tail of a black-and-white cow. A full-size cow spreads across the next double-page spread, with the answer in large type, "A cow has spots." The generous size of the book lends itself to Tafuri's pen-and-watercolor pictures, just right for using with a group as well as one-on-one. An outstanding book for involving young listeners.

Tafuri, Nancy. *This Is the Farmer.* 1994. Hardcover: Greenwillow. Ages 15 months and up.

For a story with fewer than fifty words, this packs a lot of action into its large pages. It's morning on the farm, and the rooster is crowing as the farmer pulls on his rubber boots. The words proclaim, in a rhythm used throughout the book, "This is the farmer / who kisses his wife / who pats the dog." The dog's flea lands on the cat, the cat chases a mouse, and the chase startles the geese. Each of the expansive pen-and-watercolor illustrations focuses on an animal or two but also includes other animals in the background. Each page could serve as a chance to name animals, and add their noises, or simply as another link in this fine barnyard story.

Taylor, Ann. *Baby Dance.* Illustrated by Marjorie van Heerden. 1999. Board book: HarperCollins. Ages 3 months and up.

Adapted from a longer poem, the words in this lovely board book sing along from beginning to end. A loving black father is frolicking with his baby girl as Mama and the cat snooze on a nearby couch. "Dance, little baby, move to and fro," reads one page, followed by, "Coo and crow, baby, there you go." A glowing, deep red background surrounds the father and baby as he swoops her high and low, to her obvious delight. They dance and twirl and sing, finally ending up on the couch with the father looking tired and the baby wide awake. This puts into highly readable words the joy of dancing around with a beaming, bouncing baby. With so many books that show mother and baby, it's gratifying to see dads get in on the good times.

Thomas, Joyce Carol. *Cherish Me*. Illustrated by Nneka Bennett. 1998. Hardcover: HarperCollins. Ages 2 years and up.

"I sprang up from mother earth / She clothed me in her own colors," begins this poetic celebration of a young African American girl. With brown skin, which glows above an orange shirt, and her hair in cornrows, she jumps and swings, then stops to sit thoughtfully. The final words, "Cherish me," show her gathered into the arms of a caring adult, perhaps her grandmother. The warm, textured illustrations add actions to the lyrical text, which may be too abstract for some young listeners. However, enthusiastic parents who are moved by this expression of love will enjoy sharing it with their children. The pictures also offer possibilities for imitating the movements, including some lively dancing.

Thomas, Joyce Carol. *You Are My Perfect Baby*. Illustrated by Nneka Bennett. 1999. Board book: HarperCollins. Ages newborn through 18 months.

Parents of newborns will love this poem that celebrates babies. The soft-edged, realistic illustrations show a very young African American baby whose parents are depicted vaguely in the background. But the parents' voices come through in the words: "You are a perfect baby / with perfect arms and perfect lips / and tiny fingers / and perfect hips." The tone continues to express love and delight in everything about the baby's body as well as the baby's laughter. Adults reading it to babies will inevitably play with the child's "twinkling toes" and "wiggly waist," touching hands, knees, and "perfect face" as they are named in the short verses. Just right for babies and their adoring relatives.

Thong, Roseanne. *Round Is a Mooncake: A Book of Shapes*. Illustrated by Grace Lin. 2000. Hardcover: Chronicle. Good for groups. Ages 2 years and up.

Fresh illustrations in charming patterns grace this book

about circles, squares, and rectangles. The young narrator sees shapes in her own world, which combines U.S. culture, Chinese American culture, and nature. She notices the roundness of the moon, Chinese lanterns, rice bowls, and a pebble. After several pages, she suggests that listeners look closely at the picture and around them for other round things. Next, she goes to square things—a checkerboard, pizza box, and tofu and radish cakes. Then, rectangular things, including books in the last picture, where her mother is reading to her in bed. A delightful cross-cultural concept book.

Titherington, Jeanne. *Pumpkin Pumpkin.* 1986. Paperback: Mulberry. Good for groups. Ages 2 years and up.

Lovely colored-pencil illustrations combine with large type and a simple story line to create an appealing book. A boy plants a pumpkin seed and watches carefully as it slowly grows. In most of the large pictures, a different animal appears along with the boy (or his hand) and the pumpkin plant. Eventually, the pumpkin he is watching grows so large that he can sit on it. Grinning, he picks it and pulls it in his red wagon to be carved for Halloween. Read this for the holiday or at any time of year to celebrate the cycle of plant life, a concept emphasized when he saves seeds from his carved pumpkin to plant in the spring.

***Touch and Feel Kitten/Touch and Feel Puppy.* 1999. Hardcover: DK. Ages 9 months through 2 years.**

These two small books in a popular series allow children to stroke different textures that are incorporated into cute photographs of kittens and puppies. For the cats, children can feel the rough tongue, a yellow plastic bowl, and the weave of its straw basket. The dog variation features a fuzzy blue slipper, a rubber ball, and the dog's silky fur. The quality of the photographs is unusually good, while the puppies and kittens are irresistible. Other books in the series include farm items, baby animals, and more.

Tracy, Tom. _Show Me!_ Illustrated by Darcia Labrosse. 1999. Board book: HarperCollins. Ages newborn through 18 months.

Many parents automatically play the kind of simple game the mother plays in this board book, where she points out her baby's nose, cheek, chin, tummy, knees, toes, and arms, playing with each one in turn. "Show me your nose! Is _that_ where it grows? I'm gonna nuzzle that nose," the brief text begins. Pictures of a smiling mother and baby in pastel colors, with simplified features, carry out the actions in the words. It ends with a snuggly hug from the baby's arms and the mother's.

Twinem, Neecy. _Bug Hunt: A Lift-the-Flap Book._ 1999. Paperback: Grosset & Dunlap. Ages 2 years and up.

With the dozens of flap books that hide familiar animals, it's refreshing to find one where the flaps conceal something unusual. A girl with a magnifying glass goes on a bug hunt, asking a similar question on every page: "Let's look behind a big leaf, a big leaf. What could be hiding there?" The leaf is a flap that, when lifted, reveals "a creeping crawling caterpillar." Although the artwork is utilitarian, the flaps are integrated into the setting well, with flowers hiding a butterfly, a dry leaf hiding a worm, grass hiding a grasshopper, and more.

Uff, Caroline. _Hello, Lulu._ 1999. Hardcover: Walker. Good for groups. Ages 9 months and up.

Simplicity is the keynote of this large, warm book. Lulu and her family smile out from the pages, bathed in luminous colors, with little dot eyes and round, pink cheeks. The words introduce Lulu along with the people and things in her everyday life: "This is Lulu. Hello, Lulu. This is Lulu's house. 'Come in!' says Lulu." Lulu's mother has light skin and blond hair; her father has brown skin and dark hair. Lulu looks most like her father, her little brother looks like their mother, and her older sister, like both. The illustrations offer chances to name familiar items, including a car, dog, rabbit, fish, cupcakes, pizza, and fruit. With a generous size and attractive, fuzzy-edged pictures, this welcomes young children to Lulu's world and the world of books. One in a series.

Van Fleet, Matthew. *Fuzzy Yellow Ducklings*. 1995. Hardcover: Dial. Ages 9 months and up.

For children who like "touch-and-feel" features, this little book provides seven different patches of material to feel, starting with the fuzziness of a yellow duckling. Each double-page spread starts with words about texture, color, and shape, such as "fuzzy yellow circle." The right-hand page has the circle to touch, with a flap that opens to show a group of ducklings. The format, which is the same throughout, is likely to amuse those who aren't ready to learn shapes but who will want to reach out to touch the scratchy, sticky, and scaly textures.

Van Laan, Nancy. *So Say the Little Monkeys*. Illustrated by Yumi Heo. 1998. Hardcover: Simon & Schuster. Paperback: Simon & Schuster. Good for groups. Ages 2 years and up.

A talented writer and illustrator come together to create a crowd-pleasing story about some carefree monkeys. Most pages have special sounds to make that infuse the reading with energy. "Jump, Jabba Jabba, / Run, Jabba Jabba, / Slide, Jabba Jabba, / Tiny, tiny monkeys having fun." The adorable monkeys, with curly tails and big grins, know they should build themselves some shelter. Whenever it gets cold and rainy, they envy the other animals. But the moment the sun comes out, they just want to play. Fresh, whimsical illustrations take you to a frolicking world of monkeys in trees where swinging, shouting, and sliding are the order of the day.

Van Laan, Nancy. *Tickle Tum!* **Illustrated by Bernadette Pons. 2001. Hardcover: Atheneum. Good for groups. Ages 18 months and up.**

Before the story starts in this delightful book, the author writes a personal note to parents about little games she played with her own children to make mealtime more enjoyable. She describes the motions that go with two such games, including the "chin chopper" one that appears in the story. Then on to a mother rabbit chanting a rhyme to her baby about mealtime. She tries techniques like using the spoon as a bird to swoop food into the baby's mouth and then as a choo-choo train and a dump truck. Nevertheless, food flies everywhere, and when the mother puts the baby rabbit down for a nap near the end, she says, "Off you go, little bird, up to your nest. / Time for a nappy so Mama can rest." The large watercolor-and-pastel illustrations show a lot of smiles during mealtime and afterward.

Verboven, Agnes. Translated by Dominic Barth. *Ducks Like to Swim.* **Illustrated by Anne Westerduin. 1997. Hardcover: Orchard. Good for groups. Ages 9 months and up.**

The short text of this Belgian import translates well into English, inviting young children to make animal noises. Paintings with thick brushstrokes and a rich palette show a mother and baby ducks standing by a pool without enough water to swim. "Mother duck quacks for rain. Quack! Quack! Who will help?" Each following double-page spread features a barnyard animal pitching in with a characteristic sound: "Rooster crows.

Cock-a-doodle-doo!" The animals accumulate in the illustrations until eight enthusiastic animals plus the ducks are creating a cacophony together and succeeding at bringing down rain. Prepare for lots of noise as you read this over and over.

Vigna, Judith. *Boot Weather*. 1989. Hardcover: Albert Whitman. Good for groups. Ages 2 years and up.

Snow means boot weather to Kim, and off she goes on adventures. Her real pastimes, playing in the snow and on playground equipment, take place side by side with imaginary escapades. When she climbs up a slide, she pictures herself mountain climbing. Zooming down the slide, she sees herself sledding down the steep mountain. She imagines herself as an astronaut, a hockey player, a construction worker, and an explorer. She gets shot from a cannon and takes off with Santa in his sleigh. A brief text and appealing watercolor pictures convey her morning of fun.

Waddell, Martin. *Can't You Sleep, Little Bear?* Illustrated by Barbara Firth. 1992. Hardcover: Candlewick. Paperback: Candlewick. Ages 2 years and up.

This is a warm story about a little bear and his loving father. Big Bear tucks Little Bear in one evening in their homey cave, then starts to read a book by the fire. But Little Bear is scared of the dark, so Big Bear gets him a little lantern. The next request brings a bigger lantern, and then the Biggest Lantern of Them All. Restless, Little Bear claims to be scared of the dark outdoors. But when Big Bear patiently takes him outside, they find a huge yellow moon and twinkly stars, and Little Bear finally falls asleep. The soft watercolors, full of rounded shapes, reflect the loving way that Big Bear treats his child's nighttime fears and wiggles in this simple bedtime story. The first in a wonderful series.

Waddell, Martin. *Owl Babies.* **Illustrated by Patrick Benson. 1992. Hardcover: Candlewick. Paperback: Candlewick. Board book: Candlewick. Good for groups. Ages 2 years and up.**

In this charming book, three baby owls worry one night when they wake up and find their mother gone. Throughout the short book, they wonder where she is and if she is coming back. Of course, she does, swooping down to ask, "What's all the fuss?" Sarah, Percy, and Bill, as they are named, glow white against the dark background of night as they perch on a tree in the forest in effective ink-and-watercolor illustrations. Their faces and bodies convey their emotions well, positively tingling with delight when their mother returns. The story's message, which will be unmistakable to adults, reassures children that parents who have gone out will return, so children needn't worry. No need to hammer it home, though. It's pleasure enough to meet this owl family.

Waddell, Martin. *Webster J. Duck.* **Illustrated by David Parkins. 2001. Hardcover: Candlewick. Good for groups. Ages 2 years and up.**

As this sweet story starts, a scruffy duckling named Webster emerges from his egg and thinks, "Where is my mother?" He quacks to call her, but no one comes, so the little duck goes off with the grass towering above him to find his mother. He first encounters a dog and asks, "Quack-quack?" But when the dog answers "Bow-wow," Webster knows it cannot be his mother, because she would quack as he does. The same is true of the sheep and cow, leaving Webster so discouraged that he starts to cry. The three animals try to help, though their loudness scares him, and behold, Webster's mother shows up. Webster's expressive face and postures create a personable hero for this satisfying story.

Wallace, Nancy Elizabeth. *Rabbit's Bedtime.* **1999. Hardcover: Houghton. Good for groups. Ages 12 months and up.**

"Bedtime. What was good about today?" What a wonderful question to ask before a child—or in this case, a rabbit—goes to sleep at night. In the crisp, cut-paper illustrations, a parent and child rabbit nestle together on a bed. Thinking back, they remember that there was time to work, shown in a picture of them sweeping the kitchen floor, and time to play, with the child playing dress-up. A few words on each page celebrate other aspects of the day, such as dancing and singing, laughing and giggling, being alone and being with friends. A particularly warm and thoughtful bedtime book.

Walsh, Ellen Stoll. *Hop Jump.* **1993. Hardcover: Harcourt. Paperback: Harcourt. Good for groups. Ages 2 years and up.**

Playful collage illustrations abound with energy in this book about a frog who is an artist and a dancer. Betsy is a blue frog, surrounded by green frogs who always go "Hop jump, hop jump." To Betsy, "It's always the same." She prefers to try different moves, imitating floating leaves, twisting and turning gracefully. Her new movement proves irresistible, and soon the green frogs switch to dancing. An outstanding picture-story book with a simple text about dance.

Walsh, Ellen Stoll. *Mouse Paint.* **1989. Hardcover: Harcourt. Paperback: Harcourt. Board book: Harcourt. Good for groups. Ages 2 years and up.**

This deceptively simple book tells of three white mice who find three jars of paint, red, yellow, and blue. When each climbs in one color and then drips paint on white paper, the puddles provide an enjoyable lesson in mixing colors. The red mouse jumps in the yellow puddle, and on the next page, you can see that the puddle has turned orange. They try all the combinations of the three colors, delighted with the results. The exquisite book design and illustrations combined with the well-written text make this an outstanding picture book. While toddlers probably won't understand combining colors, they will love the little mice and bright pictures. Also look for *Mouse Count*, a similar story about counting.

Walsh, Melanie. *Big and Little/What's There?* 2001. Board book: Candlewick. Ages 18 months and up.

Walsh's fine design sense makes excellent use of flaps in these two board books. Simple pictures with rich colors and clean lines illustrate basic opposites in *Big and Little*, although children will be more interested in the flaps than the concepts. On one page, bottom and top take the form of a child at the bottom of a ladder. The narrow vertical flap opens well above the book's top, to show the top of the ladder. Another on a black page has only the white word *dark*, opening to a sunny scene and the word *light*. *What's There?*, while not as clever, hides animals under all the flaps, except the last two, which hide children. Both are unusually attractive, well-crafted board books.

Walsh, Melanie. *Do Pigs Have Stripes?* 1996. Hardcover: Houghton. Board book: Houghton. Good for groups. Ages 12 months and up.

"Does a bird have a big black wet nose?" is the question on the first page of this beginning quiz book. A partial picture of a dog's head, showing the nose, fills the opposite page, giving toddlers a hint of the right answer. Turn the page and find the dog, with the comment "No, a dog does." Flat, childlike paintings in solid colors provide the clues and answers, showing a crocodile, an elephant, a cow, an anteater, and a deer. After a series of questions for which the response is "no," the final response is "yes" to the question "Does a giraffe have a long thin neck?" A book that pulls in young children, this is a good idea, well executed. It's followed by *Do Monkeys Tweet?* and *Do Donkeys Dance?* The board books work well, thanks to the simplicity of the art.

Walter, Virginia. "Hi, Pizza Man." Illustrated by Ponder Goembel. 1995. Hardcover: Orchard. Paperback: Orchard. Good for groups. Ages 18 months and up.

A young girl playing with her blocks and toy train announces to her mother, "I'm hungry!" Although we don't see her mother until the final page, we hear her voice as she skillfully distracts the girl. She tells her that the pizza man will be here soon and asks what the girl will say when he arrives. "Hi, pizza man!" The mother follows her first question by asking what the girl would say if the pizza were delivered by a woman, a cat, a dog, and so on. Children listening can join in the obvious replies while laughing at the absurd pizza delivery animals. Combining humorous pictures, an invitation to join in, and the popular topic of pizza, this is a real winner.

Walton, Rick. *My Two Hands/My Two Feet.* Illustrated by Julia Gorton. 2000. Hardcover: Putnam. Good for groups. Ages 2 years and up.

When you've read through the first story, "My Two Feet," flip this book upside down and start again at the other end. The stories about two girls who appear to be sisters run along the same lines, beginning in the morning and going through the day to bedtime. Stylized artwork using airbrushed acrylic elegantly combines flat colors and attractive patterns, such as stripes and plaids. The older girl celebrates her hands and all the things they can do—cupping water, hiding a butterfly, holding hands with another while walking. The younger sister expresses emotions through her feet: "When I am happy / My feet dance / Like ponies as they / Kick and prance." At the center of the book, when each story has reached bedtime, the two sprawl together, asleep.

Walton, Rick. *So Many Bunnies: A Bedtime ABC and Counting Book.* **Illustrated by Paige Miglio. 2001. Hardcover: HarperCollins. Paperback: HarperCollins. Ages 18 months and up.**

Old Mother Rabbit may have twenty-six children, but she knows what to do with them come bedtime in her shoe-shaped house. She feeds them broth and tucks them in, each into its own spot. Their names span the alphabet, and she says good-night to them from one to twenty-six, as told in the rhyming couplets: "5 was named Ellis. / He slept on the trellis. / 6 was named Frankie. / She slept on a hankie." A flower-filled garden and cozy house full of snug places to sleep provide an idyllic setting for the little rabbits clad in old-fashioned clothes. Children will get a kick out of all the places the bunnies sleep as they study the details in the pictures. This is one in a series for those who favor a homespun look to their books.

Wardlaw, Lee. *First Steps.* **Illustrated by Julie Paschkis. 1999. Board book: HarperCollins. Ages 12 months through 2 years.**

In this charming celebration of a child learning to walk, a pink-cheeked, round-bottomed baby starts with a routine of pulling herself up: "Creep, crawl, pull up tall. Giggle wiggle waggle." Then, realistically, she falls on her bottom, looking very surprised. She gives it another try at the coffee table, with some success, then stops by a chair and is lured on by an adult holding a teddy bear. For a short text, this one bebops along nicely to match the child's energetic efforts in a well-illustrated board book.

Wattenberg, Jane. *Mrs. Mustard's Baby Faces*. 1989. Board book: Chronicle. Ages 6 months through 2 years.

In an unusual format, this book opens accordion style and can be stood up on a shelf or table. Opened all the way, each side measures about thirty inches and shows seven babies' faces, set against different patterned backgrounds. On one side, the babies smile and laugh. The first page, which has the only text for that side, has words scattered on it, including *happy*, *jolly*, and *beaming*. Turn the long book around and seven babies are "crying," "cranky," and "crabby." They have frowns, tears forming in their eyes, and faces scrunched up in unhappiness. Why it's called "Mrs. Mustard's" is anyone's guess, but it is followed by *Mrs. Mustard's Beastly Babies*.

Weeks, Sarah. *Oh My Gosh, Mrs. McNosh!* Illustrated by Nadine Bernard Westcott. 2002. Hardcover: HarperCollins. Good for groups. Ages 2 years and up.

When Nelly McNosh takes her dog George for a walk in the park, the action accelerates when his leash breaks. "He zipped through the flowers / and skipped through the trees, / barking at bicycles, babies, and bees," sings the snappy rhyme, which keeps up a fast pace from beginning to end. Candy-colored pictures crowded with humor show Mrs. McNosh reaching for George and catching other things instead, like a trout, a wedding bouquet, a fly ball, and a bad cold. Discouraged at last, Mrs. McNosh drags herself home to find a happy surprise—"Oh, my gosh!"

Weiss, Nicki. *Where Does the Brown Bear Go?* 1989. Hardcover: Greenwillow. Good for groups. Ages 12 months and up.

What a splendid bedtime book this is, combining a soothing, repetitive text with nighttime illustrations that are still bright enough to reveal many animals. Starting with a cat and monkey, each animal appears as night is falling, with questions like, "Where does the white cat go, honey? Where does the white cat go?" The answer comes after several animals and is repeated later: "They are on their way. They are on their way home." Together, the words and colored-pencil illustrations create a feeling of peace and comfort, culminating in the picture of a child tucked into bed, surrounded by stuffed animals. An enduring gem to read at the end of the day.

Wells, Rosemary. *Max's Bath/Max's Bedtime/Max's Birthday/Max's Breakfast/Max's First Word/Max's New Suit/ Max's Ride/Max's Toys*. 1998. Board book: Dial. Ages 12 months and up.

Max has gained ground over the years to become one of the best-loved characters in books for the very young. These board books were originally published in smaller format with somewhat different pictures but do quite well in their current larger size. Max, a plump bunny, must contend with his bossy older sister, Ruby, but he always comes out a little ahead due to his persistence. In *Max's First Word*, she tries to get him to expand beyond his first word, "Bang." But he continues to say "Bang" when she tells him the right words for cup, pot, and more. He won't say "apple," but when he eats it, he surprises her by saying, "Delicious." Wells, who makes good use of the board book format, has other books about Max and Ruby, but these board books are a great place to start getting to know this stellar duo.

Wells, Rosemary. *Max's Dragon Shirt*. 1991. Hardcover: Dial. Paperback: Penguin. Good for groups. Ages 2 years and up.

With a text longer than the board books, this story about Max starts with how much he wants a Dragon Shirt. But when his older sister, Ruby, takes him to a big department store, she insists he buy new pants instead. When Ruby stops to try on dresses, Max falls asleep in the dressing room, then wakes up and goes looking for her. He finds a Dragon Shirt on his way. Meanwhile, Ruby goes looking for Max. She finds him eating ice cream, having dripped so much ice cream on his shirt that they must buy it, leaving no money for new pants. Irresistible pictures of plump rabbits fill the pages of this satisfying story. One in a delightful series.

Wells, Rosemary. *McDuff Comes Home*. Illustrated by Susan Jeffers. 1997. Hardcover: Hyperion. Good for groups. Ages 2 years and up.

McDuff, a small, white dog, gets lost one day while chasing a rabbit and finally falls asleep in a vegetable garden. The older woman who finds him and says she'll drive him to the police station puts McDuff in the sidecar of her big red motorcycle. In response to McDuff's barking, she ends up at his owners' house, to everyone's delight. The old-fashioned pictures strike just the right note. One in a popular series.

Wells, Rosemary. *Noisy Nora*. 1999 reissue. Hardcover: Dial. Paperback: Puffin. Good for groups. Ages 15 months and up.

First published in 1973, this has been reissued with eye-catching illustrations in vibrant colors, even better than the first time around. It's a timeless story about a middle child who feels ignored. "Jack had dinner early, / Father played with Kate, / Jack needed burping, / So Nora had to wait." How does Nora cope with being overlooked? Noise! She bangs the window, slams the door, and spills her sister's marbles. And that's just her first effort at drawing attention. But it's only when she's quiet and seems to have gone away that her family reveals how much they value noisy Nora. The excellent new illustrations are a fitting accompaniment to a well-loved story.

Whybrow, Ian. *Quacky Quack-Quack!* **Illustrated by Russell Ayto. 1998. Paperback: Candlewick. Good for groups. Ages 18 months and up.**

Looking self-satisfied, a baby strolls along with a small sack of bread. It's meant for the ducks, but the baby starts to eat it himself, to the ducks' loud dismay. That is only the beginning of the noise. Geese honk. A marching band goes by. Donkeys and dogs and snakes add their voices. So do crocodiles and lions from the nearby zoo. The scraggly watercolors blast the noise out from the page with great energy. Added to the cacophony is the baby's scream when his older brother tries to take the bread. Hooray for generous older brothers—he gives the baby his ice cream and gives the animals the bread: "Yum! Yum!" Charming pictures and lots of loud animal noises add up to a good time.

Wiesner, David. *Tuesday.* **1991. Hardcover: Clarion. Paperback: Clarion. Ages 2 years and up.**

This nearly wordless book depicts a wild night when frogs rise on their lily pads and fly around a neighborhood. Hundreds of them soar higher than telephone wires, diving at birds and grinning with delight. They swoop low, straight into a clothesline, and several end up with capes made from laundry. Their beguiling adventure continues until dawn, when the magic ends, catching them by surprise and leaving lily pads all over the town. Winner of the Caldecott Medal, this is guaranteed to make you smile.

Wilkes, Angela. *My First Word Book.* **1993. Hardcover: DK. Ages 18 months and up.**

A clean design and brightly colored photographs characterize this attractive word book. Each page presents a dozen or so photographs in framed boxes with clear labels to identify each item. Grouped by theme, the subjects encompass mealtime, bedtime, animals, things that go, counting, colors, and more. The skillful use of white background space makes everything easy to see. Inevitably, sizes get confusing, so the photo of a city bus is smaller than the one of a motorcycle on the same page. However, many children will enjoy the game of pointing and naming, or having a parent do it for them.

Williams, Sam. *The Baby's Word Book.* **1999. Board book: Greenwillow. Ages 12 months through 2 years.**

All the pages of this large board book are filled with babies and toddlers with different skin colors, participating in everyday activities and playing with familiar items. Cute children with circular faces and little dots for eyes push a wagon, heft a large teddy bear, and pull on a train on one page about toys, with the toy name under each of the nine pictures on the page. Opposite, a baby demonstrates actions and emotions, such as yawning, eating, silly, and happy. As a first word book, this offers the advantages of a durable format and well-spaced pictures that won't overwhelm young children. Have fun with your child identifying the objects and animals, pointing out colors on a page, and connecting the pictures to your child's own surroundings. An attractive book to dip into rather than read from cover to cover.

Williams, Sue. *I Went Walking.* **Illustrated by Julie Vivas. 1990. Hardcover: Harcourt. Paperback: Harcourt. Board book: Harcourt. Good for groups. Ages 9 months and up.**

Delightful watercolor illustrations combine with questions and answers to make a top-notch book for the very young. A child declares, "I went walking," followed by the question

"What did you see?" The picture hints at the answer, with the first one showing a cat hidden in a bushel of logs. On the next page, the child hugs the cat, with the response, "I saw a black cat looking at me." It continues with a brown horse, red cow, green duck, pink pig, and yellow dog, all of which follow the child. Although this follows a format similar to *Brown Bear, Brown Bear, What Do You See?*, by Bill Martin, the illustrations make it well worth adding to your collection or getting from the library. Children who like this will like *Let's Go Visiting*, by the same author.

Williams, Vera B. *Lucky Song*. 1997. Hardcover: Greenwillow. Ages 2 years and up.

What makes a perfect day? For little Evie, such a day starts out with something new to wear, a pink-and-orange cap. Then she wants something new to play with, and her grandpa makes her a kite. Naturally, she wants to go out and fly it, and her legs carry her up a steep hill to do just that. With only one sentence on a page, this brief story focuses on the color-saturated pictures of a young girl having a great time. Glorious background colors frame little Evie, who glows with the joy of the day. Back home, her grandmother makes her dinner, her sister wraps her in a blanket, and her father sings her a goodnight song. What could be better?

Williams, Vera B. *"More More More," Said the Baby: 3 Love Stories*. 1990. Hardcover: Greenwillow. Paperback: Morrow. Board book: Morrow. Ages 12 months and up.

This Caldecott Honor Book shines with color and warmth. The three "love stories," illustrated with framed gouache paintings and hand-lettered text, are about toddlers and the adults who love them. In the first, Little Guy starts running and his father catches him, whirls him in the air, and kisses his perfect belly button, "Right in the middle, right in the middle, right in the middle of your fat little belly." Similarly, Little Pumpkin's grandmother catches her and kisses each of her toes. With multiethnic characters, including a white grandmother with a black granddaughter, this beautifully illustrated book speaks to universal bonds between adults and the little children they love. Some parents may find the picture of the child thrown in the air inappropriately rough, while for others, this will be a family favorite. Skip the board book version and go for the real thing in full size.

Wilson, Karma. *Bear Snores On*. Illustrated by Jane Chapman. 2001. Hardcover: McElderry Books. Good for groups. Ages 2 years and up.

The short rhyming verses in this large book about a sleeping bear dance the listener along, only slowing the pace for the repeated phrase "But the bear snores on." Bear is cuddled in a heap in his cave, protected from the snow and cold wind. As the bear sleeps, smaller animals take refuge in his lair from a snowstorm, starting with a mouse, then a rabbit, badger, gopher, mole, wren, and raven. Old friends, they share food and talk, and start dancing. But what will happen when the bear wakes up? Expansive acrylic paintings create a cast of personable animals, even the bear, who turns out to be a hospitable host. A delightful winter escapade.

Wilson, Sarah. *Love and Kisses*. Illustrated by Melissa Sweet. 1999. Hardcover: Candlewick. Board book: Candlewick. Ages 18 months and up.

Sweetness is the theme sounded in this book by its whimsical story and illustrations. A little girl romps onto the first page, blowing a kiss made up of colored hearts. It reaches a cat, with the line "Smooch and smack! You kiss your cat."

Then, surprisingly, "Your cat may kiss a cow." Small pictures in harmonious colors show the cow kissing a goose, the goose kissing a fish, and more unlikely kisses that will make your child laugh. The circular story returns to the girl, who now gets a kiss from the cat. "Kisses! Kisses! Smooch and Smack! You'll have your love and kisses back!"

Wishinsky, Frieda. *Oonga Boonga*. Illustrated by Carol Thompson. 1999. Hardcover: Dutton. Paperback: Puffin. Ages 2 years and up.

Oonga boonga are the magical words that finally get baby Louise to stop crying. All the family members, and even some neighbors, have tried to quiet the screaming infant, singing, rocking, and playing the harmonica. But "Louise kept on crying until her wails shook the pictures off the walls." Large, amusing illustrations with a nice variety of framed pictures and text show Louise's older brother coming to the rescue with the funny phrase "Oonga boonga." Everyone repeats it, inviting listeners to join in, too. But when the brother goes off to play, the words quit working, until he returns with a new silly refrain. A favorite for library storytimes, this was first published in 1990, now reissued with pictures by a different illustrator.

Wolff, Ashley. *Stella and Roy*. 1993. Hardcover: Dutton. Paperback: Puffin. Ages 18 months and up.

Younger siblings will cheer on Roy in this story about a boy and his older sister racing in the park. Exquisite block prints hand-tinted with watercolors show Stella taking off on a path around a lake, pedaling a large tricycle. Roy, in contrast, coasts along on a wooden four-wheeler. When Stella challenges Roy to a race, she shows her overconfidence by stopping often along the way. As in "The Tortoise and the Hare," slow and steady proves to be a winning formula as Roy rolls "right on by" with his father strolling behind him. After Stella climbs a tree, admires goldfish, picks flowers, and talks to a policewoman on a horse, she finds that she reaches the goal, a popcorn stand, after her brother, who yells, "Rotten egg!" with great glee. Stella concedes graciously when Roy shares his popcorn, a satisfying end to a memorable book.

Wong, Janet S. *Buzz*. Illustrated by Margaret Chodos-Irvine. 2000. Hardcover: Harcourt. Paperback: Harcourt. Ages 18 months and up.

It's morning, and a young boy is looking out a window at a bee, which makes the first of many buzzing sounds in a busy morning. The next buzz comes from the boy's snoring parents, "BUZZZbuzzzBUZZZbuzzz." Then, "BUZZZZ. Hooray for the alarm clock!" Soon the father's electric razor buzzes, and so does a lawn mower outside. The buzzing sounds continue through a hectic breakfast, his parents' departure for work, and his grandmother's arrival for the day. The spacious illustrations, which sport a retro look, show a Caucasian father and a mother of Asian descent rushing through their morning as so many working parents do. After hearing this ingenious book, young children will start listening more closely to the sounds around them, especially the ones that buzz.

Wong, Janet S. *Grump*. Illustrated by John Wallace. 2001. Hardcover: McElderry Books. Ages 9 months and up.

Anyone who has experienced how tiring it can be to care for a toddler will love this book. "Look how tired this Mommy is. Tired and frumpy. Grouchy chumpy. Oh, what a grump!" A tired mother holds a mop and pail, almost lost in the surrounding white space. What is Baby's next move? Mixing applesauce and ketchup and dumping it on his head. For once in a children's book, the mother looks disgusted as she sweeps and scrubs the floor. "Mommy's slumping. Mommy's tired. Thump thump thumping up the stairs." The irresistible rhythm will captivate even babies, while older children may recognize the toddler's role as their own. The mother optimistically puts her "little lump" down for a nap and, when he can't sleep, reads to him. The amusing end will come as no surprise to parents. Between the apt theme, the bouncing text, and the delightful watercolors, this is not to be missed.

Wood, Audrey. *King Bidgood's in the Bathtub*. Illustrated by Don Wood. 1985. Hardcover: Harcourt. Ages 2 years and up.

"King Bidgood's in the bathtub and he won't get out. Oh, who knows what to do? Who knows what to do?" King Bidgood plans to spend the day in his bathtub. When one courtier suggests he get out to fish, the bathtub becomes wreathed with water plants and filled with fish. Another who says it's time to lunch finds the tub bedecked with an astonishing array of food. Superb illustrations create magical effects, with the bathtub transformed into delightfully detailed scenes. Children will want to listen to this Caldecott Honor Book, which also has an outstanding text, again and again.

Wood, Audrey. *The Napping House*. Illustrated by Don Wood. 1984. Hardcover: Harcourt. Paperback: Harcourt. Board book: Harcourt. Ages 18 months and up.

"There is a house, a napping house, where everyone is sleeping," starts this terrific book. In a bouncing, cumulative verse, different people and creatures pile up on a bed and sleep—a granny, a child, a dog, a cat, and a mouse. But just when listeners get used to the story's pattern and think they know what's next, a "wakeful flea" upsets the routine. Wildly frantic pictures show all of the sleepers tossed into the air as they wake up. While the very young will be more interested in the catchy rhythm, they will soon also enjoy the splendid pictures in this modern classic.

Wood, Audrey. *Quick as a Cricket*. Illustrated by Don Wood. 1982. Hardcover: Child's Play. Paperback: Child's Play. Good for groups. Ages 18 months and up.

"I'm as quick as a cricket, / I'm as slow as a snail, / I'm as small as an ant, / I'm as large as a whale," begins this well-loved book, with one sentence per large picture. A boy brings the text to life, leapfrogging over a huge cricket, lying languidly by a snail, standing the same height as red ants in the undergrowth. He's nice as well as mean, cold as well as hot, weak as well as strong in the slightly surreal, colorful pictures. At the end, the boy stands admiring his bulletin board, which is crowded with pictures of animals, and declares, "Put it all together, / And you've got ME!" A tribute to the imagination and the different selves a child can be.

Wood, Audrey. *Silly Sally*. 1992. Hardcover: Harcourt. Board book: Harcourt. Good for groups. Ages 2 years and up.

For a goofy good time, open up this large book and follow Silly Sally into town. How does she go? "Walking backwards, upside down." Zany cartoonlike pictures show her with wild red hair and frilly pantaloons, walking on her hands. She meets a number of animals, as told in the rhyming text: "On the way she met a pig, a silly pig, they danced a jig." The pig, dog, and loon join her, proceeding upside down, too. But when they meet a sheep, they fall asleep, until Neddy Buttercup tickles them all awake. The final scene shows them all walking on their hands into town and the townspeople imitating them. Expect your child to try walking upside down after listening to this popular book.

Wood, Audrey, and Don Wood. *Piggies*. 1991. Paperback: Voyager. Board book: Red Wagon. Ages newborn and up.

This completely delightful book turns a baby's fat hands into a romping ground for ten wonderful piggies, using a short, rhythmic text. (Try to get this in the large size, rather than the board book, so you and your child can enjoy the piggies' cunning costumes.) "Sometimes they're hot little piggies," dressed for the beach, "and sometimes they're cold little piggies," bundled up and playing on mitten-clad hands. They also splash in bubbles and play in mud, in spectacular illustrations. Most of the pages offer strong possibilities for adding actions, counting fingers, and skipping them down to baby's toes. Likely to become a family favorite for years as your child grows from liking the sounds to being mesmerized by the details in the pictures.

Wood, Don and Audrey. *The Little Mouse, the Red Ripe Strawberry, and the Big Hungry Bear*. Illustrated by Don Wood. 1984. Hardcover: Child's Play. Paperback: Child's Play. Board book: Child's Play. Good for groups. Ages 12 months and up.

A personable little mouse with a round belly and perky ears carries a ladder out of its house. A voice is speaking to it: "Hello, little Mouse. What are you doing?" The mouse approaches a huge, hanging strawberry, and the voice says, "Oh, I see. Are you going to pick that red, ripe strawberry?" When the voice warns the mouse about the big, hungry bear who loves strawberries, the mouse gets more and more worried until it's shaking all over. The mouse tries to bury, chain, and disguise the strawberry with no success, until the voice suggests a solution. Oversize illustrations paint a luxuriant green world of undergrowth and a snug mouse home cluttered with furniture. Lots of humor softens the tension in this popular read-aloud. You'll want the full-size edition, not the board book, to get the most out of this wonderful story and its pictures.

Wormell, Christopher. *Blue Rabbit and Friends*. 2000. Hardcover: Phyllis Fogelman Books. Paperback: Penguin. Good for groups. Ages 2 years and up.

This beautifully designed book tells a simple story of a rabbit, bear, goose, and dog looking for new homes and happily trading places with one another. Blue Rabbit, who doesn't like his home, encounters Bear sitting in a pool. Bear offers Blue Rabbit the pool as a home, but the rabbit declines. They set off together to find something better. Each animal finds the perfect new home, except Blue Rabbit, who decides he prefers adventure and sets off on his bike to see the world "with the open sky above and the wind in his face." The large, childlike block prints in saturated colors have an old-fashioned look that suits the story. Followed by *Blue Rabbit and the Runaway Wheel*.

Yaccarino, Dan. *Good Night, Mr. Night*. 1997. Hardcover: Harcourt. Paperback: Harcourt. Ages 2 years and up.

In this somewhat surrealistic bedtime book, night takes the form of a star-covered man who wears a bowler hat. "When the sun slowly falls just over the hill, Mr. Night wakes," starts the poetic text. With his black figure stark against bright colors, he walks through trees and closes flowers for the night. Stroking farm animals, he calms them, and wading through the ocean, he quiets the waves. Inside a warmly lit house, a boy sees Mr. Night through a window and knows it's time for bed. Mr. Night leans gently over the boy and closes his eyes. Flowing lines with heavy brushstrokes and muted colors add to the dreamy nature of this story, which ends with the boy's waking and bidding Mr. Night a good-night.

Yaccarino, Dan. *So Big!* 2001. Paperback: HarperCollins. Good for groups. Ages 12 months and up.

A simple format and good use of flaps characterize this playful book. Each double-page spread asks a question and then, under the flap, receives the same answer, "Sooo Big!" The question is always the same, except for the animal named: "How big is a baby giraffe?" On the left is an adult giraffe, and on the right, a young one with its head down. The flap opens upward in this case, to show the baby at its full height. For the baby owl, the flap opens to the right and the owlet spreads its wings. After five animals, the question is, "How big are YOU?" with three children answering, "I'm sooo big!" Nicely constructed on a topic children care about.

Yaccarino, Dan. *Zoom! Zoom! Zoom! I'm Off to the Moon!* 1997. Hardcover: Scholastic. Paperback: Scholastic. Good for groups. Ages 18 months and up.

With entertaining, retro illustrations, this high-energy book travels to the moon and back. "Zoom! Zoom! Zoom! I'm off to the moon. / Up, up, and away, I'm leaving today," says a boy as he dashes out the front door toward a rocket ship. He dons an enormous, rounded space suit plus space boots, and he's ready to head for the moon. Turn the book sideways to get a long picture of this rocket and the countdown from 5 to 0, and liftoff. Short, punchy phrases carry you along on the journey as the neon-colored illustrations dazzle the eye. An absolute must for kids who love outer space, but great fun even for those who don't.

Yashima, Taro. *Umbrella*. 1958. Paperback: Puffin. Good for groups. Ages 2 years and up.

In this exquisite book, a young Asian American girl named Momo gets an umbrella and red rubber boots for her third birthday. She is extremely pleased with the presents but disappointed that a series of sunny days means she doesn't need them. One morning before going to nursery school, Momo decides she needs the umbrella to keep the sun out of her eyes, but her mother disagrees. Finally the morning comes when it's raining. Under her umbrella, Momo hears the "raindrops make a wonderful music she never had heard before— *Bon polo, bon polo, ponpolo ponpolo.*" Mixed-media artwork with a scratchy texture creates an urban setting from a child's perspective in this wonderful Caldecott Honor Book.

Yee, Wong Herbert. *Here Come Trainmice/Hooray for Truckmice*. 2000. Board book: Houghton. Ages 18 months and up.

These small, original board books are a treat to look at. Yee uses geometric blocks of bright colors to form trucks and trains, with tiny, clothed mice acting like people. A short, rhyming text in *Here Come Trainmice* describes a passenger's train journey and different train cars. In *Hooray for Truckmice*, the verses focus on different kinds of trucks and what they do. The jaunty mice do a lot of waving, and in the truck book, a small mouse frequently calls out, "Hooray for Truckmice!" A fine combination of appealing pictures and topics.

Yolen, Jane. *How Do Dinosaurs Say Good Night?* Illustrated by Mark Teague. 2000. Hardcover: Blue Sky Press. Good for groups. Ages 18 months and up.

"How does a dinosaur say good night when Papa comes in to turn off the light? / Does a dinosaur slam his tail and pout? /

Does he throw his teddy bear all about?" So begins this priceless good-night book filled with misbehaving dinosaurs trying to delay bedtime. The simple rhyming text flows naturally from beginning to end, providing funny premises for the rounded pictures of dinosaurs in child-sized beds. The huge creatures, shown from different perspectives, cry and moan and stamp their feet but, in the end, hug and kiss the human parents good-night. Don't miss the endpapers, with their pictures of each dinosaur on a bed, labeled with their scientific names. A superb variation on the bedtime theme, destined to be well loved.

Young, Ed. *Seven Blind Mice*. 1992. Hardcover: Philomel. Ages 2 years and up.

Exquisite illustrations and a simple text make this a superb book. Seven blind mice are curious about the new Something that has come to their pond. Each day, a mouse of a different color sets forth to determine what It is. Each one touches one part of the Something but misinterprets what he feels. One mouse, for example, reports that the ear is a fan. The seventh and cleverest mouse puts all the clues together and, after she has made her excursion, reveals what the Something is. Set against a black background, the collage artwork uses handmade papers to create a stunningly beautiful book. A Caldecott Honor Book.

Young, Ruth. *Golden Bear*. Illustrated by Rachel Isadora. 1992. Paperback: Puffin. Good for groups. Ages 12 months and up.

Even before the story begins, the cuddly golden bear announces his presence, first on the title page, then doing a handstand on the dedication page. This large, fetching teddy bear belongs to a young African American boy and accompanies him everywhere, as if the bear were alive. They skate, read, and play the violin together. The textured illustrations, infused with warmth, show the sturdy young boy and his life-size companion sharing their days and, on the last page, tucked into bed and dreaming. A charming story about the companionship of imaginary friends.

Ziefert, Harriet. *No Kiss for Grandpa*. Illustrated by Emilie Boon. 2001. Hardcover: Orchard. Ages 2 years and up.

Louie, a young cat absorbed in looking at a book, is not pleased to be interrupted by his grandfather's visit. When his mother asks, "Do you have a kiss for Grandpa?," in true child-like fashion, Louie answers, "No kiss." He and his grandfather walk to the beach, where everything that Grandpa suggests gets a negative reply. Grandpa's a little hurt, but he hangs in there, following Louie's lead. Things only come right when they get back home and Grandpa proposes that they read to-gether. Finally, as Grandpa is leaving, Louie has a kiss for him. Cheerful, uncluttered pictures help tell this realistic story, which ends on a happy note.

Ziefert, Harriet. *Train Song*. Illustrated by Donald Saaf. 2000. Hardcover: Orchard. Good for groups. Ages 2 years and up.

"Chug-a-chug-chug and clickety-clack . . . Freight train must be coming back," read the words under a little boy and his toy train, outdoors on a hill. He's looking down to where a real train is coming over a railroad bridge. With the refrain of "chug-a-chug-chug and clickety-clack," the train passes slowly, with time to look at each car. Cars carry three cows, three pigs, and sixteen geese and roosters and hens—a count-ing opportunity for older preschoolers. With no effort to be re-alistic, this train closely resembles a toy train with its bright colors and smiling animals. Finally, it disappears around a hill, leaving the little boy with the consoling thought, "Tomorrow when it's almost ten, / Freight train will be back again."

Zion, Gene. *Harry the Dirty Dog*. Illustrated by Margaret Bloy Graham. 1956. Hardcover: HarperCollins. Paperback: HarperCollins. Ages 2 years and up.

This old favorite continues to captivate young listeners with its well-paced story and dynamic illustrations. Harry, a white dog with black spots, likes everything—except getting a bath. One morning, he buries the scrubbing brush from the bathtub and runs away for the day, getting dirtier and dirtier as he plays. When he returns home, the family doesn't recognize him, because he has turned into a black dog with white spots. Only by digging up the brush and begging for a bath does Harry solve his problem. Children respond sympathetically to Harry's dilemma and enjoy his outings as much as he does. The first in a series.

Zolotow, Charlotte. *Some Things Go Together*. Illustrated by Ashley Wolff. 1999. Hardcover: HarperCollins. Good for groups. Ages 18 months and up.

A smiling pig and one of its offspring grace the cover of this lyrical book about natural pairs. "Peace with dove / Home with love," it begins, followed by, "Gardens with flowers / Clocks with hours." The couplets return more than once to the words "You with me," accompanied by a picture of an adult and a child in a happy scene. The warmly colored paintings, which use black outlines to good effect, mostly show idyllic outdoor settings, ending with one of a mother and child in a field of flowers. A comforting book with a sentiment parents will like.

Zolotow, Charlotte. *William's Doll*. Illustrated by William Pène du Bois. 1972. Hardcover: HarperCollins. Paperback: HarperCollins. Ages 2 years and up.

This modern classic gives voice to a feeling boys have that's often ignored. William would like to have a doll: "He wanted to hug it and cradle it in his arms . . ." His older brother makes fun of him when he sees William pretending to care for a baby doll, while their father hopes to dispel his son's interest in dolls with a basketball and an electric train, both of which William likes. But he still wants a doll, and when his grandmother visits, she understands and buys him one. Upset, the father exclaims, "He's a boy," but the grandmother explains that William needs the doll so that when he's a father, he will know how to take care of his baby. In a small format, with apt illustrations, this is a wise, warmhearted book that imparts an important message.

3

Resources and Tips for Parents

Favorite Picks

Here, divided into categories, are books that were recommended to me time and time again by different parents and librarians. The final list, "Preschool Books in Series to Try with Two-Year-Olds," is for parents whose toddlers are ready for longer books—the books are not included in this guide. All the other lists are drawn from the books annotated in this guide.

Baby Shower Gifts

Brown, Marc, *Finger Rhymes* (see page 41)
Dunn, Opal, *Hippety-Hop, Hippety-Hay: Growing with Rhymes from Birth to Age Three* (see page 47)

Dyer, Jane, *Animal Crackers: A Delectable Collection of Pictures, Poems, and Lullabies for the Very Young* (see page 47)

Emerson, Sally, *The Kingfisher Nursery Rhyme Songbook* (see page 48)

Hoban, Tana, *Black on White/White on Black* (see page 162)

Lobel, Arnold, *The Arnold Lobel Book of Mother Goose* (see page 55)

Manning, Jane, *My First Baby Games* (see page 57)

Opie, Iona, editor, *My Very First Mother Goose* (see page 59)

Oxenbury, Helen, *All Fall Down/Clap Hands/Say Goodnight/Tickle, Tickle* (see page 215)

Favorite Bedtime Books

Bang, Molly, *Ten, Nine, Eight* (see page 80)

Brown, Margaret Wise, *Goodnight Moon* (see page 95)

Fleming, Denise, *Time to Sleep* (see page 139)

Fox, Mem, *Time for Bed* (see page 141)

Katz, Karen, *Counting Kisses* (see page 182)

Long, Sylvia, *Hush Little Baby* (see page 56)

McBratney, Sam, *Guess How Much I Love You* (see page 200)

Melmed, Laura Krauss, *I Love You as Much . . .* (see page 205)

Weiss, Nicki, *Where Does the Brown Bear Go?* (see page 269)

Books for Older Siblings of a New Baby

Falwell, Cathryn, *We Have a Baby* (see page 134)

Harris, Robie H., *Happy Birth Day!* (see page 154)

Keats, Ezra Jack, *Peter's Chair* (see page 182)

Meyers, Susan, *Everywhere Babies* (see page 205)
Scott, Ann Herbert, *On Mother's Lap* (see page 236)
Steptoe, John, *Baby Says* (see page 251)

Old Favorites

Brown, Margaret Wise, *Goodnight Moon* (see page 95)
Brown, Margaret Wise, *The Runaway Bunny* (see page 96)
Freeman, Don, *Corduroy* (see page 142)
Johnson, Crockett, *Harold and the Purple Crayon* (see page 178)
Krauss, Ruth, *The Carrot Seed* (see page 186)
Kunhardt, Dorothy, *Pat the Bunny* (see page 186)
Sendak, Maurice, *Where the Wild Things Are* (see page 238)
Seuss, Dr., *Green Eggs and Ham* (see page 239)
Slobodkina, Esphyr, *Caps for Sale* (see page 246)
Wright, Blanche Fisher, *The Real Mother Goose* (see page 68)

Books That Inspire Movement

Brown, Marc, *Play Rhymes* (see page 42)
Burns, Kate, *Jump Like a Frog!/Snap Like a Crocodile!* (see page 101)
Carle, Eric, *From Head to Toe* (see page 105)
Carter, David A., *If You're Happy and You Know It, Clap Your Hands: A Pop-Up Book* (see page 43)
Cauley, Lorinda Bryan, *Clap Your Hands* (see page 110)
Gardiner, Lindsey, *Here Come Poppy and Max* (see page 144)
Newcome, Zita, *Toddlerobics* (see page 211)
Rosen, Michael, *We're Going on a Bear Hunt!* (see page 230)

Books That Invite Verbal Participation

Charlip, Remy, *Fortunately* (see page 110)

Davis, Katie, *Who Hops?* (see page 120)

Martin, Bill, Jr., *Brown Bear, Brown Bear, What Do You See?* (see page 194)

Miller, Margaret, *Where Does It Go?* (see page 207)

Shaw, Charles G., *It Looked Like Spilt Milk* (see page 242)

Tafuri, Nancy, *Spots, Feathers, and Curly Tails* (see page 256)

Westcott, Nadine Bernard, adapter, *The Lady with the Alligator Purse* (see page 67)

Williams, Sue, *I Went Walking* (see page 273)

Favorite Flap Books

Campbell, Rod, *Dear Zoo* (see page 103)

Cimarusti, Marie Torres, *Peek-a-Moo!* (see page 112)

Elgar, Rebecca, *Is That an Elephant over There?* (see page 129)

Hill, Eric, *Where's Spot?* (see page 159)

Leslie, Amanda, *Flappy Waggy Wiggly* (see page 188)

MacLeod, Elizabeth, *I Heard a Little Baa* (see page 192)

Rowe, Jeannette, *Whose Ears?/Whose Feet?/Whose Nose?* (see page 232)

Books with Multiethnic Groups of Children

Appelt, Kathi. *Toddler Two-Step* (see page 76)

Calmenson, Stephanie. *Good for You: Toddler Rhymes for Toddler Times* (see page 42)

Cauley, Lorinda Bryan. *Clap Your Hands* (see page 110)

Hindley, Judy. *Eyes, Nose, Fingers, and Toes: A First Book All about You* (see page 160)

Hudson, Cheryl Willis, and Bernette G. Ford. *Bright Eyes, Brown Skin* (see page 169)

Newcome, Zita. *Toddlerobics* (see page 211)

Newcome, Zita. *Toddlerobics: Animal Fun* (see page 212)

Oxenbury, Helen. *All Fall Down/Clap Hands/Say Goodnight/ Tickle, Tickle* (see page 215)

Preschool Books in Series to Try with Two-Year-Olds

(Not annotated in this guide)

Bemelmans, Ludwig, *Madeline*

Brown, Marc, *Arthur's Nose*

Havill, Juanita, *Jamaica Tag-Along*

Henkes, Kevin, *Chester's Way*

Hoban, Russell, *A Birthday for Frances*

Lobel, Arnold, *Days with Frog and Toad*

Marshall, James, *George and Martha*

McPhail, David, *Pig Pig Grows Up*

Meddaugh, Susan, *Martha Calling*

Rey, H. A., and Margret Rey, *Curious George*

Williams, Vera B., *A Chair for My Mother*

Tips on Reading Aloud

Reading aloud well does not come naturally to everyone. Here are techniques you can practice until they come easily. *The Read-Aloud Handbook,* by Jim Trelease, offers more ideas on how to go about it, as well as numerous reasons that reading aloud is beneficial.

- If you haven't read the book already, scan it to get a sense of its content before you start reading aloud.
- Choose books you are excited about or your child is excited about. It is hard to read a book you don't enjoy.
- Read with expression. A monotone is hard to listen to. Children need to hear changes in your voice to indicate when you are reading dialogue. Vary your pace, too. Slow down to build up suspense and speed up during exciting scenes.
- Create voices for different characters if you enjoy it, but it isn't necessary for a good reading. A story can be read effectively in a straightforward manner as long as you have expression and enthusiasm.
- Read at a moderate pace, not too fast. Listening is a challenge for many children, and you don't want to leave them behind as you speed ahead. Picture-story books require time for enjoying the illustrations.
- Feel free to stop and discuss the book if you and your listener want to. Answer questions as they come up. How much you want to stop and explain new words is up to you. Stopping too often to explain can undermine the story's impact.
- Keep in mind that children can look bored or restless and

still be listening. Some children need to be moving around or fidgeting with something. The real question is, are they also enjoying the book? If so, let them squirm and play with toys as they listen.

- If your child is not enjoying a book, you are not obliged to finish it. Nor must you read a book word for word, especially if your toddler is happily turning the pages too quickly for you to keep up. Sometimes you might want to concentrate on looking at the pictures and maybe talking about them. As always, the goal is to have fun, not to force a reluctant listener to listen.

Reading aloud has a host of educational benefits, but it works best if it isn't approached as an educational exercise. Parents have been known to have children repeat each word after them, as a device to teach reading. Such a tedious approach is more likely to dampen enthusiasm for books than to promote learning. Just enjoy the books together; all the aspects of "reading readiness," such as learning vocabulary and becoming familiar with books, will follow naturally.

Activities with Books

Books stand on their own as art and entertainment, and sometimes the best approach is simply to read a book and savor it. In other cases, talking while you read the book enriches the experience. But it can also be fun to pair books with simple activities. The more active suggestions are geared toward toddlers, while reading with infants can be enriched with simple items like toys or food that correspond to what's shown in a book. Brainstorm about other possibilities, with the goal, as always, of making reading a wonderful experience.

- When reading infants *Red, Blue, Yellow Shoe* (see page 164), find some of the items shown in the photographs and have them for your child to see and touch, such as a purple flower, an orange, and a green maple leaf. The board book *I Touch* (see page 216) includes an illustration of a beach ball; compare the picture to the real thing with your baby.
- Teddy bears and dolls appear in lots of books, such as *Golden Bear* (see page 284) and *My Doll, Keshia* (see page 150). Read a book like one of these and explore together how the toy in the book is like your child's toy.
- *Pots and Pans* (see page 166) invites a session for a one-year-old of banging around on your kitchen floor like the child in the book. Similarly, *Wrapping Paper Romp* (see page 168) is aimed at the same age child and could lead to a session of playing with old wrapping paper, which makes a fine, if short-lived, toy.
- *Bubbles, Bubbles* (see page 75), *Max's Bath* (see page 270), and *King Bidgood's in the Bathtub* (see page 278) are three

of several books related to bath time that might make reluctant bathers more interested in the task.

- In the mood to move? Read a dance book, put on some
  music, and shake a leg with your baby or toddler. Try *Baby
  Dance* (see page 257), *Dance* (see page 179), *Hop Jump*
  (see page 265), or *Watch Me Dance* (see page 219).
- Tie a book in with the weather. If you live where it snows,
  read *The Snowy Day* (see page 183) in the winter. Read
  Boot Weather (see page 263) before or after a walk through
  puddles. The quartet of books by Anna Grossnickle Hines,
  with titles like *What Can You Do in the Rain?* (see page
  161), also explore ideas for rain, wind, and sun.
- Read a book in conjunction with a field trip. *Sam Who
  Never Forgets* (see page 225) and *Good Night, Gorilla* (see
  page 223) are set at a zoo, while Tom Paxton's *Going to the
  Zoo* (see page 61) is a song to sing on the way. Take a city
  bus ride and tie it to the wonderful pop-up book *The
  Wheels on the Bus* (see page 69) or the parody, *The Seals on
  the Bus* (see page 51).
- Young vehicle fans can always find real-life equivalents to
  what they see in books about trucks, heavy building machinery, trains, and planes. Bring a vehicle book along in
  the car in case you can stop at a construction site or see a
  train go by. Toy trucks and other toy vehicles can also be
  compared to photographs and illustrations in books.
- Going on a plane trip? Read *First Flight* (see page 203) or
  Miss Mouse Takes Off (see page 214) ahead of time and
  maybe take the books with you on the flight.
- Concept books that explore colors and shapes lend themselves naturally to follow-up activities. Reading *Is It Red?
  Is It Yellow? Is It Blue? An Adventure in Color* (see page
  163) can send you and your child on a hunt for those same
  colors in your house. *What Is Round?* (see page 124) sug-

gests looking around in everyday life for round objects. Or page through a magazine together with lots of color photographs to find colors and shapes.

- Eating and cooking are natural follow-ups to books like *Pancakes, Pancakes!* (see page 106) or *Growing Vegetable Soup* (see page 128). *Peanut Butter and Jelly: A Play Rhyme* (see page 67) suggests it's time for a sandwich, and even *The Lady with the Alligator Purse* (see page 67) includes pizza in its final scenes. *If You Give a Mouse a Cookie* (see page 213) cries out for a cookie and a glass of milk to go with it.

- Make sure your toddler has easy access to paper, crayons, pens, pencils, markers, rubber stamps, and any other tools that will encourage written expression and artwork. A child's first attempts at scribbling and telling stories through pictures are important steps for the process, much later, of learning to print and learning to create written stories.

- Make a book about your child's life. Mount photographs of your child, family, and familiar items and places, and cover them with plastic wrap or insert them in plastic sleeves for protection.

- Two very attractive magazines are aimed at very young children. If you think it would excite your child to receive a magazine in the mail, *Babybug* is for children six months to two years and *Ladybug* for those two to six years. Both offer high-quality stories, poems, and illustrations. For more information, see *www.cricketmag.com*.

- Alert baby-sitters or other caregivers to books that your child especially enjoys. Perhaps donate a copy to the child-care center your child attends. Find out what books the caregiver recommends.

Music Resources

Listening to music is another enrichment activity related to singing and reading aloud. Although songbooks are described in the first chapter, it is beyond the scope of this guide to annotate musical recordings. The following book and Web sites will lead parents to recommended recordings for very young children and information on introducing children to music.

Reid, Rob. *Children's Jukebox: A Subject Guide to Musical Recordings and Programming Ideas for Songsters Ages One to Twelve.* **1995. American Library Association.**
This book, which will guide you to musical recordings for children, is arranged by subject and annotates more than four hundred songs.

Association for Library Service to Children (a division of the American Library Association). *www.ala.org/alsc*
This Web site has an annual list of "Notable Children's Recordings," which includes music and recorded books; lists from previous years are also available.

Best Children's Music. *www.bestchildrensmusic.com*
A useful commercial Web site that includes lists of recommended cassettes and CDs, organized by age groups, with links to reviews and information about awards.

Children's Music Web. *www.childrensmusic.org*
A nonprofit that promotes good music for children, this organization sponsors a music award for which children help

choose the recipient. The Web site provides useful links, including radio stations with children's programming.

Music Education for Young Children. *www.music4kidson line.com/meyc*
A Web site about music for ages birth through eight with information about child development and music, and recommended recordings and books.

Music for Little People. *www.mflp.com*
This commercial site offers a wonderful selection of music for children, with an emphasis on alternative and multiethnic recordings. You can request its extensive catalog at the Web site, too.

Books in Spanish

Many young children in this country speak Spanish as their first or second language, and an increasing number of children's books originally written in English are being translated into Spanish. However, the translations vary significantly in quality. Below I have listed books included in the body of this guide that have been translated from English or published with Spanish and English printed side by side. You will find annotations for them on the pages indicated.

Each book below appeared on one (or both) of two recommended lists from reliable sources. One source is the Los Angeles Public Library, where a longer list of Spanish titles is available at *www.lapl.org/kidspath* by following the links to "Recommended Reading" and then "Español." The other source is the Association for Library Service to Children, a division of the American Library Association; you can find a longer list of Spanish titles at *www.ala.org/alsc* by searching the Web site for "Spanish Born to Read." Another on-line source is Lectorum, a publisher and distributor of Spanish books (*www.lectorum.com*). Its New York City store is the largest Spanish-language store in the United States.

Books Translated into Spanish from English

Alborough, Jez, *¿Dónde está mi osito?/Where's My Teddy?* (see page 73)

Brown, Margaret Wise, *Buenas noches, luna*/Goodnight Moon (see page 95)

Brown, Margaret Wise, *El gran granero rojo*/Big Red Barn (see page 94)

Browne, Anthony, *Cosas que me gustan*/Things I Like (see page 97)

Carle, Eric, *La oruga muy hambrienta*/The Very Hungry Caterpillar (see page 106)

Frasier, Debra, *El día en que tú naciste*/On the Day You Were Born (see page 141)

Galdone, Paul, *Los tres chivitos gruff*/The Three Billy Goats Gruff (see page 143)

Guarino, Deborah, *¿Tu mamá es una llama?*/Is Your Mama a Llama? (see page 151)

Hague, Michael, *Mama gansa: una colección de rimas infantiles clásicas*/Mother Goose: A Collection of Classic Nursery Rhymes (see page 49)

Hill, Eric, *¿Dónde está Spot?*/Where's Spot? (see page 159)

Hutchins, Pat, *Llaman a la puerta*/The Doorbell Rang (see page 171)

Keats, Ezra Jack, *La silla de Pedro*/Peter's Chair (see page 182)

McBratney, Sam, *Adivina cuánto te quiero*/Guess How Much I Love You (see page 200)

McDonnell, Flora, *Quiero a los animales*/I Love Animals (see page 200)

Numeroff, Laura Joffe, *Si le das una galleta a un ratón*/If You Give a Mouse a Cookie (see page 213)

Rosen, Michael, *Vamos a cazar un oso*/We're Going on a Bear Hunt! (see page 230)

Sendak, Maurice, *Donde viven los monstruos*/Where the Wild Things Are (see page 238)

Seuss, Dr., *Huevos verdes con jamón*/Green Eggs and Ham (see page 239)

Shannon, David, *¡No, David!/No, David!* (see page 241)

Slobodkina, Esphyr, *Se venden gorras: La historia de un vendedor ambulante, unos monos y sus travesuras/Caps for Sale: A Tale of a Peddler, Some Monkeys and Their Monkey Business* (see page 246)

Waddell, Martin, *Las lechucitas/Owl Babies* (see page 264)

Wells, Rosemary, *Nora la revoltosa/Noisy Nora* (see page 271)

Wood, Don and Audrey, *El ratoncito, la fresa roja y madura y el gran oso hambriento/The Little Mouse, the Red Ripe Strawberry, and the Big Hungry Bear* (see page 280)

Zion, Gene, *Harry, el perrito sucio/Harry the Dirty Dog* (see page 286)

Books with Side-by-Side Spanish and English

Delacre, Lulu, *Arroz con leche: Popular Songs and Rhymes from Latin America* (see page 46)

Emberley, Rebecca, *My Colors/Mis colores; My Numbers/Mis números; My Opposites/Mis opuestos; My Shapes/Mis formas* (see page 131)

Griego, Margot C., et al., *Tortillitas para Mamá: And Other Nursery Rhymes, Spanish and English* (see page 48)

Jaramillo, Nelly Palacio, *Grandmother's Nursery Rhymes/Las nanas de Abuelita* (see page 52)

Orozco, José-Luis, *De colores and Other Latin-American Folk Songs for Children* (see page 60)

Orozco, José-Luis, *Diez deditos: Ten Little Fingers & Other Play Rhymes and Action Songs from Latin America* (see page 60)

Locating Books

Libraries

Public libraries are a great resource for parents. They are free and typically offer a broader and deeper range of books than bookstores do. Libraries are good places to find books that are out of print, an important service because many children's books go out of print quickly. Libraries are also more likely than bookstores to carry books from smaller presses.

Good libraries are increasingly easy to use, with computerized catalogs that tell if a book is on the shelf or in a nearby library. Many public library catalogs can be accessed from home through the Internet. Many libraries are part of a branch system or a large cooperative system, so you can use your card at more than one library. In such cases, you can usually return books to the library closest to you, even if you checked them out elsewhere. Most libraries have book drops so that you can return books when the library is closed.

Interlibrary loan (ILL) is a convenient way to get access to many more books than your local library has in its collection. In many libraries, borrowing a book through ILL is free, although some public libraries charge a small fee per book. Some computerized catalogs allow you to input your library card number if you want to request a book from another library. Your local library will call, E-mail, or send a notice through the mail when it arrives, often in a few days.

While you are signing out books, find out what other programs and services your local library offers. You may discover storytimes—often called lapsits—for you and your baby, toddler storytimes, programs on parenting, and more.

Bookstores and Catalogs

Bookstores vary enormously in their selections of children's books. Some offer a wide array of books, usually with an emphasis on paperbacks. Others have only a small selection or carry mostly books in popular series. Some cities have bookstores devoted just to children's books, a treat for children's book lovers. The quality of advice from booksellers varies enormously. If you are lucky, someone at your local bookstore knows about children's books. More likely, staff at superstores and even smaller bookstores don't know enough to make good suggestions, although that may not stop them from giving advice.

Most bookstores will order a book for you for no charge if the store doesn't carry it but can get it easily from another source. If you don't see the book you want, ask about placing such a special order. Bookstores are increasing the services they offer for families, adding storytimes, author book signings, and other programs.

On-line bookstores such as *amazon.com* and *barnesand noble.com* are increasingly popular. They are especially helpful for getting obscure books that a local store might not carry or for people who don't live near a bookstore. Their Web sites offer an easy way to survey what books an author has written and if they are available for purchase. They may also offer a used book service to get out-of-print books that a publisher no longer supplies.

Take the recommendations of on-line bookstores and the information they provide with caution, too. While some of the recommendations come from knowledgeable staff, others seem to be ads disguised as neutral advice. Note, too, that "subject" searches on *amazon.com* to find books on topics like dinosaurs or songbooks in no way sort the books for excellence. Television and other commercial tie-ins figure heavily in the books that appear, even for babies and toddlers.

Most catalogs and book clubs typically offer a small selection of good children's books. One exception is *Chinaberry Books*, an outstanding catalog of more than five hundred children's books, with thoughtful descriptions of each title. It covers toddlers through adolescents, with a section on parenting books and a small selection of novels for adults. Chinaberry Books, 2780 Via Orange Way, Suite B, Spring Valley, CA 91978; (800) 776-2242; *www.chinaberry.com*.

Keeping Up with What's New in Children's Book Publishing

If you are interested in keeping up with what's new in children's books, here are some recommended magazines, review journals, and Web sites. Also check your local newspaper, which may have regular or occasional articles on new children's books. Many libraries provide booklists that highlight recent recommended books. For example, each year the American Library Association publishes an annotated list of approximately seventy-five Notable Children's Books, a useful resource available in most libraries and on the American Library Association Web site, listed below.

The Horn Book Magazine is a well-established, bimonthly journal about children's books. It prints insightful reviews of recommended books and well-written articles about children's literature. Available at bookstores and libraries, and by subscription.
(800) 325-1170; *www.hbook.com*

Book Links is an attractive, useful magazine of great interest to children's librarians and educators, published by the American Library Association six times a year. It highlights books on selected topics and authors, geared toward curriculum needs. Available by subscription and in many libraries.
(888) 350-0950; *www.ala.org/BookLinks*

BOOK: *The Magazine for the Reading Life* is a glossy bi-monthly magazine aimed at the general public that carries a column and a limited number of reviews of children's books, both written by Kathleen Odean.
(800) 317-2665; *www.bookmagazine.com*

The Children's Literature Web Guide from the University of Calgary is an outstanding site that provides information as well as links to many other good sites.
www.ucalgary.ca/~dkbrown

The Fairrosa Cyber Library of Children's Literature Web site is an enthusiastic collection of information, links, and booklists.
www.fairrosa.info

The American Library Association Web site provides links to ALA journals, Web site picks for families, booklists, award information, and a limited number of book reviews.
www.ala.org

Organizations and Web Sites Concerned with Babies, Toddlers, and Books

Association for Library Service to Children (a division of the American Library Association). *www.ala.org/alsc/born.html*
A Web site with lots of useful information and links for parents, including advice on reading to the very young.

Beginning with Books. *www.beginningwithbooks.org*
This nonprofit affiliate of the Carnegie Library of Pittsburgh offers low-income parents the books, information, and encouragement to read aloud to their young children. The Web site includes an annual "Best Books for Babies" list of ten books.

Children's Book Council. *www.cbcbooks.org*
This nonprofit, whose members are publishers, is dedicated to encouraging literacy and the use and enjoyment of children's books. The Web site has information about new books, useful booklists, and more about keeping up with publishing.

I Am Your Child. *www.iamyourchild.org*
I Am Your Child is a national public awareness and engagement campaign to make early childhood development a top priority in the United States. The Web site has tips and advice for parents of young children as well as information about the campaign.

National Association for the Education of Young Children (NAEYC). *www.naeyc.org*

This Web site for the professional organization of early childhood educators provides a list for parents of all early childhood programs currently accredited by NAEYC.

National Child Care Information Center. *www.nccic.org*

A project of the Child Care Bureau of the U.S. Department of Health and Human Services, this Web site gives advice on finding good child care and a lot of other useful information for parents and educators.

National Network for Child Care. *www.nncc.org*

This Web site is a source of extensive information and links about early childhood education.

Reach Out and Read. *www.reachoutandread.org*

The Web site of a project that involves pediatricians giving children's books to young patients.

Reading Is Fundamental. *www.rif.org*

Founded in 1966, RIF develops and delivers children's and family literacy programs that help prepare young children for reading and motivate school-age children to read regularly.

Read to Me. *www.readtomeprogram.org*

An organization devoted to encouraging young mothers to read to their babies. The Web site has an outstanding "frequently asked questions" section on reading to the very young.

Zero to Three. *www.zerotothree.org*

An organization dedicated to improving the first three years of children's lives. The Web site offers helpful information and resources for parents and child-care providers.

Further Reading for Parents

Here are some recommended books about babies, toddlers, books, and language.

Butler, Dorothy. *Babies Need Books*. 1998 revised edition. Heinemann.
A New Zealand writer makes a plea for the importance of children's books, with lists of recommended titles for newborn through six years, many of which are not easily available in the United States.

Golinkoff, Roberta Michnick, and Kathy Hirsh-Pasek. *How Babies Talk: The Magic and Mystery of Language in the First Three Years of Life*. 1999. Dutton.
A fascinating discussion of how babies and toddlers acquire language, with interactive exercises to understand your child's language development better.

Gopnik, Alison, Andrew N. Meltzoff, and Patricia Kuhl. *The Scientist in the Crib: Minds, Brains, and How Children Learn*. 1999. Morrow.
This readable book reveals remarkable new information about how young children learn and how scientists study the topic.

Horning, Kathleen T. *From Cover to Cover: Evaluating and Reviewing Children's Books*. 1997. HarperCollins.
This outstanding guide to evaluating children's books for all ages explains clearly what elements make a good children's book.

Odean, Kathleen. *Great Books about Things Kids Love: More Than 750 Books for Children 3 to 14.* 2001. Ballantine.
An annotated guide by subject to recommended picture books, novels, biographies, informational books, folklore, and poetry.

Odean, Kathleen. *Great Books for Boys: More Than 600 Books for Boys 2 to 14.* 1998. Ballantine.
An annotated guide to recommended picture books, novels, biographies, informational books, folklore, and poetry.

Odean, Kathleen. *Great Books for Girls: More Than 600 Recommended Books for Girls Ages 3–14.* 2002 revised edition. Ballantine.
A 417-page annotated guide to books with strong female characters for children ages three to fourteen.

Rand, Donna, Toni Trent Parker, and Sheila Foster. *Black Books Galore: Guide to Great African American Children's Books.* 1998. Wiley.
An excellent resource for finding books with positive African American characters, for babies through ninth graders.

Trelease, Jim. *The Read-Aloud Handbook.* 2001 fifth edition. Penguin.
This useful book argues effectively for reading aloud to children from newborns through teens.

Further Reading for Librarians

Over the last twenty years, public libraries have increasingly offered storytimes for the very youngest children and their parents. Not only does this begin to familiarize the children with the library and books in a positive way, it's also a wonderful way to introduce parents to excellent books, helpful practices like fingerplays and action rhymes, and the various resources the library has to offer. It encourages parents and, later, their children to make the public library a vital part of their lives for years to come.

The following books provide practical advice on running programs, with specific suggestions for books, music, and fingerplays and other activities, often grouped around themes. The suggestion lists include many out-of-print books that libraries may have in their collections, which this guide does not list because of its emphasis on books parents can buy if they choose.

Butler, Dorothy. *Babies Need Books.* 1998 revised edition. Heinemann.
Davis, Robin Works. *Toddle On Over: Developing Infant & Toddler Literature Programs.* 1998. Alleyside Press.
DeSalvo, Nancy N. *Beginning with Books: Library Programming for Infants, Toddlers and Preschoolers.* 1993. Library Professional Publications.
Ernst, Linda L. *Lapsit Services for the Very Young: A How-to-Do-It Manual.* 1995. Neal-Schuman.

Ernst, Linda L. *Lapsit Services for the Very Young II: A How-to-Do-It Manual.* 2001. Neal-Schuman.

Greene, Ellin. *Books, Babies, and Libraries: Serving Infants, Toddlers, and Their Parents & Caregivers.* 1991. ALA.

Jeffery, Debby Ann. *Literate Beginnings: Programs for Babies and Toddlers.* 1995. ALA.

Nespeca, Sue McCleaf. *Library Programming for Families with Young Children: A How-to-Do-It Manual.* 1994. Neal-Schuman.

Nichols, Judy. *Storytimes for Two-Year-Olds.* 1998 2d edition. ALA.

Author and Illustrator Index

Acredolo, Linda, 72
Adinolfi, JoAnn, 245
Ahlberg, Allan, 72
Ahlberg, Janet, 72
Alborough, Jez, 72, 73, 300
Aliki, 74
Allen, Pamela, 74
Appelt, Kathi, 75, 76, 291
Apple, Margot, 242
Archambault, John, 195
Arnosky, Jim, 76
Aruego, Ariane, 149
Aruego, Jose, 149, 185
Asch, Frank, 77
Ayliffe, Alex, 143, 199
Ayto, Russell, 272
Azarian, Mary, 234

Baer, Gene, 78
Baker, Alan, 78
Baker, Keith, 79
Baker, Liza, 79
Bang, Molly, 80, 81, 289

Banks, Kate, 82
Barner, Bob, 82
Barrett, Mary Brigid, 83
Barth, Dominic, 262
Barton, Byron, 83, 84, 85, 86, 148, 180
Barton, Jill, 158
Bauer, Marion Dane, 86
Beaton, Clare, 40, 86, 90
Beddows, Eric, 176
Beeke, Tiphanie, 98
Benjamin, Floella, 40
Bennett, David, 87
Bennett, Nneka, 258
Benson, Patrick, 264
Berends, Polly Berrien, 87
Berger, Barbara, 88
Bishop, Nic, 115
Blackstone, Stella, 89, 90
Blos, Joan, 91
Bond, Felicia, 94, 213
Boon, Emilie, 285
Bornstein, Ruth, 91

AUTHOR AND ILLUSTRATOR INDEX

Bowie, C. W., 92
Boynton, Sandra, 92
Brennan, Linda Crotta, 93
Brett, Jan, 54
Brown, Marc, 41, 42, 62, 93, 288, 290
Brown, Margaret Wise, 94, 95, 96, 289, 290, 300
Brown, Ruth, 96, 97
Browne, Anthony, 97, 300
Bruss, Deborah, 98
Buck, Nola, 98
Buckley, Helen, 99
Burningham, John, 100, 101
Burns, Kate, 101, 290
Burton, Jane, 102
Butler, John, 102
Bynum, Janie, 103, 208

Cabrera, Jane, 103
Calmenson, Stephanie, 44, 292
Campbell, Robert, 103, 291
Carle, Eric, 104, 105, 106, 107, 194, 290, 300
Carlstrom, Nancy White, 107, 108
Carr, Jan, 109
Carter, David A., 43, 109, 290
Cauley, Lorinda Bryan, 110, 290, 291
Cepeda, Joe, 116
Chandra, Deborah, 110
Chapman, Jane, 229, 275
Charlip, Remy, 110, 111, 291
Cheon, Winnie, 254
Chodos-Irvine, Margaret, 277
Chollat, Emilie, 75
Chorao, Kay, 43
Christelow, Eileen, 111
Chwast, Eve, 83
Cimarusti, Marie Torres, 112, 291
Coalson, Glo, 236
Cole, Joanna, 44
Collicutt, Paul, 112
Conteh-Morgan, Jane, 191
Cony, Frances, 45
Cooke, Andy, 87

Cooney, Barbara, 48
Cornell, Laura, 119
Cousins, Lucy, 45, 113, 114
Cowell, Cressida, 114
Cowen-Fletcher, Jane, 115
Cowley, Joy, 115
Coy, John, 116
Craig, Helen, 156
Crebbin, June, 116
Crews, Donald, 117, 118, 181
Crews, Nina, 118
Cummings, Pat, 119
Curtis, Jamie Lee, 119

Dabcovich, Lydia, 120
D'Allancé, Mireille, 214
Davis, Katie, 120, 291
Day, Alexandra, 120
de Groat, Diane, 166
Degen, Bruce, 107, 108, 121
Delacre, Lulu, 46, 302
Demarest, Chris, 121, 122
dePaola, Tomie, 46, 122, 217, 241
Dijs, Carla, 123
Dodds, Dayle Ann, 123
Donohue, Dorothy, 109
Dotlich, Rebecca Kai, 124
Downey, Lynn, 124
Doyle, Charlotte, 125
Dunn, Opal, 47, 288
Dyer, Jane, 47, 141, 190, 248, 289

Eastman, P. D., 125
Ehlert, Lois, 34, 78, 126, 127, 128, 129, 195
Eitan, Ora, 155
Elgar, Rebecca, 129, 130, 291
Elivia, 52
Ellwand, David, 130
Emberley, Ed, 131
Emberley, Michael, 154
Emberley, Rebecca, 131, 302
Emerson, Sally, 48, 289
Eriksson, Eva, 190
Ernst, Lisa Campbell, 132, 167
Euvremer, Teryl, 250

Falconer, Ian, 132
Falwell, Cathryn, 133, 134, 289
Faulkner, Keith, 134
Feiffer, Jules, 135
Fernando, Denise, 89
Firehammer, Karla, 124
Firth, Barbara, 263
Flack, Marjorie, 135
Fleming, Denise, 136, 137, 138, 139, 289
Ford, Bernette G., 169
Ford, George, 168, 169
Ford, Miela, 139, 140
Fox, Christyan, 140
Fox, Diane, 140
Fox, Mem, 140, 141, 289
Frasier, Debra, 141, 300
Frazee, Marla, 205
Freedman, Claire, 142
Freeman, Don, 142, 290
French, Vivian, 143

Galdone, Paul, 143, 300
Gammell, Stephen, 196
Gardiner, Lindsey, 144, 290
Gentieu, Penny, 72, 144
George, Kristine O'Connell, 145
Geras, Adèle, 145
Gershator, Phillis, 146
Gerth, Melanie, 146
Gibbons, Gail, 147
Gilchrist, Jan Spivey, 150, 151
Ginsburg, Mirra, 148, 149
Gliori, Debi, 149
Godon, Ingrid, 114
Goembel, Ponder, 267
Gomi, Taro, 150
Goodwyn, Susan, 72
Gorton, Julia, 267
Graham, Margaret Bloy, 286
Granström, Brita, 160
Greenfield, Eloise, 150, 151
Griego, Margot C., 48, 302
Grossman, Bill, 151
Guarino, Deborah, 152, 300

Hague, Kathleen, 152
Hague, Michael, 49, 152
Haines, Mike, 152
Hale, Sarah Josepha, 50
Hall, Zoe, 153
Hallensleben, Georg, 82
Halpern, Shari, 52, 153, 253
Hargrove, Linda, 153
Harper, Isabelle, 154
Harris, Robie H., 154, 289
Harris, Trudy, 155
Harter, Debbie, 90
Hathon, Elizabeth, 155
Hawkes, Kevin, 151
Hayashi, Nancy, 233
Hayes, Sarah, 156
Hazen, Barbara Shook, 157
Heap, Sue, 157, 229
Henkes, Kevin, 157, 158
Heo, Yumi, 261
Hest, Amy, 158, 159
Hible, Paula, 213
Hill, Eric, 159, 291, 300
Hill, Susan, 160
Hillenbrand, Will, 50
Hindley, Judy, 160, 292
Hines, Anna Grossnickle, 161, 162
Hines-Stephens, Sarah, 162
Ho, Minfong, 51
Hoban, Tana, 162, 163, 164, 165, 289
Hom, Nancy, 247
Horenstein, Henry, 165
Hort, Lenny, 51
Hubbell, Patricia, 166, 167, 168
Hudson, Cheryl Willis, 168, 169
Huliska-Beith, Laura, 146
Hunter, Sally, 169
Hurd, Clement, 95, 96
Hurd, Thacher, 170, 171
Hutchins, Pat, 171, 172, 173, 300

Imershein, Betsy, 174
Inkpen, Mick, 174, 175
Intrater, Roberta Grobel, 176
Isadora, Rachel, 284

Jam, Teddy, 176
James, Synthia Saint, 146
Janovitz, Marilyn, 177
Jaramillo, Nelly Palacio, 52, 302
Jeffers, Susan, 271
Jenkins, Steve, 230
Jeram, Anita, 159, 177, 200
Johnson, Crockett, 178, 186, 290
Jonas, Ann, 178
Jones, Bill T., 179
Joosse, Barbara M., 179
Jorgensen, Gail, 180

Kalan, Robert, 180, 181
Karas, G. Brian, 51, 65, 250
Kasza, Keiko, 181
Katz, Karen, 182, 289
Keats, Ezra Jack, 25, 52, 182, 183,
    289, 300
Keller, Holly, 183, 227
Kellogg, Steven, 152
Kenyon, Tony, 53
Kim, Joung Un, 153
Kirk, Daniel, 53, 189
Kitamura, Satoshi, 184
Kleven, Elisa, 60
Kliros, Thea, 161
Koide, Tan, 184
Koide, Yasuko, 184
Kopper, Lisa, 185, 189
Kosaka, Fumi, 75
Kraus, Robert, 185
Krauss, Ruth, 186, 290
Kuklin, Susan, 179
Kunhardt, Dorothy, 186, 290
Kvasnosky, Laura, 187

Labrosse, Darcia, 260
Lambert, Jonathan, 134
Lambert, Sally Anne, 47
Lambert, Stephen, 91
Lamont, Priscilla, 54
Lavallee, Barbara, 179
Lawrence, Michael, 187
Lawston, Lisa, 188
Lear, Edward, 54

Leslie, Amanda, 188, 291
Levine, Pamela, 188
Lewin, Hugh, 189
Lewis, Kevin, 189
Lewis, Rose, 190
Lin, Grace, 258
Linch, Tanya, 55
Lindgren, Barbro, 190
Litzinger, Rosanne, 125
Lobel, Arnold, 55, 289
London, Jonathan, 191
Long, Sylvia, 56, 57, 289
Losordo, Stephen, 191

Maccarone, Grace, 192
MacCarthy, Patricia, 193
Maclean, Colin, 48
Maclean, Moira, 48
MacLeod, Elizabeth, 192, 291
Mahy, Margaret, 193
Mallat, Kathy, 194
Manning, Jane, 57, 58, 289
Marshall, James, 58, 220
Martin, Bill, Jr., 194, 195, 291
Martin, Rafe, 196
Marzollo, Jean, 196, 197
Mayer, Mercer, 198
Mayo, Margaret, 199
McBratney, Sam, 200, 289, 300
McCarthy, Patricia, 193
McDonnell, Flora, 200, 201, 300
McEwen, Katharine, 116
McFarland, Jim, 201
McFarland, Lyn Rossiter, 201
McGee, Marni, 202
McKee, David, 202
McMillan, Bruce, 50
McPhail, David, 79, 203, 204
Meade, Holly, 51
Meddaugh, Susan, 204
Melling, David, 152
Melmed, Laura, 205, 289
Meyers, Susan, 205, 290
Miglio, Paige, 268
Milanowski, Stephanie, 188
Miller, Margaret, 206, 207, 291

Miller, Virginia, 207
Minters, Frances, 208
Morgan, Mary, 208
Moser, Barry, 154
Most, Bernard, 209
Moxley, Sheila, 40
Mullins, Patricia, 140, 180
Munsinger, Lynn, 212
Murphy, Jill, 209
Murphy, Mary, 210

Narahashi, Keiko, 110, 210, 211, 238
Newcome, Zita, 211, 212, 290, 292
Noll, Sally, 140
Numeroff, Laura Joffe, 212, 213, 300

O'Book, Irene, 213
O'Brien, Patrick, 214
Ochiltree, Dianne, 214
Opie, Iona, 59, 289
Ormerod, Jan, 36, 99, 214, 215, 256
Orozco, José-Luis, 60
Oxenbury, Helen, 215, 216, 230, 289, 292

Pandell, Karen, 217
Paparone, Pamela, 98
Parkins, David, 264
Parr, Todd, 217
Paschkis, Julie, 268
Paul, Ann Whitford, 218
Paxton, Tom, 61
Peek, Merle, 61, 64
Pene Du Bois, William, 287
Phillips, Louise, 192
Pilkey, Dav, 218
Pinkney, Andrea, 219
Pinkney, Brian, 219
Plecas, Jennifer, 168
Pluckrose, Henry, 219
Pomerantz, Charlotte, 220
Pons, Bernadette, 262
Prater, John, 220, 221

Prelutsky, Jack, 62
Priddy, Roger, 221

Raffi, 63
Rand, Ted, 195
Raschka, Chris, 222, 223
Rathmann, Peggy, 223, 224
Ray, Mary Lyn, 224
Raymond, Victoria, 94
Regan, Laura, 197
Rex, Michael, 191
Rice, Eve, 224, 225
Richards, Laura E., 225
Riley, Linnea, 226
Robbins, Ken, 226
Rockwell, Anne, 227, 228
Rockwell, Harlow, 228
Roddie, Shen, 228
Root, Barry, 160
Root, Phyllis, 229
Rose, Deborah Lee, 230
Rosen, Michael, 230, 290, 300
Roth, Susan L., 231
Rounds, Glen, 231
Rowe, Jeannette, 232, 291
Royen, Mary Morgan Van, 157
Russo, Marisabina, 232
Ryder, Joanna, 233
Rylant, Cynthia, 233

Saaf, Donald, 285
Saul, Carol P., 234
Savadier, Elivia, 245
Sayles, Elizabeth, 243
Scarry, Richard, 234
Schindel, John, 235
Schmidt, Karen, 61
Schumaker, Ward, 76
Schwartz, Amy, 64, 235
Schwartz, Roslyn, 236
Scott, Ann Herbert, 236, 290
Seeger, Laura Vaccaro, 64
Sendak, Maurice, 237, 238, 290, 300
Serfozo, Mary, 238
Seuss, Dr., 239, 240, 290, 300

AUTHOR AND ILLUSTRATOR INDEX

Shannon, David, 241, 302
Shapiro, Arnold, 241
Shaw, Charles G., 242, 291
Shaw, Nancy, 242
Shea, Pegi Deitz, 243
Siddals, Mary McKenna, 243
Siebert, Diane, 244
Simmons, Jane, 244
Singer, Marilyn, 245
Sís, Peter, 246
Slobodkina, Esphyr, 246, 290, 302
Smith, Charles R., Jr., 247
Smith, Maggie, 145
Sneed, Brad, 87
Sorensen, Henri, 205
Spagnoli, Cathy, 247
Spinelli, Eileen, 248
Spowart, Robin, 249
Stadler, John, 249
Steen, Sandra, 250
Steen, Susan, 250
Steig, William, 250
Steptoe, John, 251, 290
Stickland, Henrietta, 252
Stickland, Paul, 251, 252
Stinchecum, Amanda Mayer, 150
Stoeke, Janet Morgan, 253
Stringer, Lauren, 224
Sturges, Philemon, 253
Suen, Anastasia, 254
Sweet, Melissa, 166, 275

Taback, Simms, 65, 255
Tafuri, Nancy, 148, 255, 256, 257, 291
Takabayashi, Mari, 93, 167, 196
Takahashi, Hideko, 248
Taylor, Ann, 257
Teague, Mark, 283
Thomas, Joyce Carol, 258
Thompson, Carol, 228
Thong, Roseanne, 258
Tiegreen, Alan, 44
Titherington, Jeanne, 66, 259
Tracy, Tom, 260
Twinem, Neecy, 260

Uff, Caroline, 260

Van Fleet, Matthew, 261
Van Heerden, Marjorie, 257
Van Laan, Nancy, 261, 262
Verboven, Agnes, 262
Vere, Ed, 188
Vigna, Judith, 263
Vivas, Julie, 273

Waddell, Martin, 263, 264, 302
Wallace, John, 277
Wallace, Nancy Elizabeth, 265
Walsh, Ellen Stoll, 265
Walsh, Melanie, 266
Walter, Virginia, 267
Walters, Catherine, 145
Walton, Rick, 267, 268
Wardlaw, Lee, 268
Washburn, Lucia, 243
Watson, Mary, 161
Wattenberg, Jane, 269
Weeks, Sarah, 269
Weiss, Nicki, 269, 289
Wells, Rosemary, 59, 66, 270, 271, 302
Westcott, Nadine Bernard, 63, 67, 218, 269, 291
Westerduin, Anne, 262
Whybrow, Ian, 272
Wiesner, David, 272
Wilkes, Angela, 272
Williams, Garth, 62
Williams, Sam, 192, 202, 225, 273
Williams, Sue, 273, 291
Williams, Vera B., 274
Willingham, Fred, 92
Wilson, Karma, 275
Wilson, Sarah, 275
Wimmer, Mike, 244
Winter, Jeanette, 68
Wishinsky, Frieda, 276
Wisniewski, David, 243
Wolff, Ashley, 95, 233, 276, 286
Wong, Janet S., 277
Wood, Audrey, 278, 279, 280, 302

AUTHOR AND ILLUSTRATOR INDEX

Wood, Don, 278, 279, 280, 302
Wormell, Christopher, 281
Wright, Blanche Fisher, 68, 290

Xiong, Blia, 247

Yaccarino, Dan, 124, 281, 282
Yashima, Taro, 283
Yee, Wong Herbert, 283

Yolen, Jane, 283
Young, Ed, 284
Young, Ruth, 284

Zahares, Wade, 254
Zelinsky, Paul O., 23, 69
Ziefert, Harriet, 285
Zion, Gene, 286, 302
Zolotow, Charlotte, 286, 287

Title Index

10 Minutes till Bedtime, 224
17 Kings and 42 Elephants, 193
A Is for Amos, 110
Across the Stream, 148
Again!, 220
Airport, 83
All Fall Down, 35, 215, 289, 292
Alligators All Around: An Alphabet, 237
Altoona Baboona, 103
Animal Crackers: A Delectable Collection of Pictures, Poems, and Lullabies for the Very Young, 47, 289
Animal Sounds, 168
Are You My Mommy?, 123
Arf! Beg! Catch! Dogs from A to Z, 165
Arnold Lobel Book of Mother Goose, 55, 289
Arroz con leche: Popular Songs and Rhymes from Latin America, 46, 302

Ask Mr. Bear, 135
At the Beach, 228
Away We Go!, 124

Baboon, 82
Baby Dance, 257, 296
Baby Faces, 206
Baby Loves, 187
Baby Rock, Baby Roll, 89
Baby Says, 251, 290
Baby Signs at Mealtime, 72
Baby Sleeps, 72
Baby! Talk!, 144
Baby's Boat, 66
Baby's Word Book, 273
Backyard Bedtime, 160
Bark, George, 135
Barn Cat, 234
Barn Dance!, 195
Barnyard Banter, 136
Bean Soup, 162
Bear at Home, 90
Bear Play, 139

TITLE INDEX

Bear Snores On, 275
Bear Went Over the Mountain, 66, 221
Bear's Bargain, 77
Bear's Day, 132
Beast, 204
Bedtime, 40
Bedtime!, 91
Benny Bakes a Cake, 15, 224
Big & Little, 217
Big and Little, 266
Big Book of Baby Animals, 88
Big Book of Beautiful Babies, 130
Big Book of Things That Go, 89
Big Dog and Little Dog, 218
Big Dog and Little Dog Getting in Trouble, 218
Big Dog and Little Dog Going for a Walk, 218
Big Fat Hen, 79
Big Friend, Little Friend, 150
Big Red Barn, 94, 301
BINGO, 66
Black & White, 217
Black on White, 162, 289
Blue Buggy, 72
Blue Hat, Green Hat, 92
Blue Rabbit and Friends, 281
Boats, 84
Boo Hoo Boo-Boo, 245
Book!, 145
Book! Book! Book!, 98
Boom, Baby, Boom, Boom!, 193
Boot Weather, 263, 296
Bouncing Time, 166
Boy, a Dog and a Frog, 198
Brave Bear, 194
Bright Eyes, Brown Skin, 169, 292
Brown Bear, Brown Bear, What Do You See?, 25, 33, 194, 291
Brown Sugar Babies, 247
Bubbles, Bubbles, 75, 295
Bug Hunt: A Lift-the-Flap Book, 260
Bugs! Bugs! Bugs!, 82
Building a Road, 219
Bumble Bee, 94

Bunny Bungalow, 233
Busy Penguins, 235
Busy Toes, 92
But Not the Hippopotamus, 92
Buzz, 277

Can I Have a Hug?, 149
Can You Hop?, 188
Can't Sleep, 222
Can't You Sleep, Little Bear?, 263
Caps for Sale: A Tale of a Peddler, Some Monkeys and Their Monkey Business, 24, 246, 290, 302
Car Wash, 250
Carrot Seed, 25, 186, 290
Cat Is Sleepy, 184
Cat's Pajamas, 170
Cat's Play, 132
Charlie Parker Played Be Bop, 25, 222
Cherish Me, 258
Chick and the Duckling, 149
Chicka Chicka Boom Boom, 25, 195
Chicken Soup with Rice: A Book of Months, 237
Children's Zoo, 163
Child's Good Night Prayer, 192
Chugga-Chugga Choo-Choo, 189
Clap Hands, 35, 215, 289, 292
Clap Your Hands, 110, 290, 291
Cock-a-Doodle-Moo!, 209
Color Farm, 126
Color Zoo, 34, 126
Come Along, Daisy, 244
Come Back, Hannah!, 232
Construction Trucks, 174
Corduroy, 142, 290
Countdown to Bedtime, 152
Counting Kisses, 182, 289
Country Animals, 113
Cow Moo Me, 191
Cowboy ABC, 121
Cowboys, 231
Cows in the Kitchen, 116
Crocodile Beat, 180
Crunch Munch, 191

TITLE INDEX

D.W. Rides Again!, 93
Daddy and I, 150
Daisy Dare, 177
Dance, 179, 296
Dappled Apples, 109
Dark, Dark Tale, 28, 96
De Colores and Other Latin-American Folk Songs for Children, 60, 302
Dear Zoo, 23, 103, 291
Diez deditos: Ten Little Fingers & Other Play Rhymes and Action Songs from Latin America, 60, 302
Dig Dig Digging, 199
Dinosaur Roar!, 252
Dinosaur Stomp! A Monster Pop-Up, 23, 251
Dinosaurs, Dinosaurs, 84
Do Pigs Have Stripes?, 266
Do You Know New?, 196
Do You Want to Be My Friend?, 22, 104
Dog Is Thirsty, 184
Doll and Teddy, 72
Doorbell Rang, 171, 301
Down by the Bay, 63
Down by the Station, 50
Duck Is Dirty, 184
Ducks Like to Swim, 262

Each Living Thing, 233
Eat Up, Gemma, 156
Elmer's Colors, 202
Elmer's Day, 202
Elmer's Friends, 202
Elmer's Weather, 202
Emma's Pet, 203
Everyone Poops, 150
Everything Book, 136
Everywhere Babies, 205, 290
Eyes, Nose, Fingers, and Toes: A First Book All About You, 160, 292

Fall Leaves Fall!, 153
Farm Animals, 113
Feast for 10, 133

Feathers for Lunch, 127
Finger Rhymes, 41, 288
Fire Engines, 227
Fire Fighter Piggy Wiggy, 140
Fire Truck, 246
First Flight, 203, 296
First Steps, 268
Fish Eyes, 127
Five Little Monkeys Jumping on the Bed, 111
Flannel Kisses, 93
Flappy Waggy Wiggly, 188, 291
Flea's Sneeze, 124
Flower in the Garden, 113
Foot Book: Dr. Seuss's Wacky Book of Opposites, 239
Fortunately, 110, 291
Fred's Bed, 245
Freight Train, 117
From Head to Toe, 24, 105, 290
Fuzzy Yellow Ducklings, 261

Garden Animals, 113
Gentle Rosie, 35, 208
Geraldine's Blanket, 183
Gigantic! How Big Were the Dinosaurs?, 214
Go Away, Big Green Monster!, 131
Go, Dog, Go!, 125
Going to Bed Book, 92
Going to the Zoo, 61, 296
Golden Bear, 284, 295
Good-bye, Hello!, 228
Good Dog, Carl, 120
Good Dog, Daisy!, 185
Good for You: Toddler Rhymes for Toddler Times, 42, 292
Good Morning, Baby, 168
Good Morning, Chick, 148
Good Night, Baby, 168
Good Night, Gorilla, 22, 223, 296
Good Night, Mr. Night, 281
Good Night, Owl, 172
Goodnight Moon, 19, 95, 289, 290, 301

Grandfather and I, 99
Grandfather Twilight, 88
Grandmother and I, 99
Grandmother's Nursery Rhymes/Las
    Nanas de Abuelita, 52, 302
Green Eggs and Ham, 26, 239, 290,
    301
Greetings, Sun, 146
Grey Lady and the Strawberry
    Snatcher, 80
Growing Like Me, 227
Growing Vegetable Soup, 25, 128,
    297
Grump, 277
Guess How Much I Love You, 200,
    289, 301

Hand Rhymes, 41
Happy Birth Day!, 154, 289
Harold and the Purple Crayon, 178,
    290
Harry the Dirty Dog, 286, 302
Hat for Minerva Louise, 253
Hattie and the Fox, 140
Have You Seen My Duckling?, 255
Hello Toes! Hello Feet!, 218
Hello, Lulu, 260
Hen on the Farm, 113
Here Come Poppy and Max, 144,
    290
Here Come Trainmice, 283
"Hi, Pizza Man," 267
Hide and Seek, 253
Hippety-Hop Hippety-Hay: Growing
    with Rhymes from Birth to Age
    Three, 47, 288
Honk!, 122
Hooray for Snail!, 249
Hooray for Truckmice, 283
Hop Jump, 265
Hop on Pop, 240
How a Baby Grows, 98
How Do Dinosaurs Say Good Night?,
    283
Hug, 72
Humphrey's Corner, 169

Humpty Dumpty and Other Nursery
    Rhymes, 45
Humpty Dumpty and Other Rhymes,
    59
Hungry Monster, 229
Hush: A Thai Lullaby, 51
Hush, Little Alien, 53
Hush Little Baby, 56, 289
Hush, Little Baby, 52
Hushabye, 100

I Can, 216
I Had a Rooster: A Traditional Folk
    Song, 64
I Hear, 216
I Heard a Little Baa, 192, 291
I Heard Said the Bird, 87
I Know an Old Lady Who Swallowed
    a Fly, 65
I Love Animals, 200, 301
I Love Trains!, 253
I Love You As Much, 205, 289
I Love You Because You're You, 79
I Love You Just the Way You Are,
    207
I Love You Like Crazy Cakes, 190
I Love You, Sun, I Love You, Moon,
    217
I Make Music, 150
I See, 216
I See Me, 243
I Spy Little Animals, 197
I Spy Little Wheels, 197
I Touch, 216, 295
I Want To Be an Astronaut, 85
I Went Walking, 273
If You Give a Mouse a Cookie, 213,
    297, 301
If You're Happy and You Know It,
    Clap Your Hands: A Pop-Up
    Book, 43, 290
I'll Play with You, 243
In My New Yellow Shirt, 248
In the Night Kitchen, 237
In the Rain with Baby Duck, 158
In the Small, Small Pond, 20, 137

In the Tall, Tall Grass, 137
Into the A, B, Sea, 230
Is It Red? Is it Yellow? Is it Blue?: An
  Adventure in Color, 163, 296
Is That An Elephant Over There?,
  129, 291
Is That Josie?, 210
Is Your Mama a Llama?, 152, 301
It Looked Like Spilt Milk, 242, 291
Itsy Bitsy Spider, 66, 68

Jack and Jill and Other Nursery
  Rhymes, 45
Jack: It's Bathtime, 130
Jack: It's Bedtime, 130
Jack: It's Playtime, 130
Jafta, 189
Jamberry, 121
Jesse Bear, What Will You Wear?,
  107
Jesse Bear's Tum-Tum Tickle, 108
Jiggle Joggle Jee!, 225
Joseph Had a Little Overcoat, 255
Jump, Frog, Jump!, 180
Jump Like a Frog!, 101, 299
Just Like Daddy, 21, 77

King Bidgood's in the Bathtub, 278,
  295
Kingfisher Nursery Rhyme Songbook,
  48, 289
Kipper, 26, 174
Kipper's Book of Colors, 175
Kipper's Book of Numbers, 175
Kipper's Book of Opposites, 175
Kipper's Book of Weather, 175
Kiss Good Night, 159
Knock at the Door and Other Baby
  Action Rhymes, 43

Lady with the Alligator Purse, 22, 67,
  291, 297
Leaf Baby, 83
Let's Count, 168
Little Boy Blue and Other Rhymes, 59
Little Cloud, 105

Little Donkey Close Your Eyes, 95
Little Gorilla, 91
Little Miss Muffet and Other Nursery
  Rhymes, 45
Little Mouse, the Red Ripe
  Strawberry, and the Big Hungry
  Bear, 280, 302
Little Rabbit's First Word Book, 78
Look Out, Bird!, 177
Love and Kisses, 275
Lucky Song, 274
Lunch, 138

Maisy Drives, 26, 114
Mama Cat Has Three Kittens, 138
Mama, Do You Love Me?, 179
Mama Don't Allow, 170
Mama Mama, 197
Mama Zooms, 115
Mary Had a Little Lamb, 50
Mary Wore Her Red Dress and Henry
  Wore His Green Sneakers, 61
Max's Bath, 270, 295
Max's Bedtime, 270
Max's Birthday, 270
Max's Breakfast, 270
Max's Dragon Shirt, 34, 270
Max's First Word, 270
Max's New Suit, 270
Max's Ride, 270
Max's Toys, 270
May We Sleep Here Tonight?, 184
Maybe My Baby, 213
McDuff Comes Home, 271
Mice Squeak, We Speak, 241
Miss Mouse Takes Off, 214, 296
Miss Mouse's Day, 214
Mole Sisters and the Piece of Moss,
  236
Mole Sisters and the Rainy Day, 236
Moo, Baa, La La La, 92
Moosey Moose, 223
"More More More," Said the Baby: 3
  Love Stories, 274
Morning Song, 243
Mother for Choco, 181

Mother Goose: A Collection of
  Classic Nursery Rhymes, 49, 301
Mother Goose Remembers, 40
Mouse Mess, 226
Mouse Paint, 265
Mr. Brown Can Moo! Can You?: Dr.
  Seuss's Book of Wonderful Noises,
  240
Mr. Gumpy's Motor Car, 100
Mr. Gumpy's Outing, 15, 101
Mrs. Mustard's Baby Faces, 269
My Aunt Came Back, 119
My Baseball Book, 147
My Basketball Book, 147
My Best Friend, 172
My Big Book of Everything, 221
My Car, 85
My Cats Nick and Nora, 154
My Colors/Mis Colores, 131, 302
My Doll, Keshia, 150, 295
My First Baby Games, 57, 289
My First Baby Signs, 72
My First Songs, 57
My Football Book, 147
My Kitten Friends, 102
My Little Sister Ate One Hare, 151
My Love For You, 231
My Mother is Mine, 86
My Numbers/Mis Numeros, 131, 302
My Opposites/Mis Opuestos, 131,
  302
My Own Big Bed, 161
My Puppy Friends, 102
My Shapes/Mis Formas, 131, 302
My Soccer Book, 147
My Two Feet, 267
My Two Hands, 267
My Very First Mother Goose, 59, 289
My Very First Word Book, 20, 272

Napping House, 278
Nicky & Grandpa, 133
Night Cars, 176
Nine-in-One, Grr! Grr!, 247
No, David!, 241, 302
No Kiss for Grandpa, 285

Noisy Nora, 271, 302
Now I'm Big, 206
Number One, Tickle Your Tum, 221

Of Colors and Things, 164
Oh, Baby!: A Touch-and-Feel Book,
  155
Oh My Gosh, Mrs. McNosh!, 269
Oh No, Anna!, 21, 143
Old MacDonald, 15, 64, 66
Old MacDonald Had a Farm, 45
Old Mother Hubbard and Her
  Wonderful Dog, 58
Olivia Counts, 132
Olivia's Opposites, 132
On Mother's Lap, 236, 290
On the Day You Were Born, 141,
  301
One Cow Moo Moo!, 87
One Duck Stuck, 229
One Hot Summer Day, 118
One Little Spoonful, 74
One Moose, Twenty Mice, 86
One Was Johnny: A Counting Book,
  237
Oonga Boonga, 276
Opposites, 92
Over in the Meadow, 52
Owen's Marshmallow Chick, 157
Owl and the Pussycat, 54
Owl Babies, 264, 302

Pancakes for Breakfast, 122
Pancakes, Pancakes!, 106, 297
Panda Big and Panda Small, 103
Papa Papa, 197
Parade, 117
Pat-a-Cake, 53
Pat-a-Cake and Other Play Rhymes,
  44
Pat the Bunny, 23, 186, 290
Peace at Last, 209
Peanut Butter and Jelly: A Play
  Rhyme, 67
Peek-a-Boo!, 176, 215
Peek-a-Boo, You!, 176

Peek-a-Moo!, 112, 291
Pet Animals, 113
Peter's Chair, 182, 287, 301
Pierre: A Cautionary Tale in Five
    Chapters and a Prologue, 237
Piggies, 280
Piggy in the Puddle, 220
Pigs Aplenty, Pigs Galore, 204
Pillow Pup, 214
Pippo Gets Lost, 216
Planes, 84
Planting a Rainbow, 128
Play Rhymes, 42, 290
Playgrounds, 147
Playtime, 40
Playtime, Maisy!, 114
Playtime Rhymes, 54
Pots and Pans, 25, 166, 295
Pretty Brown Face, 219
Pumpkin Pumpkin, 259
Pussycat Pussycat and Other Rhymes,
    59

Quackety Quack Quack!, 272
Quick as a Cricket, 279

Rabbits & Raindrops, 76
Rabbit's Bedtime, 265
Raffi Children's Favorites, 63
Rain, 181
Rain Dance, 75
Rainy Day, 253
Read-Aloud Rhymes for the Very
    Young, 62
Real Mother Goose, 68, 290
Red, Blue, Yellow Shoe, 164, 295
Red-Eyed Tree Frog, 115
Red Rubber Boot Day, 224
Richard Scarry's Best Word Book
    Ever, 234
Ride a Purple Pelican, 62
Roll Over: A Counting Song, 64
Rosie's Walk, 173
Round Is a Mooncake: A Book of
    Shapes, 25, 258
Runaway Bunny, 9, 96, 290

Sam Who Never Forgets, 225,
    296
Sam's Cookie, 190
Sam's Teddy Bear, 190
Say Goodnight, 35, 215, 289, 292
Says Who?: A Pop-up Book of
    Animal Sounds, 109
School Bus, 118
Sea, Sand, Me!, 167
Seals on the Bus, 51, 296
See the Rabbit, 72
See You Later, Alligator, 187
Seven Blind Mice, 284
Shake Shake Shake, 219
Sheep in a Jeep, 242
Sheila Rae's Peppermint Stick, 158
Show Me!, 260
Sidewalk Trip, 25, 167
Silly Little Goose!, 256
Silly Sally, 279
Sing, Sophie!, 123
Skidamarink: A Silly Love Song to
    Sing Together, 65
Skip Across the Ocean: Nursery
    Rhymes From Around the World,
    40
Sleep Tight, Ginger Kitten, 145
Sleepy Baby, 188
Sleepy Bear, 120
Sleepytime Rhyme, 111
Smile!, 176
Snacktime, Maisy!, 114
Snaily Snail, 223
Snap Like a Crocodile!, 101, 299
Snow Baby, 83
Snowballs, 129
Snowy Day, 25, 183, 296
So Big!, 282
So Many Bunnies: A Bedtime ABC
    and Counting Book, 268
So Say the Little Monkeys, 261
Some Things Change, 210
Some Things Go Together, 286
Soup Too?, 162
Soup's Oops!, 162
Splash!, 201

TITLE INDEX

Spots, Feathers, and Curly Tails, 22, 256, 291
Squirrel Is Hungry, 184
Stella and Roy, 276
Sunflower, 140
Sylvia Long's Mother Goose, 56

Teddy Bear, Teddy Bear, 49
Teddy in the House, 113
Teeny Tiny Baby, 235
Tell Me Again About the Night I Was Born, 119
Ten Little Bears: A Counting Rhyme, 152
Ten Little Bunnies, 249
Ten Little Ladybugs, 146
Ten Seeds, 25, 97
Ten Terrible Dinosaurs, 252
Ten, Nine, Eight, 80, 289
There's a Cow in the Cabbage Patch, 33, 90
There's an Alligator Under my Bed, 198
Things I Like, 97, 301
Things That Go, 227
This Is the Bear, 156
This Is the Farmer, 257
This Little Piggy, 58
This Train, 112
Three Bears, 86
Three Billy Goats Gruff, 143, 301
Three Little Kittens, 55
Thump, Thump, Rat-a-Tat-Tat, 78
Tickle, Tickle, 35, 215, 289, 292
Tickle Tum!, 262
Tickly Under There, 149
Time for Bed, 141, 289
Time to Sleep, 139, 289
Titch, 173
Toby, Where Are You?, 250
Toddler Two, 254
Toddler Two-Step, 76, 291
Toddlerobics, 24, 211, 290, 292
Toddlerobics: Animal Fun, 212, 292
Tom and Pippo Go for a Walk, 216
Tom and Pippo Read a Story, 216

Tom and Pippo's Day, 216
Tomie dePaola's Mother Goose, 46
Too Big, Too Small, Just Right, 208
Tortillitas para Mama: And Other Nursery Rhymes, Spanish and English, 48, 302
Touch and Feel Kitten, 259
Touch and Feel Puppy, 259
Train Song, 244, 285
Trains, 84
Trucks, 84, 174
Trucks: Giants of the Highway, 226
Tuesday, 272
Twinkle Twinkle Little Star, 15, 68
Twinkle, Twinkle, Little Star: A Traditional Lullaby, 57
Two Bear Cubs, 178
Two Girls Can, 211

Umbrella, 283
Up Bear, Down Bear, 155

Very Busy Spider, 106
Very Hungry Caterpillar, 106, 301
Very Quiet Cricket, 107
Vroomaloom Zoom, 116

Wake Up, Me!, 202
Watch Me Dance, 219, 296
Water, Water, 151
We Have a Baby, 134, 289
Webster J. Duck, 264
Wee Willie Winkie and Other Nursery Rhymes, 45
Wee Willie Winkie and Other Rhymes, 59
Welcome, Little Baby, 74
We're Going on a Bear Hunt!, 230, 290, 301
Whaley Whale, 223
What Can You Do in the Rain?, 161, 296
What Can You Do in the Snow?, 161
What Can You Do in the Sun?, 161
What Can You Do in the Wind?, 161
What is Round?, 25, 124

What Is That?, 165
What Mommies Do Best/What
    Daddies Do Best, 212
What Shall We Do With The Boo-
    Hoo Baby?, 114
What Shall We Play?, 157
What's On My Head?, 206
What's There?, 266
Wheels on the Bus, 23, 69, 296
When Mama Comes Home Tonight,
    248
When Sophie Gets Angry—Really,
    Really Angry . . . , 81
Where Do Bears Sleep?, 157
Where Does It Go?, 207, 291
Where Does the Brown Bear Go?,
    269, 289
Where is Baby's Belly Button?, 182
Where the Wild Things Are, 238, 290,
    301
Where's My Teddy?, 73, 300
Where's Spot?, 23, 28, 159, 291, 301
Where's Your Smile, Crocodile?, 142
White on Black, 162, 289
Who Are They?, 165
Who Hops?, 22, 120, 291
Who Said Red?, 238
Who Sank the Boat?, 74
Whose Baby Am I?, 102
Whose Ears?, 232, 291

Whose Feet?, 232, 291
Whose Mouse are You?, 185
Whose Nose?, 232, 291
Whose Shoe?, 207
Wibbly Pig Can Make a Tent, 175
Wibbly Pig Is Happy, 175
Wibbly Pig Likes Bananas, 175
Wibbly Pig Opens His Presents, 175
Wide-Mouthed Frog: A Pop-Up Book,
    134
Widget, 201
Wiggle Waggle Fun: Stories and
    Rhymes for the Very Very Young,
    199
Wild Rosie, 35, 208
William's Doll, 287
Will's Mammoth, 196
Window Music, 254
Wings Across the Moon, 153
Wormy Worm, 223
Wow! Babies, 144
Wrapping Paper Romp, 168, 295

Yellow Ball, 81
You Are My Perfect Baby, 258
You Can't Catch Me, 125

Zoom City, 171
Zoom! Zoom! Zoom! I'm Off to the
    Moon!, 282

Subject Index

action rhymes, 43, 44, 47, 48, 49, 53, 58, 110, 199
activities with books, 24–26, 295–297
adoption, 119, 181, 190
Africans, 189
age ranges, 10–15, 33–35
airplanes, 83, 84, 203, 214
alligators, 67, 170, 198, 237
alphabet books, 110, 121, 165, 195, 230, 237, 268
American Library Association, 298, 300, 306, 307, 308
anger, 81
Asian-Americans, 190, 254
Asians, 247, 258, 277, 283
Association for Library Service to Children, 298, 300, 308
astronauts, 85, 282
autumn, 109, 139, 153

Babies Need Books, 9, 310, 311
babies, 98, 130, 141, 154, 182, 205, 213, 235, 236, 247, 269, 276
faces, 144, 176, 206
language acquisition, 4–5
newborn and older sibling, 134, 141, 182, 236, 251, 289
baboons, 82, 103
baby animals, 88, 102
baby shower gifts, 288
baking, 224
bands, 78
barnyard, 64, 90, 94, 113, 136, 140, 148, 173, 195, 209, 256, 257, 281
baseball, 147, 249
basketball, 147
baths, 75, 130, 270, 278
beach, 81, 167, 228, 285
bears, 86, 90, 107, 120, 132, 139, 152, 157, 178, 194, 207, 209, 221
bears, polar, 139
bears, teddy, 49, 73, 142, 156, 284
beds, 161, 245

333

bedtime, 17, 52, 56, 57, 80, 88, 91, 95, 100, 111, 139, 141, 153, 157, 159, 160, 188, 192, 205, 222, 223, 224, 245, 263, 265, 268, 269, 281, 283, 289
bees, 94
Beginning with Books, 308
Beginning with Books, 312
Best Children's Music, 298
bicycles, 93, 276
Big Book format, 94, 128, 141, 171, 263, 265, 273, 278, 279
birds, 127
birthdays, 61, 91, 110, 224, 270
black-and-white illustrations, 12, 162, 165
Black Books Galore, 311
blacks, 50, 99, 116, 118, 119, 133, 146, 156, 168, 169, 172, 179, 182, 183, 189, 219, 222, 247, 251, 257, 258, 284, 311
blankets, 183
Blue's Clues, 27
boats, 66, 74, 84, 100, 101, 227
body, human, 13, 92, 105, 150, 160, 182, 218
Book Links, 306
Book Magazine, 307
books, 98, 145
Books, Babies, and Libraries, 313
books that invite movement, 23–24, 290
books that invite participation, 21–24, 290–291
bookstores, 304–305
bunnies, 76, 95, 96, 184, 186, 233, 249, 268
buses, 51, 69, 118
Butler, Dorothy, 310
butterflies, 106

cardboard books, 12
cars, 85, 100, 116, 171, 176, 250
caterpillars, 106
cats, 55, 102, 132, 138, 145, 154, 162, 170, 201, 234, 259

chickens, 79, 148, 149
Children's Book Council, 308
Children's Jukebox, 298
Children's Literature Web site, 307
Children's Music Web, 298
chimpanzees, 72, 97
Chinaberry Books, 305
Chinese Americans, 190
cloth books, 12, 113, 114
clothes, 61, 92, 107, 207, 253, 270
clouds, 105, 242
colors, 61, 106, 138, 163, 164, 175, 202, 217, 238, 248, 265
concept books, 15, 258. (*see also* alphabet, colors, counting, opposites, shapes)
cooking, 106, 122, 133, 224
counting, 13, 29, 52, 64, 76, 80, 86, 97, 111, 127, 131, 132, 151, 152, 168, 175, 182, 188, 221, 229, 234, 237, 249, 252, 268, 280
courage, 73, 161, 177, 194, 198, 263
cowboys, 110, 121, 231
cowgirls, 110
crickets, 107
crocodiles, 142, 180

dance, 76, 179, 195, 219, 265
Davis, Robin Works, 312
DeSalvo, Nancy N., 312
dinosaurs, 84, 214, 251, 252, 283
disabilities, 115
dogs, 58, 120, 135, 162, 165, 185, 201, 214, 218, 222, 259, 269, 271, 286
dolls, 72, 150, 193, 287
drums, 193
ducks, 149, 158, 229, 244, 255, 262, 264, 272

Easter, 157
elephants, 193, 201, 202
emergent literacy, 5–8
Ernst, Linda L., 312, 313

SUBJECT INDEX

Fairrosa Cyber Library of Children's
  Literature Web site, 307
farms, 64, 90, 94, 113, 136, 140,
  148, 173, 195, 209, 256, 257, 281
fathers, 53, 61, 77, 116, 150, 197,
  200, 212, 257
fear, 73, 161, 177, 194, 198, 263
feet, 92, 218, 239, 267
fingerplays, 11, 14, 24, 31, 41, 42,
  43, 44, 47, 54, 57, 199
fire engines, 246
fire fighters, 140, 227
first word books, 14, 78, 221, 234,
  272, 273
fish, 127, 230
flaps, books with, 23, 30, 45, 65,
  101, 103, 109, 112, 122, 129,
  130, 143, 152, 159, 176, 182,
  188, 192, 215, 232, 254, 260,
  266, 282, 291
flowers, 97, 113, 128, 140
folktales, 86, 143, 246, 247
food, 67, 74, 106, 133, 138, 156,
  213, 226, 256, 262
football, 147
Foster, Sheila, 311
foxes, 148
friendship, 77, 162, 172, 211, 216,
  218, 261
frogs, 115, 134, 180, 272
From Cover to Cover: Evaluating and
  Reviewing Children's Books, 310

games, 43, 44, 46, 61, 76, 110, 207
gardening, 97, 113, 128, 140, 259
geese, 122, 256
gender roles, 211, 287
gifts, 59, 288
Golinkoff, Roberta Michnick, 4, 5,
  310
Gopnik, Alison, 4, 10–12, 310
gorillas, 91, 223
grandfathers, 88, 99, 133, 220, 285
grandmothers, 91, 99, 287
Great Books About Things Kids Love,
  34, 311

Great Books for Boys, 34, 311
Great Books for Girls, 34, 311
Greene, Ellen, 313
Griffin, Mary Lee, 7
growing, 91, 227
guessing games, 72, 112, 120, 152,
  163, 188, 192, 207, 232, 256
guitar music, 63

Halloween, 109, 259
hamsters, 224
hand signs, 72
hands, 72, 267, 280
Hirsh-Pasek, Kathy, 4, 5, 310
Hmong, 247
Horn Book Magazine, 9, 306
Horning, Kathleen T., 310
horses, 110, 121
How Babies Talk, 4, 5, 310

I Am Your Child, 308
ice cream, 167
insects, 82, 107, 260
interracial families, 181, 190, 277

Jeffry, Debby Ann, 313
jump rope rhymes, 67

kings, 193, 278
kittens, 55, 102, 138, 145, 259
Kuhl, Patricia, 4, 10–12, 310

labeled pictures, 14, 78, 221, 234,
  272, 273
ladybugs, 146
lambs, 50
language acquisition, 4–5
Laos, 247
Lapsit Services for the Very Young,
  312
Lapsit Services for the Very Young II,
  313
Latinos, 60
Library Programming for Families with
  Young Children, 313
libraries, 30–31, 98, 298, 300, 303

Los Angeles Public Library, 300
lullabies, 47, 51, 52, 56, 57, 60, 66

magazines, 297, 306–307
Meltzoff, Andrew N., 4, 10–12, 310
mice, 138, 158, 177, 185, 208, 213,
    214, 226, 265, 280, 283, 284
monkeys, 111, 216, 241, 261
monsters, 131, 143, 204, 229, 238
morning, 243
mothers, 77, 86, 115, 152, 179, 181,
    185, 193, 197, 205, 212, 236,
    248, 277
mothers, animal, 152
motorcycles, 271
movement, books that invite,
    23–24, 290
multicultural books, 291–292
Music Education for Young
    Children, 299
Music for Little People, 299
music, 63, 150, 193, 219, 222,
    298–299

National Association for the
    Education of Young Children
    (NAEYC), 309
National Child Care Information
    Center, 309
National Network for Child Care,
    309
Nespeca, Sue McCleaf, 313
Nichols, Judy, 313
nursery rhymes, 11, 14, 15, 17, 40,
    45, 46, 47, 48, 49, 52, 53, 55, 56,
    58, 59, 68, 79

ocean, 81, 228, 230
Odean, Kathleen, 311
opposites, 92, 125, 131, 132, 162,
    175, 208, 217, 239, 252, 266
owls, 54, 172, 264

pancakes, 106, 122
pandas, 103
pans, 166

parades, 78, 117
Parker, Toni Trent, 311
participation, books that invite,
    21–24, 290–291
penguins, 235
pets, 203
piano music, 63
pigs, 58, 132, 140, 175, 204, 220,
    280
plants, 97, 128, 140, 186, 259
play rhymes, 67
playgrounds, 147
poetry, 47, 54, 62, 199
ponds, 137, 255
pop-up books, 23, 43, 69, 109, 134,
    251
pots, 166
prayers, 192
pumpkins, 77, 259
puppies, 102, 135, 159, 185, 214,
    259

rabbits, 76, 95, 96, 184, 186, 233,
    249, 268
rain, 75, 76, 118, 158, 181, 224,
    236, 253, 283
Rand, Donna, 311
Reach Out and Read, 309
Read-Aloud Handbook, The, 28, 293,
    311
Read to Me, 309
reading aloud, 2–3, 293–294,
    age ranges for, 10–15, 33–35
    difficulties in, 28–30
    emotional benefits, 8–9
    how to, 19–21
    when to, 16–18
    where to, 16–18
Reading Is Fundamental, 309
Reid, Rob, 298
rereading, 26–28
resources for parents, 288–307
rockets, 53, 282

scary stories, 80, 96, 143, 198, 238,
    252

Scientist in the Crib, The, 4, 10–12, 310
sea animals, 230
seasons, 83, 153
shapes, 105, 124, 126, 131, 242, 258
sheep, 242
shoes, 207, 218
snow, 83, 93, 129, 161, 183, 253, 263, 275
soccer, 147
songs, 15, 43, 46, 47, 48, 51, 57, 60, 61, 63, 64, 65, 66, 68, 69, 170, 255
soup, 128, 237
Spanish, books in, 300–302
special needs, children with, 10
spiders, 106
sports, 147
Storytimes for Two-Year-Olds, 313
sunflowers, 140

teddy bears, 49, 73, 142, 156, 284
textures in books, 155, 186, 259, 261
Thai, 51
Toddle on Over, 312
toes, 92

toilet training, 150
touch and feel books, 155, 186, 259, 261
trains, 50, 84, 112, 117, 189, 225, 244, 253, 254, 283, 285
Trelease, Jim, 28, 293, 311
trucks, 84, 174, 176, 199, 219, 226, 227, 246, 283

vehicles, 13, 84, 114, 118, 124, 199, 227
Voigt, Cynthia, 9

weather, 75, 76, 83, 93, 118, 129, 158, 161, 175, 181, 183, 202, 224, 236, 243, 253, 263, 275, 283
Web sites, 306–309
winter, 83, 93, 120, 129, 161, 183, 253, 263, 275
wooly mammoths, 196
word books, 14, 78, 221, 234, 272, 273
wordless books, 22, 80, 113, 114, 120, 122, 164, 198, 223, 272

Zero to Three, 309
zoo, 61, 139, 163, 166, 223, 225

KATHLEEN ODEAN has been a children's librarian for seventeen years in public and school libraries. She chaired the 2002 Newbery Award Committee and has served on a previous Newbery Committee, the Caldecott Award Committee, and the American Library Association's Notable Children's Books Committee. Her other three guides to children's books are *Great Books for Girls: More than 600 Recommended Books for Girls Ages 3 to 14*, *Great Books for Boys: More than 600 Books for Boys 2 to 14*, and *Great Books About Things Kids Love: More than 750 Recommended Books for Children 3 to 14*.

Ms. Odean is a contributing editor for *BOOK: The Magazine for the Reading Life* as well as a reviewer for *Kirkus Reviews* and *Booklist*. She frequently speaks to parent and teacher groups about books for children and teens, and how to promote reading. She lives in Barrington, Rhode Island, with her husband, Ross Cheit.